LONDON BY GASLIGHT

TITLES BY THE AUTHOR

Novels

Weep for Lycidas
Spring in Tartarus
All the Trees Were Green
Vernal Equinoz
What Are We Waiting For?
Battered Caravanserai
So Linked Together
Treadmill
There's Glory For You!
Long Vacation
The Dividing Stone
The Brain
A Hansom to St James's

The "Rocester" Novels

Higher Things
The House in Fishergate
Sinecure
The Darkened Room

Biography

Gambler's Glory (*John Law of Lauriston*)
Count Cagliostro: "Nature's Unfortunate Child. . ."
They Would Be King (*Lambert Simnel, King Theodore, Bernadotte, Henry Christophe*)
Prince of Hokum (*Peter Cheyney*)
Charles Dickens: A Sentimental Journey in Search of an Unvarnished Portrait
Rosa (*Rosa Lewis of the Cavendish Hotel*)
Lord of London (*2nd Duke of Westminster*)
Clarence (*HRH the Duke of Clarence & Avondale*)

Historical and Paranormal

Airborne at Kitty Hawk (*The Wright Brothers*)
The History of the Hat
London by Gaslight: 1861–1911
London Growing: The Development of a Metropolis
Mulberry: The Return in Triumph (*Prelude to D-Day*)
The London That Was Rome
Fantare of Strumpets
The Roots of Witchcraft
Fire from Heaven (*Spontaneous combustion*)
Vanishings

The Sherlock Holmes Monographs

Theatrical Mr Holmes
Decorated Mr Holmes
Cynological Mr Holmes

The Sherlock Holmes Commentaries

In the Footsteps of Sherlock Holmes
The London of Sherlock Holmes
The World of Sherlock Holmes
I, Sherlock Holmes
A Study in Surmise: The Making of Sherlock Holmes

Philately

Mauritius 1847
A New Approach to Stamp Collecting (*with Douglas B. Armstrong*)

Cuisine

Beer Cookery

Short Stories

Transit of Venus
Exploits of the Chevalier Dupin (USA only)
Murder in the Rue Royale, and Other Exploits of the Chevalier Dupin

Advertising

Technical and Industrial Publicity

LONDON BY GASLIGHT
1861–1911

MICHAEL HARRISON

Revised and Expanded

GASOGENE PRESS, Ltd.
Dubuque, Iowa

PUBLICATION STAFF

Managing Editor, Jean R. Starr
Compositor, Carlisle Graphics
Printing and Binding, Thomson-Shore

Library of Congress Catalogue Number: 86–083423

Copyright © 1963, 1987 by Michael Harrison. All rights reserved

ISBN 0-938501-04-6

No part of this publication may be reproduced, stored in a retrieval system, or transmitted, in any form or by any means, electronic, mechanical, photocopying, recording, or otherwise, without the prior written permission of the author and publisher.

Printed in the United States of America

10 9 8 7 6 5 4 3 2 1

For MARYVONNE
'Her' Book

*... and now, revised and
fully illustrated, still 'her' book*

C·O·N·T·E·N·T·S

P·A·R·T O·N·E
The First Decade 1

P·A·R·T T·W·O
The Second Decade 49

P·A·R·T T·H·R·E·E
The Third Decade 91

P·A·R·T F·O·U·R
The Fourth Decade 131

P·A·R·T F·I·V·E
The Fifth Decade 169

Index 195

I·L·L·U·S·T·R·A·T·I·O·N·S

Her Majesty Queen Victoria, 1887	G-1
Trial-trip of the world's first Underground Railway, the Metropolitan, 1862	G-2
John Wiggins, one of the last to be hanged publicly in Britain	G-3
'Skittles': the 'Fair but Frail' Catherine Walters, Meretrix and Fashion-Dictatrix	G-4
Agnes Willoughby, the impudent ruin of an ancient House	G-5
Laura Bell, the Evangelical Harlot	G-6
Mrs Edward ('Lillie') Langtry: generous with her expensive favours	G-7
President Abraham Lincoln, greatly indebted to the Prince Consort	G-8
Lord Lytton, Viceroy and Psychic Investigator	G-9
Louis Pasteur, seeking a germ-free environment	G-10
George, Duke of Cambridge, Commander-in-Chief	G-11
Lord Randolph Churchill	G-12
Gustave Eiffel, famed French Tower-builder, 1889	G-13
Colonel Valentine Baker, of the Tenth Hussars	G-14
Eugen Sandow, the Strong Man—with stooge	G-15
Cecil Rhodes, Empire-builder	G-16
His Royal Highness the Prince of Wales	G-17
The Peers of Britain, stripped of all political power	G-18
Victorian tea-shop of the grander class	G-19
London's first telephone-exchange, 1879.	G-20
London celebrates its first Bank Holiday, 1871	G-21
Great Western Royal Hotel, Paddington, 1852	G-22
The Apogee of Empire, 1897	G-23
The Prince wins the 1896 Derby with his *Persimmon*	G-24
An Era's end: the dead King lies in State	G-25
A Bethnal 'sweat-shop' of 1863	G-26
Salvation Army women's night shelter, 1895	G-27
The Cycling Craze: late 'Nineties	G-28
Mrs. William ('Mary') Cornwallis West	G-29
An elderly Suffragette is arrested	G-30
'Jack the Ripper' murders—Police warning-poster	G-31
Crosby Hall, a surviving Mediaeval mansion	G-32
Thames Embankment first lit by electricity, 1897	G-33
London by gaslight	G-34

P·A·R·T O·N·E

The First Decade

The ten-year span from 1861 to 1871 was the most revolutionary in the history of Britain—revolutionary in the social sense; though in other countries it was 'revolutionary' in the literal sense as well. Almost everything happened in that world-changing decade to alter the existing social pattern. The year 1861 saw so many changes— so many "firsts"—of fundamental social influence, that it is hard to state which was the most important. There was the first electromagnetic telephone of the obscure German schoolmaster, Johan Philipp Reis; the incandescent electric lamp (which made Underground railways and flame-free mining possible) of Joseph Swan; the opening of the Aerated Bread Company's chain of "respectable" tea-shops was of vital importance in the emancipation of Woman; and—all this in 1861—the dying Prince Consort, husband of Queen Victoria, used all his diplomatic skill to avoid war between Great Britain and the government of President Lincoln, thus leaving "Honest Abe" to fight, and eventually to conquer, the rebellious South.

The Sixties had begun with a Civil War in North America; the decade ended with a bloodless but perhaps even more fundamental revolution in London: the last vestiges of Ecclesiastical power were swept away; the purchase of military commissions was also abolished; and entry to both the Army and the Civil Service was, henceforth, to be by written examination. An Education Act provided for free, compulsory, nation-wide education in those 'Board Schools' which so impressed Sherlock Holmes a decade later.

of Wales (the future King Edward the Seventh) began to display his undisciplined sexual tastes even as the decade began, and that Father was still alive. Before the decade's end, he had appeared in the witness-box in one of the filthiest divorce-cases on record. In the Birkenhead yards, the Manchester Cotton Kings had the commerce-raider Alabama built to break the North's blockade of the cotton-producing South—a gesture which was to cost Great Britain in 1873, £3,000,000 in compensation to the now secure Union. Everywhere there was change—and, as one looks back—it is hard to deny that most of it was change for the better.

In 1861, in the dreary northern town of Newcastle-on-Tyne, an event of—literally—world-changing significance took place.

An industrial exhibition was being held in Newcastle, and among the exhibits was an electric lamp of unprecedented principle: the invention of a young civil engineer, Joseph Swan.

Mr Swan had taken a strip of oiled paper, coated it thickly with powdered graphite, enclosed the loop of paper within a glass bulb, exhausted the air from the glass bulb so that a near-perfect vacuum was obtained, and passed an electric current through the graphite on the oiled paper. As the electric current flowed, the graphite began to heat up. From dull red it became bright red, and from bright red it became golden.

The interested visitors to the exhibition were the first members of the public privileged to see an incandescent electric lamp—actually working.

If Joseph Swan realized the significance of his invention, there were very few others who did. Above slum- and rustic cottage-level, every house in the United Kingdom was illuminated with gas, and a vast industry had been built up, not only on the nation-wide use of gas as an illuminant, but on the assumption that, in achieving gas-lighting, mankind had found the ultimate in illuminants.

Gas-stoves had been shown at the Great Exhibition, held in Hyde Park, London, in 1851—so that it was obvious that gas would enjoy a still greater use, since it was destined to be utilized as a source of both light and heat.

But in that first experimental lamp, shown by Swan at Newcastle in 1861, the doom of the Age of Gas was irrevocably pronounced—and the Age of Gas was something a good deal more than the prismatic glitter of the lustre gasolier in the middle-class drawing-room or in Simpson's Coffee Divan in the Strand; something more than the demoniac blue flicker of the fish-tail burner in a Lyceum dressing-room or in a servant's bedroom, high in a tall stucco-fronted house in Lancaster Gate. The colour of a gas-flame, whether in pendant lustre or in wire-caged fish-tail burner, in a globular Thames Embankment street-lamp or—a nearly invisible blue—in the burner of a Bunsen whose heat, in a thousand laboratories, incubated our 'scientific' world, is the characteristic colour of the Victorian Age—an age which, for all the strange talk of the Victorians' 'stuffiness', is outstanding as the most innovating age in the world's long history.

Other ages have dreamed, have planned, have developed: but only in the Victorian Age did they do all these things—and innovated, too.

Other ages have been as restless, as filled with energy; but no other age has had the will and the power to translate that energy into achievements which had to meet the exacting demands of the Victorians' standards of practicality.

Practical. . .? Well, I have always thought that the story of how William Thompson, later Lord Kelvin, solved the problem of reception of the trans-Atlantic telegraph signals may well stand as the epitome of all that we think of as Victorian practicality—and the mental attitudes of which that practicality was the summing-up.

When the electrical impulses were received at Valentia from Newfoundland, they were too weak. They were able to move the needle of the telegraph instrument so little that the telegraph-clerk could hardly detect the movement. He certainly could not read a message from the movements of the needle.

Yet the needle moved. If, Thompson reasoned, a means could be found to magnify that movement, the signals could be read.

Accordingly, he attached a small mirror to the recording-needle, and, darkening the room, directed a beam of light on to the mirror.

This beam, reflected on the mirror, moved through many degrees of arc, no matter how small the vibrations of the needle, and the receiving-clerk could then read clearly the variations of the needle.

And the small mirror—small and *light* enough to be stuck on to the needle of the receiving instrument? A sequin dropped from Mrs Thompson's dress. . . .

We think complacently of our Electrical-passing-into-Atomic Age; and those who take a pride in living in a world of telephones and radio-telephones, of cinemas and television, of vacuum-sweepers and refrigerators, of automobiles and aeroplanes, mostly feel that 'we' have produced these things; and produced the age of which they are the characteristics and character-makers.

But each age is the product, not of itself, but of the age which preceded it—and it was in the Victorian Age, the Age of Gas, that this modern Electrical-Atomic Age of ours was produced.

There is not an invention of which the presence patterns our living which was not invented in Victorian days, and realized at least in experimental form—even the history of the development of atomic energy begins with J. J. Thomson's sudden interest in the Geissler tube, that scientific toy which so interested Frederick the Great, more than two centuries ago.

Perhaps, for all that the electric telegraph, the electric lamp, the telephone, the motor-car and the cinema were realized practically before the end of the Victorian Age, the full development of electricity's resources was held back by the persistence of what, for want of a more accurate term, we may call the Mentality of Gaslight.

It is a fact hard to accept, but it is a fact nevertheless, that modern Paris, the Paris of Haussmann, owes its inspiration to the London which was modern in 1860. It was Haussmann's ambition to create, in the Paris that he was commissioned to reconstruct, the counterpart of those town-planned sections of London with which the name of Thomas Cubitt is most generally associated.

Travellers from London, sighing with relief to find themselves in civilized Paris, may well look for the resemblance between the soot-laden, man-hating dreariness of modern London, and the warm-hearted elegance of Paris. All the same, it was only Haussmann's innate Frenchness which enabled him so to improve upon his model—but his model was London, no doubt of it.

Yet, at the beginning of our period, London was not quite the desolate, despairing compromise with reality that it is to-day.

We hear about the enormous wealth that we have created, read in the newspapers of the billions of pounds sterling spent at this Bank Holiday or that Christmas—as though the activity of the rotary-presses churning out bank-notes was any indication of a nation's true wealth. We hear how every family has a refrigerator, a television set. Has every family, too, a house of its own, and at least one servant? The Victorians had—all but the derelicts at the very bottom.

In the golden glow of gas there were many emotions that the Victorians shared with us—for they, too, were human beings.

But they lacked something that we have—which poisons us. Which has not only caused us to give up our empire and our ancient capital city; but which has almost caused us to give up altogether.

They lacked self-doubt.

The builders of London reflected the spirit of their age—and though it was an empire-building age, it was a very parochial age, too. There is not, there never was, a Versailles or a Schoenbrunn or a Pardo or an Amalienborg in London. When the dubious financier, 'Baron' Albert Grant, to whom we do at least owe the gardens in Leicester-square, put up his hundred-roomed mansion, Kensington House, in 1873, at a cost of

£250,000, it fetched, on his failure, the trivial sum of £10,461, and was pulled down in 1883, just ten years after its completion. A square of houses—Kensington Court—was erected on its site. So much for what London thought of palaces. . . .

There was, indeed, nothing 'imperial' about London, in the continental, autocratic interpretation of that word. Foreign architects came to London, of course, as they went to St. Petersburg and Dresden, Würzburg and Berlin—but what grandiose ideas they brought with them they had either to modify or have modified for them.

They might have come to build palaces; they stayed to design desirable middle-class family residences—even for Town-dwelling dukes.

The Polish architect, Michael Novosielski, provides us with an illuminating example of what happened to foreign architects coming to practise in this country.

Novosielski was working in Rome when he met Sir William Chambers, who invited him to London, to act as consultant architect in the building of Somerset House. Novosielski stayed in England, and went into business on his own, as both architect and speculative builder: as the latter, he erected a terrace of small houses in the then out-of-town village of Brompton—Michael's Grove; as the former, he was associated with Nash in the development of Waterloo-place, Pall Mall and the Haymarket, being mostly responsible for the old Haymarket Opera House.

Now there are two surviving examples of Novosielski's work to be seen in London: one is the stone-fronted house, No. 105 Piccadilly, from the balcony of which the Emperor Alexander of Russia (who was then staying at the nearby Pulteney Hotel) received the acclamations of the crowd after the first defeat of Napoleon; the other is the Royal Opera Arcade, that enchanting passage of Regency shops, half of which has survived the demolition of the Carlton Hotel.

The modesty of these two buildings—the first was Lord Barrymore's Town house—testifies to the effect that the character of London and Londoners had upon even a Rome-trained Polish architect, working for the virtual ruler of an empire greater and infinitely richer than Russia's.

The truth is, that though the aristocrats and manufacturers with incomes of anything up to £500,000 a year—and there were many who touched this figure—would not have recognized the word, they liked to be 'cozy'. Those who envy them their country mansions, full of servants, should interpret their actions: they disliked the windy, comfortless vastness of their 'country places,' and they found an excess of retainers irksome. They kept up the country houses, and staffed them with servants, because, by so doing, they supported the rural population. Given an opportunity to escape the tyranny of the big house and its big staff, they eagerly accepted the proffered freedom. They commissioned houses in London which were so small that only a skeleton staff could find accommodation there.

With the rise of the middle class, Cubitt cashed in by planning and building miles of streets which were lined with three-, four- and five-storey houses which were modelled on the pattern already made fashionable by the Best (as well as the Richest) People: the Cubitt houses of Belgrave-road, Pimlico, are not any smaller than the Adam houses of the Adelphi or the Nash houses of Regent's Park: and—save for the stucco Corinthian decorations of the latter—all were based on the flat-fronted, one-family-and-a-few-servants houses which had sprung up in the City of London after the Great Fire of 1666.

The pattern which is being effaced today was a pattern which persisted in London for three hundred years: the pattern based on the private dwelling. It is over a century ago that the flat came to London—and the alacrity with which the middle-class families snapped up the £300-a-year flats in order to 'solve the servant problem', was a sure pointer to the pattern of living that the future would establish.

Yet, as the blocks of flats went up in newly built Victoria-street and elsewhere, the houses went up in vastly greater quantities. The house was not to give in to the flat without a struggle, which is why to-day, for all the extensive demolition of houses, London is still a city of houses, doomed though every one of them is.

Were one to return to the London of 1860, what would one see?

Contemporary photographs are unreliable; contemporary drawings even more so. The photographs have faded to a yellow-brown, and give the scene an impression of dinginess that, save in the dock areas and slums that Doré drew, could not have existed. The hastily produced woodcuts of the period convey an equally unfortunate impression of shadowed gloominess; but this is the inherent fault of the woodcut process. Only in the lithographs of Thomas Shotter Boys does the graphic process have the power of indicating the sunny brightness and spick-and-span cleanliness of the early Victorian scene.

London has always had fogs, long before there were fires in domestic grates or chimneys to carry the smoke into the overhead mist.

It should not be forgotten that Industry, which necessitated factories (with, naturally, factory chimneys), did not come to London in any important degree until the very end of the 19th century, and Manufacture moved south from the Midlands and North only because of the influx of a huge population of workless and work-hungry from the 'depressed areas' of Ireland and Poland. Man-power, hungry and hopeful, poured into London: Industry went to meet it and use it.

But this development did not take place until the 19th century was almost at an end.

In consequence, if we wish to look for striking dissimilarities between the London of 1860 and the London of to-day, we shall find those dissimilarities in the East End of the city. The slums have gone—or are going—but much of what could never have been other than slum property still exists: that is to say, property which, not inherently (for the bricks are good, and well laid), but by reason of its intended use, could never have had a chance of escaping the descent into slumdom.

But in 1860 London stopped at Mile End—hence the name—and beyond that, the villages of Bow and Stratford were set among the market-gardens which supplied London with its fresh vegetables.

Even in so old a suburb as Islington, there were farms from which the milk travelled in to the centre of the capital—the last of such farms survived, strange to say, as late as 1927—and letters addressed to a point a few hundred yards beyond Harrods were all marked 'Brompton', and not 'London S.W.'.

Chain-reaction is a permanent condition in human affairs, and not merely an induced condition in certain elements. When Czar Alexander II abolished serfdom throughout the Russian Empire in 1861, he set in train vast population-movements which have not yet ceased to keep the world's racial boundaries in a fluid state.

Free to leave their lord's estate, the Russian serfs came to the cities, driving out all but the most securely established. Those driven out looked west, to America; and they came to London as the first stopping-place on their way to New York or Boston.

Most of these refugees from Russian economic pressures continued their journey, but tens of thousands got no farther than London; to stay, to settle down, to change their names, to put up the fees of public schools, to become English middle-class traders, country gentlemen, even peers; to talk, with good-humoured self-depreciation, of the way 'we British always seem to muddle through'.

All this had not happened by 1860. London was growing, but the expansion was not yet to the east. It was west and north-west that London was to send out rootlets and roots in the shape of streets, so soon to be followed by bus- and tram-routes which would fill in the spaces between each pair of streets, and link up the suburb thus created with the metropolitan centre.

Beyond Aldgate, the straight, broad street was lined with 16th-, 17th- and 18th-century houses, some of which still survive: but what we call the

East End today was the nearest part of Town to the market-garden of nearer and farther Essex.

Along the high road, at Bow, there was a 'superior' settlement, with prim, three-storey houses built in terraces, and, here and there, the 18th-century house in which some merchant, with business at the docks, still lived. Some of these old mansions, too, survive.

But it was in the west that the great changes were taking place; and here were being built those parts of London—Pimlico, Lancaster Gate, Notting Hill, Bayswater—which, because they still survive almost unchanged from that day to this, would give to the traveller of those days so vivid an impression of modernity in the London of 1860.

But if the houses of London's West End are still pretty much as they were in 1860—the fine, stone-built, 'French' houses of Grosvenor-gardens were not built until 1868—what of the people? What of those smaller things which mark the subtle yet striking differences between the familiar things in a familiar setting, and the unfamiliar things in a familiar setting— just such a difference as we see when an American film-producer dresses his 'London' crowds in American clothes?

I think that the first thing to strike the traveller-back would not be the presence of so much horse-drawn traffic—after all, there is even now quite a lot about; and a pony-drawn United Dairies milk-float was until very recent years a matutinal commonplace—as a difference in the *shape* of men and women. The men, because they would all be wearing tall hats, from the beggar and the crossing-sweeper to the masher and the toff, would look, somehow, taller; while, since all the women, save paupers, would be wearing crinoline, the women would seem to be fantastically wider—'bottom heavy', if I may invert a common expression.

There would be no noticeable thinning of the traffic; and the noise might or might not seem to our traveller to be excessive—certainly the Victorians thought it was. Excessive or not, the noise would be there: not the noise of maladroit gear-changing or of revving engines, naturally, but the noise of a hundred different street-criers, hawking their wares. Noise of area-bells, tinkling on their C-springs. Noise of the men or women selling goods and services—'Muffins!', 'Chairs to Mend!', 'Brooms and Brushes!', 'Meolc!', 'Knives to Grind!' Noise of the paper-boy, noise of the whistling tradesman's lad. But above all the noise which drove Victorians to a frenzy, and is seriously reported to have hastened—if it did not (as they claimed) exactly cause—the death of that famous sporting artist, John Leech: the noise of the hurdy-gurdy. 'The Italian Invasion', *Punch* called it, week after week, year after year—wondering how many women had died of vexation from having had to listen to the plunk-plunk of the hurdy-gurdy.

Punch would show husbands defied at their own front door as they ordered the hurdy-gurdy man away; or, Vortigern-like, buying peace, while their wives lay upstairs upon the buttoned chaise-longue, going mad.

Another thing: though the traveller's ear might not be caught by all this medley of sound, be sure that his eye would be caught by something quite different from current practice: the employment of men and boys, women and girls, to transport objects now carried by vehicle. The tinsmith's door-to-door traveller would be carrying enough pots and pans on his person to supply a dozen fair-sized kitchens; the butcher's boy would be shouldering a wooden float laden with the orders for a dozen streets; and the chair-mending man, the brush-and-broom man, and all the others would be carrying around with them what would strike our traveller as their entire stock-in-trade.

Another thing: though he would certainly not meet the itinerant tradesman in the new, 'select' streets and squares of Belgravia and Pimlico—where every area gate would bear the enamelled plate: 'No Hawkers, No Circulars', and the street itself would display, at intervals, the sign: 'No Street Noises, Hawkers' Cries or Organs—By Order'—all the other streets of that 1860 London would appear to him to be lined with kerbstone traders: each with a small tray, kept level by a string running around the back of his neck.

On dry days, the kerbstone traders would need merely their professional fortitude to stand, from early morning until late night, trying to catch the eye and touch the pocket of the passer-by; but on rainy days they would need something more than mere fortitude: an almost supernatural patience would be required to endure the discomforts of standing in a gutter which would overflow after only an hour's rain and become a raging torrent of filthy water, bearing on its surface all the rubbish which had collected in the gutters during the dry weather.

When *Punch*, in those days, was not patronizingly chiding crinoline or angrily rebuking the Italian organ-grinder, it was melodramatically attacking the fiasco of Main Drainage.

Punch's representation of Old Father Thames was of a dirty grey-beard, carrying a trident crowned with a thrown-away tea-pot, fished out of the bed of the malodorous Thames. But generally *Punch* got its artists to leave out the humorous element when dealing with the Thames, and commissioned them to show an evilly shadowed London—an effect easy to secure with a block of boxwood and an engraver's burin—as background to Death himself.

There was cause for all this attack.

What had happened was this: after the (as it turned out, last) cholera epidemic—that of 1849—the connection between proper sanitation and good health was established; and Government, under pressure from a not-altogether-disinterested group of Members, had put in hand a far-reaching scheme for abolishing the more than 300,000 cess-pits which received London's daily defecations, and replacing them with flush-closets which drained into an elaborate sewer-system: 'Main Drainage', as it was called.

There were fat contracts to be licked up in this multimillion-pound scheme, and some comfortable little sinecures, too: Dickens got Lord John Russell to give one to the husband of Dickens's sister, Laetitia. The appointment seems to have been typical of the 'personnel management' which accompanied the scheme: Alfred Austin had failed as a painter, and the *artiste-peintre manqué*, looking around for a more profitable substitute occupation, chose that of sanitary engineer. It is true that what our friends the Americans delicately call the 'toilet arrangements', were more picturesque in the 1860s than they are today: richly polished mahogany seats (they were even covered with plush at Forbes House), crowning and surrounding vast bowls decorated with transfer-printed blue Staffordshire glaze. But there is something a little unseemly in even the most unsuccessful artist's abandoning the palette for the privy.

But to get back to the Main Drainage Scheme itself.

There was one competent—if short-sighted—engineer employed on the scheme: Joseph Bazalgette, the man who was afterwards to give London its Thames Embankments.

If it is possible to succeed too well, Bazalgette did it. He dug up most of the streets of London, and laid earthenware pipes along them. He connected the privies of thousands of private houses and commercial buildings to the under-road sewers, and conducted the whole of London's waste to the Thames, where . . . it remained.

This apparent defiance of a Law of Nature so firmly accepted as fact that even sentimental poets and writers had used it as stock material for countless generations—'And even the weariest river winds somewhere safe to sea'— puzzled Lord John Russell and Bazalgette, and drove *Punch* nearly insane.

Presumably the limpid waters from the Cotswolds *did* travel to join the sea at the Thames Estuary. And presumably those waters, growing more soiled as they approached London, *did* carry the orts and ordure away with them. Salmon had been able to live in the Thames (at London Bridge) until the middle of the 18th century: not even the most repulsive crustacean could survive in the waters which now lapped the foundations of the new Parliament buildings—and what is more, in the shadow of the only-two-years-completed Victoria Tower, our legislators were angrily debating whether or not to abandon Barry's masterpiece, and move the two Houses of Parliament, lock, stock and barrel, up-river to Hampton Court Palace.

For if the stench of the Thames was insupportable as one strolled (one never dared take tea) on the Members' Terrace, the stench inside was even worse. Members of a religious cast began to wonder if some physical analogue of the back-biting and double-dealing were not making itself apparent, and that the corruption of mind was not being matched with a like corruption of the surroundings.

The fact is that an open sewer, which ran across the site of the new Houses of Parliament, had been sketchily covered up with the thinnest of stone slabs, and the gorgeous and costly edifice, made of the most perishable stone known to man, erected over the open sewer.

Bazalgette solved the problem—after his fashion. But it was to be many years, many decades, before Sun and Sewer ceased to make themselves noticeable simultaneously.

The Victorian habit of closing the windows tightly, and sealing both doors and windows with green and red baize 'sausages' filled with sand, was a habit not only deriving from, but positively commanded by, the all-pervading stench which came from the polluted river.

Not everybody, of course, lived by the river; and when the wind was not blowing from the Thames, the air was sweeter then than it is now, when even the meanest back street is reeking with the fumes of imperfectly burnt petrol or Diesel oil.

There were no mechanical substitutes for the domestic servant then, as there are to-day. No vacuum-sweepers, no patent detergents, no quick-acting scourers for bath or cooking-pot.

But there were, of course, so many domestic servants in Britain—the total is estimated at 1,000,000: five per cent of the population—that inventors could find no financial backing for most 'labour savers'.

What would have been the point in putting a patent carpetsweeper on the market? No one would have bought it.

These 'improvements' were to come later—and social changes having an economic basis brought them in. It was, as we shall see later, the Typewriter which eventually made the Vacuum Cleaner and the Refrigerator not only desirable and saleable, but necessary.

But in larger matters the Victorians' irrepressible innovating spirit was setting up the pattern for our own world.

Digging was going on in London in that year of 1860 for reasons other than those connected with the construction of the main sewers.

At night, crowds of 'loafers' used to collect at the sides of huge trenches, and watch the workmen excavating by the trembling plumes of yellow light which burst from the naphtha flares.

At the end of the preceding year, the surveyors had finished their work, and now the navvies were cutting trenches or demolishing houses, so as to cut trenches beneath. London—the world—was seeing the construction of the Metropolitan Railway, already named 'The Underground Railway' by the Londoners who gathered about the fencing which divided spectators from labourers. Some came to wonder, most came to condemn: there were grave prophecies that, even before the 'cut-and-cover archways' (as the tunnels were officially described) could be completed, the houses remaining above would collapse into the subterranean workings.

Reports of trouble at Farringdon confirmed the pessimists in their opinions. The Fleet River had overflowed into the workings, on one occasion to a depth of ten feet, and men had had to pump for days to clear the huge cutting that they had made.

For London's rapid growth had come about when the railways had linked the capital with all Britain; and cheaply and swiftly, people, seeking work or only amusement, had poured into the metropolis.

The traffic congestion had become so serious that, as early as 1845, a Royal Commission had been appointed to sit and examine proposals for a solution of the problem of getting London's traffic moving again.

Among those who came before the commission with reasonable suggestions (like all Royal Commissions, this was no exception, and all the cranks in Britain pressed forward eagerly to attend this Cranks' Sabbath) was Charles Pearson, Member of the Common Council, and Surveyor to the City of London.

The proposition which had come before the commission with the most influential backing was that a central railway-terminus should be built, to which all the main-line termini, then at what were the very outskirts of London, should be connected.

But even the commission could imagine the chaos which would render the proposed station useless for all practical purposes.

Cabs would fill the tributary streets for miles around, and even foot-passengers might have been expected to have some difficulty in reaching a station upon which all those desirous of leaving London would converge.

Charles Pearson, too, rejected the idea of a central station; but he did not reject the idea of linking up the termini.

His proposition, however, was that the main-line stations should be linked with a 'ring railway'—an 'Inner Circle'—*and that this railway should run beneath street-level.*

Charles Pearson was an influential man, and a persistent one. He knew, too, how to handle what have come to be called 'public relations', and not only did he organize and inspire a 'Ginger Group' to plead his case within the two Houses of Parliament; he pamphleteered and lectured incessantly. Best of all, he persuaded his friends in the City that the scheme would be financially profitable; and by 1853—the year in which Admiral Nachimov's destruction of the Turkish fleet at Sinope precipitated the Crimean War— the first of the two Metropolitan Railway Acts was passed.

The directors were authorized to ask for one million capital, with additional borrowing powers to increase this by a further £300,000.

Before the railway was completed, a further £200,000 was borrowed from the Common Council of the City of London; but within a year or two of the railway's opening in 1863, that sum had been repaid with a handsome interest.

It is interesting to see how the Victorians tackled a traffic problem quite as grave as that which confronts us to-day. All but the newest streets of that centuries-old London were excessively narrow; and the slow-moving and relatively unmanoeuvrable horse-traffic produced, by its very nature, traffic-blocks which could last, not for hours, but for days on end.

Nowhere does this boldly innovating spirit of the Victorians show more plainly than in the imaginative resolution with which they first worked out a solution to the problem, and then went on—against all prejudice—to apply it. Remember that there were no precedents for a subterranean railway: the gloomy prophets could well have been right—as well as gloomy. The houses *might* have collapsed, as the subsoil was cut away.

Pearson and his friends were prepared to risk a subsidence of London's houses as total as that which overtook Lisbon a century before. The possible loss of life did not worry them—or, rather, it did not deter them.

They were the characteristic products of the greatest age of experiment in the world's history. There seemed to be a promise of solving a problem which must be solved: they could not have held back from trying the solution.

Now, in the spring of 1860, crowds were gathering about the cutting: the work, by day and by night, was going on.

We take this colossal undertaking for granted: it was finished twenty-two years after the first shovelful of earth had been lifted in 1859; though the first section, from Paddington to Farringdon, was completed in just over three years. But when we take it for granted, we forget that the constructors of the world's first Underground Railway had tools no different from those with which the Romans excavated the harbour-basin at Ostia. Pick, shovel, paviour's rammer, pulley-block, tackle, shear-legs—these were all that the Romans had, and these were all that the British navvies had who built the Metropolitan Railway.

Above ground, too, work of a progressive nature was going on.

In October 1860 the first Victoria Station was opened by its proprietors, the Victoria Station and Pimlico Railway, in a collection of weather-boarded huts which were to handle passenger business for nearly fifty years, when the present handsome (though, under national ownership, sadly dingy) buildings were erected. The adjoining Grosvenor Hotel was, however, put up in the following year; and escaping the discomforts of the wooden huts, the traveller to London was assured of comfort at the Grosvenor, which had a management capable of refusing admittance to Cora Pearl, one of the most notorious of those international strumpets who were, to the sixties, what the pin-up film actress is to the present time—a means by which the deprived could enjoy, vicariously, lush living, unworked for.

Not everybody, of course, was buiding railways, either below or above ground, and though there were building activities of a non-railway nature to take the gapers to Hyde Park in 1861 (they were digging the foundations of some works in connection with the Westbourne River) the idlers (most of them) preferred to entertain themselves with a spectacle which, in the sixties, attracted both High and Low, Rich and Poor: the spectacle of Vice, brazen and unashamed. If any sight was calculated to take the force out of the Reverend Mr Spurgeon's assurances that the evildoer never prospered, it was the sight of the wealthy strumpets gathered in their carriages alongside the Achilles statue: an imposing example of sculptured masculinity which had been provided with a bronze fig-leaf only a good many years after the 'Ladies of England' had subscribed to present it to the nation, as a tribute to those who fought in the Napoleonic Wars.

'There can be no disguising the fact,' *Paul Pry* reported in 1857, 'that in the West End, at Brompton, at St John's Wood, Foley-place, Portland-road, Regent's Park, and intermediate spots, some of the most magnificent women in London live under the protection of gentlemen.'

There could hardly be any disguising of the fact, for when these 'magnificent women' were not entertaining their protectors in the prim little stuccoed villas of St John's Wood—'The Grove of the Evangelist', in Victorian upper-crust slang—they were meeting established or prospective lovers in Hyde Park, in full view, not only of the admiring, envious mob in general, but of the mothers, wives, fiancées or prospective wives of the gentlemen in question.

In the cant of the day, these well-established harlots—every one of whom could ride a horse or handle the reins with equal skill—were collectively known as 'the pretty horsebreakers', a title which seems to have been conferred upon them by the writer of a letter to *The Times*.

There was not a newspaper or magazine in England—and no exception will be made of the newly established *The Queen, The Lady's Newspaper*, produced by Samuel Orchart Beeton, at the end of 1861—which did not devote columns of type, day after day, week after week, to the activities of 'the pretty horsebreakers'.

Often this comment was presented in the form of stern denunciation, not only of the pretty horsebreakers themselves, but, more, of the standard of social values which could permit their flaunting their material success in public places.

But Mr Cyril Pearl is right in pointing out that the widespread editorial use of this phrase, 'the pretty horsebreakers', suggests—in Mr Pearl's words—'the good-humoured, even affectionate tolerance' with which, by the upper classes at least, these enterprising creatures were regarded.

Students of semantology (Mr Pearl adds) discussed the social implications of these and other coinages. 'The very fact that we have lost sight of the old-fashioned language . . . is significant,' said the *Saturday Review* in 1860. 'We purposely use the term "street-walker" just now; but nobody else uses the phrase, nor that of prostitute, to say nothing of more homely language. The term "Social Evil", by a queer translation of the abstract into the concrete, has become a personality. "Unfortunates" and "fallen sisters" are the language of the sentimental.' There was a current story of a young woman in the street who was given a tract by an evangelist, and entreated to go home and read it; she looked at him bewilderedly for a moment or two, and exclaimed, 'Lor bless you, sir, I ain't a social evil, I'm waiting for a bus.' The *Saturday Review* commented that the society that supplied these euphemisms had done something to break down the barriers of virtue.

'The straightforward names that our fathers used have been repudiated by the delicacy of the age,' the same journal commented in 1862. In coarser times, words were employed to represent facts; but in proportion as the facts became more numerous and more obtrusive, the words which represent them have become obsolete and shocking.

Many circumstances have undoubtedly been invented to describe . . . the highly-tinted Venuses who form so favourite a study of the connoisseurs of the Haymarket. . . . But on the whole, the nicest, the softest, the most poetical designation we have heard is that which the Penitentiaries have invented—"soiled doves". . . . The time will no doubt come when this, too, will be thought too coarse and too direct.'

Here the writer is merely citing the history of every euphemism, whether it applies to prostitutes or privies. It is a fact that all euphemisms tend eventually to take on the 'indelicacy' of the word that they originally displaced. Another observation that I am tempted to make is that the writer in the *Saturday Review* may well have had his indignation inspired by a little natural human jealousy. Authors and freelance fiction-writers were well paid throughout the latter half of the 19th century; but staff-journalists were not. Dickens may well have received his guinea-a-day as law-court reporter of the *Morning Chronicle* in 1827, but the Aldine Press, as late as the nineties, was setting a fair standard by paying its staff-writers at the rate of 3s. 6d. for a thousand words of copy: if the industrious hack churned out his regular 30,000 words during the week, he could expect to take home a five-pound note at the end of it.

My researches into this delicate subject of journalists' remuneration shows that the sub-editors and 'features men' of the sixties got between £2 and £3 a week: even with his great fame, George Meredith could never persuade Chapman & Hall to pay him more than £5 a week as their Chief Reader—and this when he was one of the most respected novelists and poets in the English-speaking world.

There was possibly a good deal of jealousy in these denunciations of the 'pretty horsebreakers', with their spanking turn-outs, their clothes by Worth, their jewels, their houses, their liveried servants.

It was the custom to refer to the better-known of these harpies (from the Greek, *harpázo*, to rend as a bird of prey rends) by classical or pseudo-classical pseudonyms.

George Augustus Sala, one of the better-paid of contemporary journalists (he was the star-writer who established the circulation of the newly-founded *Daily Telegraph*) fairly let himself go on the subject of the Top Tarts. George, whose huge nose had been made even huger when it was split in a fight, and stitched up in an amateurish fashion immediately afterwards, may well have been the original of 'The Dong with a Luminous Nose'—and his literary style was as roseate and ample as his conk. But, loving booze and women, gregarious to a fault, and inquisitive to a virtue, George Augustus Sala (some unkind people derived the word 'salacious' from his surname) is *the* great source of information about the *feel* of the gaslit London of a century gone. It is curious, then, that his initials spell the word 'Gas'.

Hear George on the 'pretty horsebreakers'—no jealousy here!

> The Danaës! The Amazons! The lady cavaliers! The horsewomen! Can any scene in the world equal Rotten Row at four in the afternoon and in the full tide of the season? Watch the sylphides as they fly or float past in their ravishing riding-habits and intoxicatingly delightful hats; some with the orthodox cylindrical beaver, with the flowing veil; others with roguish little wide-awakes, or pertly cocked cavaliers' hats and green plumes. And as the joyous cavalcade streams past . . . from time to time the naughty wind will flutter the skirt of a habit, and display a tiny, coquettish, brilliant little boot, with a military heel, and tightly strapped over it the Amazonian riding-trouser.

Each age has its fashions in tolerance, as it has its fashions in rebuke. To-day, Society finds it in its power to tolerate the titled or professionally successful sodomite; a century ago, Society extended an equal tolerance to the impudent, wealthy whore.

Of all these women, none was more impudent, successful, admired, envied and emulated—even by the respectable—than Catherine Walters, the bewitching 'Skittles', who can claim the unique credit of having been described in verse by a Poet Laureate.

It was no Poet Laureate, however, who wrote the following—though the jingle sums up Skittles pretty well:

> In Liverpool in days gone by,
> For ha'pence and her wittles,
> A little girl, by no means shy,
> Was settin' up the skittles.

But, if Skittles had acquired her nickname from having been a skittle-alley attendant in Liverpool, she came, according to Ralph Nevill (whose forgotten books of Victorian gossip I recommend to the curious reader) from Newcastle-on-Tyne, where her father had employment as the master of a small Tyneside collier.

Sir William Hardman, who has been called 'A Nineteenth-Century Pepys'—an exaggeration—describes Skittles in terms which show that one, at least, of the Victorians was not averse from using those old-fashioned words whose passing the writer in the *Saturday Review* deplored. Writing to his friend, Edward Holroyd, in December 1862, Hardman (who was later a Lord Lieutenant of Surrey) had this to say of Skittles:

> ' "Anonyma" is "Skittles", or according to the name on her cards, Miss Walters, of equestrienne and pony-driving celebrity. "Anonyma" was the name given to her by *The Times*: "Skittles" was bestowed upon her by equally discreditable sponsors, as follows. The fair Walters was in liquor, and being chaffed by sundry gentlemen of the baser sort, she informed them in drunken but flowing periods that "if they didn't hold their bloody row, she'd knock them down like a row of bloody skittles!" Thenceforth she was known as "Skittles". A whore, sir, much sought after by fast young swells. Well, my friend, she has bolted to that hot-bed of abomination, the City of the West, New York, to wit. Her luxuriously decorated house is in the hands of the auctioneer, but horses and carriages are sold; fair patricians, eager with curiosity to know how such a one lived, and if possible, to learn the secret of her attractions to the young men of their acquaintance, throng to the deserted halls of "Skittles", and admire *le cabaret* with its seat padded with swansdown. . . . Skittles has bolted with a man of good family. His name is Aubrey de Vere Beauclerk!'

With Skittles's combination of extraordinary good looks—but good looks which were completely feminine—superb horsemanship, and impudence which had nothing feminine in it, there is no mystery in her outstanding success as a harlot.

Ralph Nevill tells an illuminating story about this woman.

A fine rider to hounds, she was present one day when the Pytchley met. It was useless for the more respectable members of the hunt—women or men—to protest: Skittles at that time was under such exalted protection: of Lord Hartington, the future Duke of Devonshire, that no one could do otherwise than accept, with grace more or less good, the fact that Skittles was there—to stay.

But, as mile after mile of the flat, heavily fenced country was covered, and many less skilful horsemen and horsewomen had fallen out, those who rode with Skittles felt a sincere admiration for this rider as fearless as she was skilful.

At the hunt's end, one gentleman, who had not been among those who welcomed Skittles, sought to make up for his original disapproval by paying her some lightly courteous attention.

Said he: 'May I say, Miss Walters, how pleasantly the wind has brought the colour to your cheeks?'

'Oh,' Skittles replied, nonchalantly (and characteristically), 'you should see my bloody arse!'

Skittles, in fact, had made more spectacular captures than a cadet member of the ducal house of Beaufort: within a few months of her having arrived in London, without even the pretence of looking for 'honest livelihood', Skittles had been installed in a splendid house in Mayfair, with servants, horses, carriages, and an irrevocable annuity of £2,000 a year (tax-free, of course), that she was to enjoy until the end of the first World War.

The provider, in this case, was the young Marquess of Hartington, later the eighth Duke of Devonshire, and father-in-law of Mr Harold Macmillan. A statue of Spencer Compton, eighth Duke of Devonshire, stands at the junction of Horse Guards-avenue and Whitehall; and the passer-by, stopping for a moment to examine the statue recently condemned by a leader-writer in the *Daily Express*, might well look for traces, in that grave, bearded visage, of the spark who was the first notable protector that Skittles, in a lifetime of influential friendships, was to make.

Another of Skittles's distinguished friends—though one who derived his distinction from brains rather than blood—was Wilfrid Scawen Blunt, who met Skittles when he was twenty-three, and was with her that afternoon in August, 1920, when she had the stroke from which, two days later, she died.

Skittles, like all the most famous harlots of her day—save only the simian Cora Pearl—passed from harlotry to a state of intense respectability. This was as true of Laura Bell, who shook down the Nepalese Minister, Prince Jung Bahadur (who was also the brother of the King of Nepal) for a sum that rumour confidently reported to be in the neighbourhood of a quarter-million pounds sterling.

This most successful coup of Laura 'of the pretty, doll-like face' gave rise to a legend which, in its characteristic Victorianism, might belong equally well to the Reverend J. G. Wood's *Boys' Own Paper* ('With Roberts to Candahar', say) as to Lady Cardigan's racier memoirs.

The innate sentimentalizing drive of the Victorians could—and did—attach 'patriotism' equally to an heroic midshipman at Sebastopol or to a far-sighted trollop in bed at Claridge's.

This is the story. After having enjoyed Laura's company, and paid handsomely for the privilege, H.R.H. the Nepalese Minister left London to return to his mountain kingdom.

From there, by yak-express, he sent her a magnificent ring as a token of his undying esteem. (One falls into clichés when repeating this sort of story.) With the ring came the letter, in which the princely writer assured Laura that if ever she needed assistance she had only to call upon the writer to receive it.

Laura left harlotry, and with her quarter-million, found herself a respectable husband, Captain Augustus Frederick Thistlethwayte, grandson of a Bishop of Norwich. The pair set up house at 15, Grosvenor-square, and people even more respectable than Captain Thistlethwayte were pleased to accept his wife's invitations to dinner.

The Indian Mutiny broke out, and one of the guests, having heard the story of the ring and promise from Laura, got in touch with the India Office, which, by Laura's consent, despatched ring and letter to the Government of Nepal, requesting that Nepal either throw in its forces on the side of Britain, or, if that were impossible, remain neutral.

Thus Nepal did not take up arms with the rebels, and those Ghurka regiments serving under the British flag maintained their allegiance.

Unfortunately, I have read a different version of the story which begins with Laura's collaring the Prince's quarter-million.

The Prince had come to England to negotiate a treaty of amity and commerce between Nepal and British India. There was no doubt that the Nepalese were eager to sign such a treaty and secure the backing of the British Government, for they had been defeated in battle by the Tibetans, who had lured the Nepalese troops up to 18,000 feet, and then slaughtered the invaders, who could do no more than pant in the rarefied atmosphere of an altitude only 9,000 feet lower than that of Everest's peak.

Unfortunately, after having been dropped at his hotel by suave F.O. types, the Prince was picked up by Laura, and robbed of his £250,000. (In jewels, they said.)

When the suave F.O. types came on the following morning to collect the Prince for further discussion of the proposed treaty, they found an outraged Oriental just sane enough to demand that either the British Government repay him his quarter-million or he would pack his bags and take off for St Petersburg.

It says something for the Victorians that even their civil service could find cash in an emergency. The India Office paid. The treaty was signed. Nepal's neutrality was assured.

And no one could do anything about Laura. . . .

I quote the legend of the ring and the letter from Prince Jung Bahadur, not because I think there is any truth in it, but because both the invention of the story and the general contemporary belief in it are so typically, so thoroughly Victorian. All the same, 'doll-like' Laura *did* manage to acquire a lot of cash.

It need hardly be said that both Laura and Skittles—after their 'redemption', of course—were friends of Gladstone, whose partiality for even not-yet-rescued 'Social Evils' Sir Philip Magnus has described and 'explained' in the pages of his admirable life of the politician.

When, in the manner known to prima donnas and their agents, Gladstone had made innumerable 'farewell performances', allowing himself each time to sacrifice himself for a country and people who would collapse without his omniscience, he came at last to the realization that there really had to be a farewell performance which was final.

He made his decision. He announced his intention to the House, and this time all who listened to him knew that the Grand Old Man was really going to leave them. At last.

He set off for Buckingham Palace, to tender his resignation to the Queen.

But first of all, he called on Mrs Thistlethwayte, and it was she, and not her Sovereign, who first heard, from the lips of Gladstone himself, that a notable, if not very productive, parliamentary career was over. At last.

Unlike Skittles, who merely achieved respectability, Laura—Mrs Thistlethwayte—achieved both respectability (Captain Thistlethwayte and No. 15, Grosvenor-square) and something that no one could quite decide whether or not to call notoriety.

But notoriety of a vastly different kind from that which had caused everyone at the Opera to stand and watch her entrance and departure.

Laura not only 'saw the light', but—interpreting the Gospel admonition literally—went out into the highways and byways to preach the Word and call sinners to repentance. Laura's description of herself was 'A sinner saved by grace through faith in the Lamb of God'.

'Her intellectual capacity was almost phenomenal, and to this was added a very poetical imagination. Her appearance on the platform of the Polytechnic was a realization of beauty and art. Mrs Thistlethwayte was not much inferior to Spurgeon. '

'Is it not strange, ' Sir William Hardman wrote, in 1862, 'to recall the time when she was the Queen of London whoredom, and had the Nepalese ambassador in her meshes. . . . '

Strange, indeed, to Hardman, perhaps—as it is strange to us.

But not so strange to her contemporaries. They understood the pattern of their contemporary existence; and only because we understand a different, newer pattern, do we find Mrs Thistlethwayte's 'conversion' strange—and ludicrous.

The 'sinner saved by grace' gave tea-parties at her mansion in Grosvenor-square, to which the converted and the unconverted—but both highly respectable—were pleased to come. Gladstone came, and brought his wife; and the mysterious death of Captain Thistlethwayte in Diamond Jubilee Year—he was found in bed, shot by his own revolver—did not put a stop either to Mrs Thistlethwayte's evangelical work or to her friendship with the Gladstones.

But even when they did not—perhaps could not—'see the light', these high-class trollops of the Golden Age of Harlotry achieved social rank, if not social acceptance. Gentlemen of blood and fortune were prepared, not only to keep them, but to marry them—often with disastrous, but hardly surprising, results.

'Mad' Windham, squire of Felbrigg Hall, Norfold, married Agnes Willoughby, mistress of Giuglini, the famous tenor. Had that been all that scandal might have brought against Agnes, one might have forgiven Windham; but Agnes, another of the famous 'pretty horsebreakers', had known hundreds of men besides the Italian tenor; and in 1862, Felbrigg, which had been in the Windham family for many centuries, passed into the hands of Windham's creditors.

An income of £16,000 a year had been insufficient for the insatiable Agnes; but when, in order to save his inheritance, General Windham, 'Mad' Windham's uncle and heir-at-law, demanded that a commission *De Lunatico Inquirendo* should pronounce on the young man's sanity (and thus on his power to break the entail, and squander the family estates), the commission found 'Mad' Windham sane.

He had always liked to drive the Norfolk coach, collecting fares in a broad Norfolk accent, that he used 'as to the manner born'. Happy now to have disencumbered himself of his ancient heritage, Windham asked for, and got, the job of driver on the Norfolk stage. His income was £1 a week, allowed to him by the uncle whom he had robbed by his own folly and his wife's greed.

Agnes had now set up house with Giuglini, and after Windham's death from drink she left Giuglini and married George Walker, agent of the Hanworth Estate—one of the few estates left in the Windham family. Her son proved that he was, for all the gossip, the true son of his reputed father when, at his twenty-first birthday party, he lost £5,000 at a single sitting of cards.

When mother and son died in the same year—1896—the ancient family of Windham was extinct. Agnes was a little late in coming to the traditional harlot's haven of respectability, but she got there at last, and when she died, she had been respectable—after a fashion—for close on forty years.

But even royalty—albeit illegitimate royalty—was not beyond the power of these astonishing women. Kate Cook, in whose photographs one looks in vain for a trace of personal beauty, elegance or wit (she looks, in fact, just like a cook in a *Punch* drawing of the time) made the most spectacular match of all when she married the Earl of Euston, son and heir of the Duke of Grafton, a title created by Charles II for one of his several bastard sons.

We shall see later how this incredible marriage turned out—here it will suffice to record the fact that Kate, one of the grossest and least scrupulous of these strumpets, had actually managed to marry into the Blood Royal of Great Britain.

Talk of Mrs Thistlethwayte's evangelical campaign—a campaign interrupted neither by her debts nor by the suicide of her husband—reminds us that there is no scene more fittingly illuminated by gaslight than a religious meeting.

Most of Victorian religion of the 'established' sort was, like Spinoza's love of God, rather of the intellectual than of the emotional kind. The Victorians supported religion because they were able to identify it with that Order which is Heaven's First Law—but since we remarked that the Victorian was the most innovating age in history, religion did not, could not, escape the innovating influences of the age.

And not everybody found, in 'established' religion, the emotional satisfaction that a strongly mystical element in Victorianism needed.

It is no paradox to state that the Victorians, for all that they believed in the correctness of what they did, were still filled with that guilt which is the conscious emergence of an inner insecurity.

They believed that what they did was right, because they believed that they did what they did because it was right to do it. But they were already feeling insecure in relation to the stability of the system that they had maintained (there was plenty of social criticism, and ardently amateur 'reform' about), and since the Welfare State is based upon the guilt that the established feel in possessing in the midst of deprivation, we must look for the beginnings of the Welfare State, not in the Beveridge Report, nor even in the schemes of 'social insurance' that Lloyd George adapted from the German system, but in the 'good works' with which every Victorian with tuppence to put in a collecting box busied himself or herself, in a greater or a lesser degree.

'The poor ye have always with you'—but when the presence of the poor makes the rich feel somewhat uncomfortable, then it is the end of the rich, though it will not be the end of the poor.

But not everyone who feels uncomfortable—guilty—in having more than his neighbour, wishes to share it with the less well-off.

An easier solace is to 'be good', and the easiest way in which one can 'be good' is to take to religion. The rise of Victorian interest in religion is in direct proportion as the menace of the 'have-nots' pressed more strongly on the awareness of the 'haves'.

Strange faiths flourished, and because there is nothing more contagious than emotional imbalance, the 'innocent' took to religion as eagerly as did the 'guilty'.

The fashionable could gather at Lord Lytton's house in Park-lane, to commune with the spirits through the obliging agency of Daniel Dunglas Home—that reputed levitationist who convinced so hard-headed a scientist as Sir William Crookes, F.R.S., and was equally unsuccessful with the equally hard-headed Robert Browning, who savagely castigated Home as 'Mr Sludge, the Medium'.

(It says something for the value of 'religion' to a man like Home, a Scotsman of more than dubious parentage, that when he married a Russian Princess, the Emperor Napoleon III gave the happy pair a magnificent wedding-present.)

The not-so-fashionable could pay their sixpences and shillings at the door of the Polytechnic, to listen to Mrs Thistlethwayte call them to repentance through the Blood of the Lamb, or take a bus to the Elephant, to hear the same call from the Reverend Mr Spurgeon, an off-beat divine who would always endorse any patent remedy, from a hair-restorer to a laxative, for the appropriate fee.

But the poor were not neglected in this wave of revivalism. The sixties saw the rise of William Booth, the Salvation Army 'general', and the first shaky beginnings of his vast empire on which, unlike that of the now defunct British Empire, the sun never sets.

We shall consider the bizarre phenomenon of the 'General's' success later but here it must be pointed out that the Salvation Army is perhaps the one perfect manifestation, surviving to modern times, of God as Revealed by Gaslight; and if scholars—but only classical—can detect a striking resemblance between the excesses (including the peculiar terminology) of the Early Christians and the Early Salvationists, this is because both Primitive Christianity and Salvationism sprang from similar economic tensions.

Religious fervour, of course, cannot exist without violent religious prejudice; and *Punch*, already 'respectabilizing' itself, set itself up as the champion of 'sane'—that is, unemotional—religion against the assaults of corybantic Nonconformity.

To *Punch* of the sixties, Cardinal Wiseman ('The Scarlet Lady'), Pusey, Wilberforce ('Soapy Sam') and Spurgeon ('The Reverend Sturgeon') were equally detestable, and equally to be attacked—week after week. In his more solemn moments, Mr Punch would denounce Confession—beloved of Catholic and Anglican alike—in terms whose seriousness outwitted any wit.

But that Confession should have caught on, even though only with the spoilt fine lady, shows a cracking of the solid self-assurance upon which the Victorian social ethos was founded, and with whose disappearance that ethos crumbled away.

In November 1861, the Prince Consort died, after having caught a severe chill when out shooting game, or it may have been typhoid.

He had been up to Cambridge to reason with his son and heir, Albert Edward, Prince of Wales, who had already, if there be anything in the story, fathered a future eminent Assyriologist on the pretty daughter of the Prince's laundress.

But, whatever the truth of this story, it is false only in detail: the implications of the story will stand every scrutiny.

The Prince had already shown disquieting evidence of a wayward nature most disturbing to a father whose sexuality, passionate though it was, was kept strictly confined within the permissibility of marriage.

Had the Prince Consort not gone up to Cambridge to see, to admonish and to reason, plead, with his errant son, he would not after have gone shooting. And would not have caught that chill—or that typhoid—from which he died.

It was the realization of these facts, and not out of any lack of sympathy with her son's affairs, that Queen Victoria turned against Albert Edward.

In the year after his father's death, the Prince of Wales came of age, and entered into the unrestricted enjoyment of the revenues of the Duchies of Lancaster and Cornwall—a total tax-free income of more than £100,000 a year.

He was granted his own establishment, and was given Marlborough House, built by Wren for John Churchill, first Duke of Marlborough, as his private residence.

What came, somewhat notoriously, to be known as 'the Marlborough House set' dates from this year. It may be noted, in passing, that Skittles,

Laura and the rest were all accepted members of 'the Marlborough House set'.

The dying Prince Consort's last act had been to demand to see—and to revise—the stern Note that Palmerston had addressed to President Lincoln on the subject of Lincoln's high-handed arrest of the two Southern envoys, Slidell and Mason, who had been taken off a British ship as they were bound for, respectively, the Courts of St James and Fontainebleau.

Palmerston, even before drafting the Note to Lincoln, protesting against this insult to the British flag and gross violation of international law, had despatched 8,000 British troops to the Canadian-U.S. border, and both Palmerston and the British people were ripe for a punitive expedition against the 'Yankees'.

The Indian Mutiny had shocked the British out of their complacent belief that, first, 'the natives' were grateful to be ruled by the British, and that, second, 'they couldn't fight save under British officers'. They could—and did. And murderously.

Not much satisfaction, again, had come out of the Crimean War. True, peace had been signed, but our principal ally (the Turks and the Sardinians and the Piedmontese didn't count) was showing every sign, only three years after the peace, of turning against us, arming Cherbourg with the heaviest guns that the world had ever seen, and calling up military classes five years ahead of schedule.

The Chinese War, too, though fought in order to prevent the Chinese Government's preventing the import of opium, and thus ruining the economy of Bengal, had turned out to be an unsatisfactory affair; the total result of which was the acquisition of the Treaty Ports—a handsome legacy for a future sixty years away—and the personal aggrandisement of Colonel Charles Gordon, C.B., R.E.

So that the prospect of a small, victory-assured war against the Union appealed to all. Only the Prince Consort was against it, and on his deathbed he managed so to revise the Note as to save Lincoln's face.

But the British were concerned only with the martial aspects of the quarrel with America—they neither appreciated the inevitable economic consequences of the American Civil War, nor would they have cared much had those consequences been pointed out.

But there was no war, and the inevitability of one of the most single-minded imperialisms of history was assured.

But against this background of international tension it was unlikely that the opening of a tea-shop in London should have been regarded as of even greater intrinsic significance than Palmerston's sending transports full of troops racing across the Atlantic.

Yet the opening of the Aerated Bread Company's first tea-shop at No. 10, Strand, in 1861 is, to the social historian, an event of far greater significance than anything which happened in that year on the High Contracting level.

'Aerated' bread was just another of those patent semi-panaceas which were a by-product of the ceaseless Victorian experimentation.

There was always activity—mostly of a 'practical' kind—and there were always unexpected and immensely 'practical' by-products.

To take one historic example: Joule, the Manchester brewer, called in a young French chemist, Louis Pasteur, to find out why Joule's beer was going sour—and losing him customers.

Pasteur had made a study of the process of fermentation, which is why Joule had called him in. When he had traced Joule's trouble to its source, Louis Pasteur knew almost everything that there was to be known about fermentation but, in learning that, he had stumbled upon the discovery of the bacillus—and so upon the realization of the true nature of infectious disease.

Joule himself, experimenting in quite another direction, was the first to determine the mechanical equivalent of heat.*

So with 'Aerated Bread'. That, too, was a by-product of pure experiment; but once invented, it had to find itself a market. And the best way in which to get a market for bread is to make people eat it—and like it.

The tea-shop was opened to accustom eaters to the new bread.

Actually, the tea-shop did more, far more, than that. It achieved the tremendously important effect of introducing a rival to the tavern; and it marked out, as it were, a place in readiness for the 'respectable female'—as distinct from the factory-girl—who had yet to enter commerce and industry.

When, with the invention of the typewriter, the New Woman emerged, the tea-shop was ready for her; eminently respectable, 'safe', cheap—and with a 'ladies' room'. It was with the provision of a 'ladies' room', to which women could retire with modesty and there find privacy, that the tea-shop made its future certain.

And when women entered the ranks of middle-class labour, they repaid the tea-shop. We shall note later how, as the public-houses of London became 'redundant' in their tens of thousands, the tea-shops multiplied, until not only the women clerks but the men, too, gathered there. Say this of the pub: it has gone down fighting—but matched against the tea-shop, it hadn't an earthly chance.

---

*To the unit of which he gave the name, 'erg'.

The women did that.

And 1861 saw the beginning of the revolution.

If old sins cast long shadows, great events have their roots in a past more or less remote. If it was to be Sholes's invention of the typewriter and its marketing, in 1873, by the Remington Firearms Company (talk about beating swords into ploughshares!) which finally 'emancipated' the educated unmarried woman from the thrall of governess-ship or unpaid domestic drudgery, the beginnings of the movement to employ 'refined females' had already begun.

The non-employment—more particularly, the non-employability—of women of a certain education was something peculiar to the first half of the 19th century. Earlier centuries than the 19th saw no prejudice against the employment of women in skilled jobs, and without suggesting that all female craftsmen and artisans of the 18th and 17th centuries were Hester Batemans or Angelica Kauffmanns, a glance at any parish-register will show how widely women had entered into competition with men in the more gainful walks of life.

This is not the place in which to trace the influence of the reaction against the 'liberal' ideas of the French Revolution on the position of women as bread-winners; but for fifty years or so, the taboo against women's entering the better-paid employments was strong enough to keep them out.

All the same, there are always pioneers—men who can see ahead, and have the courage not to wait until the inevitable is upon them.

Such a one was the famed Thomas Holloway, who, by industry and wealth, cleared his name from the charge of quackery, and has gained for himself the immortality inherent in his having a London district named after him. (That it was so named by a sort of accident, and not by intention, is only a further proof of how far he succeeded in establishing himself among the respectable.)

Thomas Holloway's shop and warehouse in the Strand, within a few doors of Temple Bar, was one of the sights of London—a London, by the way, far more given to making pilgrimages of this sort than is the London of today.

To show their employees at work was a popular and traditional self-advertising device with the employers of labour (readers will recollect that it was his having to paste on the blacking-bottle labels *while sitting in the window* of Day & Martin's shop in Chandos-street which so disgusted the young Charles Dickens).

The Americans, always so romantically traditional, have restored this custom of exhibiting their employees behind acres of plate glass. The advantage of this custom is that it not only draws the crowds—for there is no sight more pleasing to an idler than the sight of others working—but it ropes in, as it were, the public to act as invigilators over one's own staff.

Holloway welcomed visitors to his establishment, where, in 'conditions of refined delicacy', respectable females rolled pills, boxed them, labelled the boxes, and addressed the packages which took Holloway's cure-all boluses all over the world.

Holloway was viewed with somewhat dubious eyes when he started in business, and he had to flourish exceedingly before he became, with his gift of a hospital in North London, 'accepted'.

But there is no doubt that his demonstrating that nicely-brought-up young women could be employed in conditions which exhibited neither the soul-killing drudgery of the sweat-shop nor the coarseness of the factory had a profound effect on the development of the pattern of female employment.

Since we are on the subject of sweat-shops, it should be noted here that an official enquiry into working conditions among the women not employed in such establishments as Holloway's revealed that—to take but two examples of the incredible sweating of the sixties—a woman was paid 2½d. for making a shirt, complete with frilled front, *and using her own thread,* while for trimming those delicate parasols which look so enchanting in the patent aquatint-and-oil prints of Baxter and Le Blond, the wretched sempstress received the grotesque sum of a penny-farthing.

Food was to become cheap during the 19th century: that was one of the material benefits of Empire. But cheap food had not arrived in the sixties, and living conditions, for those incapable of earning more than the starvation-rates paid to needlewomen, were appalling.

Indeed, money generally was 'tight', and credit, even within the City of London, was very, very shaky.

In 1857, there had been a spectacular crash on Wall-street: in one day, over one thousand seemingly well-established firms had collapsed; but things were hardly better in London.

Two years before, the private bank of Strachan, Paul and Bates, established, as Snow's Bank, in the reign of Charles II, had failed with liabilities of close on a million pounds. That Baron Alderson had sentenced the three partners, Sir John Dean Paul, Bart, William Strachan and Robert Makin, to fourteen years' transportation did nothing to restore credit generally. The bank had collapsed in the middle of the Crimean War, but its failure could be attributed to nothing but dishonesty on the part of the three bankers.

Strachan's Bank was a particularly notorious example of failure, but had it been the only case of failure London's banking credit might not have suffered much. Unfortunately, there were many other failures.

The whole banking system fell into discredit. Money hid itself. What, then, was left in circulation, got 'dear', and employers found themselves in the happy control of a seller's market. The less scrupulous employers took full advantage of their position.

When a middle-aged Frenchman dropped down dead in Leicester-square from starvation, the coroner's jury brought in a verdict of 'Death from Natural Causes'.

A few doors away from Holloway's establishment were the offices of Samuel Orchart Beeton—whose initials spell, significantly, the word 'S.O.B.'. Mr Beeton is better known today for having been the husband of Mrs Beeton, but he was well known in his day on his own account, as a vigorously enterprising publisher of decidedly republican sentiments. In the pages of his journals, he was constantly attacking royalty, sometimes by not-so-subtle innuendo, often in direct denunciation. The extravagance and bad choice of friends of the Prince of Wales were favourite targets of Beeton's pen; but Queen Victoria bore him no malice, and when Beeton, as part of the publicity campaign to launch *Uncle Tom's Cabin* in England, asked the Queen to grant an audience to the author, Harriet Beecher Stowe, Her Majesty graciously consented to receive the chief publicist of the Abolitionist cause.

Temple Bar was pulled down in 1878, and the scandal attaching to its removal we shall consider later; but there are still some old houses and buildings which were standing in the sixties (two of the houses date from 1629) and it is possible, for all the rebuilding which has taken place about the site of old Temple Bar, to recapture something of the *feel* of the Strand as it was in the sixties.

The great 'improvement' which was to transform the appearance of this district where the City of Westminster joins the City of London had already been put in hand; and since 1852, the old houses of Butcher's-row—a grisly huddle of decaying 17th-century lodging-houses and cut-rate bordellos—had vanished, to make way for Street's new Law Courts.

Not until 1882 were the buildings finished, and the various Courts of Justice housed within the monastic Gothic of Street's masterpiece.

All during the sixties, the site of the new Law Courts was an open space, covered with the ruins of the tumble-down houses which had been demolished in the previous decade. Surrounding this vacant site and facing it were old houses which were—literally—leaning on Temple Bar (so much so, that when the Bar was pulled down, Holloway's pill establishment collapsed into the Strand.)

Nor were the houses the flat-fronted brick of the late 17th and early 18th centuries. They belonged to an older age, and their upper storeys projected in tiers above the roadway. Old pubs abounded—notable among them the Old Cock, in Fleet-street, with its entrance in Apollo-court, and the Palsgrave's Head, in the Strand, with its entrance in Palsgrave's-place.

At the corner of Chancery-lane a huge, half-timbered, lath-and-plaster building sagged ominously over the main road: though before the sixties ended this was pulled down to make way for the flamboyantly decorated red-sandstone establishment of Messrs Attenborough, the pawnbrokers.

There is something decidedly mysterious about the design—or, more accurately, the decoration—of this handsome building, which is still standing.

In a niche cut into the Strand elevation, there is the stone statue of a somewhat effeminate youth, dressed according to a romantic Victorian's idea of late 16th-century French dress.

On the plinth on which this statue rests are cut these lines from Byron's *Lara*:

> They were not common links that formed the chain,
> That bound to Lara Kaled's heart and brain.

The proximity of three shining golden balls on an elaborate wrought-iron bracket makes this quotation all the more obscure in intention. What has such a statue, and such a couplet, to do with pawnbroking?

The statue was bought at an exhibition at Alexandra Palace, but that does not explain why it is here.

Since we are in Fleet-street, let us look east to St Paul's, and try to recapture the vision of a century ago.

Spanning the bottom of Ludgate-hill was the railway via-duct which is still offensively there today; but spanning the bottom of Fleet-street was a 'pedestrian crossing'—a bridge of iron, with lattice-work sides, to which access was gained by a curving flight of stairs rising from each pavement.

The bridge was sufficiently high for buses and the larger furniture-lorries to pass beneath it, and the only reason why it was pulled down was a matter, not of its inconvenience, but of its indelicacy.

So many males halted on their errands to cluster about the bridge, so that they might catch a glimpse of what was beneath crinoline as the female road-crossers ascended and descended the newel staircases, that the City police combined with the City employers to denounce the bridge, not only as an infernal nuisance, but as an affront to delicacy and a temptation to loose thinking.

The iron bridge has gone, and so, too, have almost all the buildings that one would have seen as one looked down Fleet-street on any day in the sixties.

Indeed, at that time, the only 'modern' building was that of Hoare's Bank, built in 1831 from the designs of Charles Parker, the architect who also designed the doomed Stamford-street Chapel.

Every other house dated from not later than the preceding century, and though there had been a certain amount of refronting (usually a stucco rendering, in the 'classical' manner of William Herbert) most of the houses in Fleet-street dated from the 17th century, and there were several dating from the 16th century.

The only other 'modern' buildings, besides Hoare's Bank, were at Ludgate-circus, where the Circus itself was ringed with elegant stucco-fronted three-storey houses, having shops on the ground floor, which were built in 1825. Buildings of this type are still to be seen in the west Strand, though again their doom has been pronounced.

Passing through Temple Bar, the antique appearance of the street was preserved into the Strand; but let us notice that in those days Fleet-street, like so many other City streets, was full of hotels, and that in Salisbury-court was one of the most modern hotels in London: the Salisbury, now a block of offices.

To digress for a moment from the consideration of the Strand, it will be recorded that the sixties were not only the decade which saw the building of London's first Underground railway and the introduction of the residential flat (based on the Viennese model), but the carrying-out of a vast programme of hotel-building.

The modern hotel dates from the 1860s, and so little have we progressed in our attainment of comfort-in-living since those days that although the population of London has more than quadrupled during the past hundred years, we Londoners have lost no fewer than *three hundred* hotels of the first class since the beginning of this century.

No wonder that the finding of decent hotel accommodation by travellers and overseas visitors is so formidable a task today! No wonder that the pirate owners of ramshackle lodgings in Ladbroke-grove and the seedier tributaries of the Vauxhall Bridge-road can hold the desperate bed-seeker up to ransom, leaving their insatiable gas-meters to collect the last few shillings that the landladies' rapacity has left to the lodger!

But in the sixties, and for many years after the decade had closed, Anderton's Hotel, in Fleet-street, charged only 2s. a night, *with* breakfast. (Included in the service was a special waking-up system devised for the convenience of reporters going on duty.)

How well I remember the last days of Anderton's!: the swing-doors of bevelled plate-glass, opening up into a long, wide entrance-hall which ran the entire depth of the building.

The sides of it were lined with comfortable basket-chairs, embowered, for privacy, in a hot-house décor of potted palms.

Service hatches opened on to this hall-way, and ancient waiters, in shiny dress coats older than themselves, moved softly about on the worn carpet, bringing tankards of beer on tin trays which boomed with a faint, elfin sadness that this writer, at least, finds unforgettable.

There was no district of London in the sixties which had not its full, rich supply of hotels. From way down east, far beyond Aldgate Pump, to the distant confines of the west, just by the new suspension bridge which had spanned the Thames at Hammersmith, the hotels clustered thick about every principal street.

The Strand was even more full of hotels than was Fleet-street; though, of all the Strand hotels, Haxell's (where the Strand Palace Hotel now stands), Horrocks's (splendidly rebuilt in the sixties, at the corner of Norfolk-street) and Morley's (South Africa House has taken its place, and blotted out its memory) were the most famous.

But it was farther west that the new, 'palace' hotels were rising: the Buckingham Palace Hotel, in Buckingham-gate; the Westminster Palace Hotel, at the corner of the recently constructed Victoria-street; the Belgravia, in Grosvenor-gardens.

These three hotels are still standing: the first, once the offices of Imperial Chemical Industries (and formerly of Nobel Explosives) is again an hotel; the second has become Abbey House, a block of offices, too; and the third, again turned into offices, houses a group of firms which make metal containers for industry.

Then the great hotels were rising above every railway terminus: Euston, King's Cross, St Pancras, Cannon-street, Charing Cross, Holborn, Victoria (the Grosvenor), Paddington. . . .

The following decade was to bring even more splendid standards in hotel-design to London, when the new road—Northumberland-avenue—was built to connect Trafalgar-square with the Embankment.

Older hotels, such as Long's (to which Byron went for a drink after he had left Mr Murray's office, around the corner, and from which his lordship was expelled for having voided into a potted palm in the entrance-hall) and Mivart's, were redecorated, and in the case of Mivart's, renamed: it has been 'Claridge's' now for a century.

But though most of the big new hotels were rising around the new street which ran from Westminster Abbey to Pimlico—Victoria-street—

other grand hotels were rising in what, to us, seem most unlikely places. One of the grandest of the new hotels was the Inns of Court, which had a frontage on Holborn, and another on Lincoln's Inn-fields.

This vast and luxuriously appointed hotel (offering far more 'amenities' than any modern hotel would—or could—offer to its patrons) boasted a palm-decorated entrance-hall almost the size of a railway terminus's. And the advertisements which appeared in such publications as Henry Herbert & Company's expensively produced, *London: A Complete Guide* show that the Inns of Court Hotel was equipped with passenger-lifts—'ascending rooms', they were called in the hotel's notices. The Lincoln's Inn-fields frontage of the Inns of Court Hotel survived until 1936, when it was pulled down to make way for a modern building.

The influence behind the building of these great hotels, with their two, three, four and five hundred rooms, as well as that behind the building of the flats which were going up along Victoria-street, was not American but European—principally Austrian. English architects, for all that they knew (if only through reading Smollett) that the Edinburgh Scots had been living in flats for a couple of centuries, did not go north to Scotland, but south-east to Vienna, for instruction in the art of designing flats and hotels.

The origin of both has now been generally forgotten, but the debt to Austria was not only acknowledged at the time, it was used as a selling point: 'Apartments on one floor, constructed upon the principles adopted with such signal success throughout the domains of the Austro-Hungarian Empire.'

I shall consider, later, the difference between what Queen Victoria really was, and what slanderers have since represented her to be. I shall emphasize the Queen's lack of snobbishness: a trait that she shared with that other maligned monarch, King George IV. Both were what, in the loose modern phrase, we call 'intensely democratic'.

But here I should like to point out that all those Great Rulers of the 19th century were—well, I shan't use that odious word, 'democratic'; but—'accessible'. Turn the pages of any popular journal of the 19th century, and see how often such-and-such a homely product, from Schweitzer's Cocatina to Mellins's Food; from Eno's Fruit Salt (*Regd.*) to Apokathartikon Cleaning Fluid for Clothes, was advertised with a glowing testimonial from some crowned head. Heaven knows how the public relations officers of those days brought off such spectacular coups, but the fact is that His Imperial Majesty the Emperor Francis Joseph seemed always to be good for a tribute to some patent food, medicine or appliance.

I have examined the records of old-established businesses, and it was a pretty struggling firm whose bill-heads could not sport at least half-a-dozen coats-of-arms, all of reigning sovereigns of the first class. One of the fables which have tended to obscure the true picture of the 19th century is that 'Trade' was despised. The middle class, climbing from the commercial to the aristocratic, may well have despised its own origins; but royalty did not. At any international exhibition (and every state, even the remote Australian ones, organized them at regular intervals) orders of chivalry, not merely gold medals and diplomas, were awarded to prize exhibitors by the sovereign or president.

Many were the manufacturers of meritorious pickles or bloater paste who returned to their factories in Bermondsey or their homes in Dulwich or Streatham, proudly sporting the button of the Legion of Honour or Isabella the Catholic or the Rose of Lippe or St Stephen or SS Lazarus and Maurice.

This aside overtook me before I had a chance to explain that the 'favourite' foreign nation with the 19th-century English was Austria.

In the previous decade, there had been the unfortunate incident of General Heynau's visit to Barclay Perkins's brewery.

The general had been responsible for putting down the Hungarian revolt of 1848, and the story had circulated in Britain that he had caused Hungarian women to be stripped to the waist and flogged in public.

Some years later General 'Hyena', as the British called him, came to England on an official visit, and one of the interesting sights that he was to be taken to see was the great brewery on the Thames.

But word had got around that the general was due at Barclay Perkins's, and when 'Hyena' and his conducting party arrived at the brewery, the draymen were waiting for him.

They mocked him, they spat on him, they pelted him with handfuls of their own dray-horses' dung, they knocked his hat down over his eyes, they stripped him of his frock coat, satin waistcoat and frilled shirt (as they believed that he had stripped the Hungarian women), they threw him headlong into the horse-trough, and they would have ended up by killing him had not the police arrived in time to save him.

The British Government apologized humbly for this unfortunate occurrence. The draymen did not.

But even General 'Hyena' did nothing to cure the British—more especially the London English—of their romantic affection for Austria and the Austrians. And when in 1861 England and Austria sent a joint naval expedition to bombard Tripoli, in Turkish Syria, all felt that the incident of General 'Hyena' was due to be forgotten.

The fact is that the Austrian cutters had the reputation, in England, of making the best ladies' 'tailor-mades' in the world. It was admitted that no one could beat the English cutter when it came to making men's clothes, nor the French couturier when it came to 'frills and furbelows'; but when it came to 'tailor-mades', then the credit must go to the Austrians.

Why the British should have thought that cutting women's suits should have been more important than cutting off Hungarians' heads is merely another of those historical mysteries with which the backward-glancer may always amuse himself in trying to solve.

Still . . . there it is: the Austrians were popular; and nothing that they have ever done to Hungarians or Czechs, Serbs or Croats, has ever quite lost them that popularity.

Austrian tailors abounded in London until the beginning of the 1914 war; but one of the vanished features of Gaslit London was the number of Austrian hotels and restaurants. They were always cheap, always well-run, and though the waltz did not come from Vienna (it was brought back by the French revolutionary armies from Germany, and given a French polish in Paris, before being exported to England after the defeat of Napoleon) the music which made the waltz popular did. In every Austrian restaurant and hotel, stringbands, often with their members dressed *à la Tzigane*, played Viennese waltzes. London got its Johann Strauss, not from such places as the St James's Hall, but from the many Austrian restaurants and hotels.

Clear-cut divisions between this period and that are all right for the history books, but such clear divisions do not occur in history itself.

With all the modernity that we find in the London of the sixties—the Underground Railway, the lift, the telephone, the incandescent electric lamp; a successful wireless transmission across the River Tweed a decade old already; proposals for television; successful aeroplane and helicopter models already old history—with all these things (I had forgotten the sewing-machine) to link the sixties with today, there were all those other things which linked the sixties with the past.

After Sir James Young Simpson, Bt, had defied the 'ethics' of the Royal College of Surgeons by administering chloroform to Queen Victoria as she was being delivered of a child, that same child was then baptized by the Archbishop of Canterbury, his head covered by a full-bottomed wig. Not until the sixties did this last vestige of the ecclesiastical wig (with a history dating back to the Sumerians) disappear.

There was nothing more 'modern' than the extensive railway system which covered Britain. But the mode of running those railways was stamped with the manners of an earlier age.

No smoking was permitted on the platforms.

When the station-master of a country town saw a gentleman light up a cigar as he stood on the platform awaiting the train, the official stalked up to the offender, snatched the cigar from his mouth, and flung it angrily on to the line.

Then—and only then—did the hireling recognize, in the smoker, the Lord Viscount Palmerston—Prime Minister, Foreign Minister: whatever he was at that moment.

'I beg your lordship's pardon,' said the now obsequious jack-in-office. 'Had I realized that it was your lordship, I . . .'

My good man,' said the imperturbable 'Pam', 'so long as I thought you were a servant of the railway, merely doing his duty, I had nothing but respect for you. I now perceive that you are nothing but a damned snob!'

And talking of railways, it was at about this time that the great House of Smith had its beginnings, when W. H. Smith, later First Lord of the Admiralty, secured a concession from various railway companies to open his book-stalls on the station. As Smith was a roaring Noncomformist, there was no need for a railway company, which thought that even smoking a cigar on the platform was corrupting morals, to insist on vetting Smith's stock. With that other book-selling pillar of Chapeldom, Mudie, Smith exercised such a tyranny over the reading public that not one of our great novelists, from Dickens to Thackeray, from Lever to Trollope, was able to approach the facts of life save through the obscurest innuendo.

But to go back to this business of that mixture of the modern and the mediaeval that we find in the sixties: as Street's steam-tram rattled up and down the length of Victoria-street, and the Atlantic Telegraph carried news of the American Civil War from New York to London, men and women were still being hanged, in public, outside the county gaols—in the case of London hangings, outside that same Newgate Prison which had fallen to the assault of Lord George Gordon's followers.

The grim old prison, with its wonderfully suitable architecture (all soot-stained vermicular rustication, iron-studded wooden doors, grilles and rusting iron spikes), vanished only in 1903, when the modern Central Criminal Court rose on its site.

Few people walk now to the Central Criminal Court by choice; but in the Sixties it was, at certain times, one of the most attractive rendezvous in London.

It is generally accepted that it is more 'civilized' to execute criminals in private: but this admission comes rather from habit than from reason. If it be not only necessary that justice be done, but that, in addition, justice should be seen to be done, then private hangings go against this ideal. Who can say that the sentence of the law was really carried out? That sheriff and governor and parson and warders and hangman were not bribed to fake a death?

Unthinkable. . . . ? Maybe. But, in the sixties, men were not only still being hanged; they were seen to be hanged—and a high old time the spectators had at the hanging, too.

The long hours of waiting for the Nine o'Clock Walk the crowd beguiled as suited its thousand individual fancies. Anyway, the pubs which are still thick about the Old Bailey opened at 6 a.m., and the upper windows were as crowded in the sixties as they had been when my Lord Tomnoddy and Sir Carnaby Jenks (of the Blues) rented a room to see a man die in his shoes.

For those tho could read, *The Times*, ever in the forefront of the educational movement, prepared lavishly illustrated 'Lives' of the more popular criminals, and these were sold at a penny.

As I write, I have before me *The Illustrated and Unabridged Edition of The Times Report of the Trial of William Palmer, for Poisoning John Parsons Cook, of Rugeley*, published by Ward & Lock, 158, Fleet-street. For a penny the book must have been wonderful value: I myself did not mind giving two guineas for it, when I saw it on Rosenthal's shelves, in Oxford.

There is, in fact, a vast literature made up of the biographies of hanged men and women, and if the presses on which this cheap literature was turned out were the latest steam-powered rotaries, the sentiment behind the writing, as well as behind the hanging, linked the sixties intimately with the London not merely of Jack Sheppard but of Guy Fawkes.

Before the last war, on the pavement outside Henekey's wine-shop in Holborn Bars, there used to sit a blind man, with a black American-cloth apron draped over legs which ended at the knees.

The serenity with which he sat and displayed, the day's long length, his little stock of bootlaces and matches and collar-studs, was of a sort which is seen only on the faces of those blind whose minds come halfway between the dull apathy of the half-wit and the restlessness of the highly intelligent.

Around his neck, suspended on a brass chain which shone as though burnished with metal-polish, he bore a black tinware placard, neatly lettered in fading white.

One day, impelled by I knew not what inquisitiveness to put aside my somewhat self-conscious youthful good manners, I stopped to read the words written on the placard.

The man was a living—but just living—link with the sixties.

For the card told how, as a boy, he had been caught in the blast of the explosion which had rocked something more than Clerkenwell Prison, and the explosion had cost him his eyes and most of his legs.

The year was 1867, and the Irish Dynamiters, supplied with money and high-explosives by O'Donovan Rossa, from his headquarters in New York, had begun that long attack upon London's Underground and most of London's public buildings and monuments which, with intervals of respite both for the public and for the dynamiters, lasted from 1867 to the year of the Diamond Jubilee, then to be resumed just before World War II, and continued ever since.

Some Irishmen—'Fenians'—arrested on pretty clear evidence of complicity in a bombing, were locked up in Clerkenwell Prison.

Their friends still at liberty determined to rescue them from the clutches of the tyrannous Sassenach, and dynamite being in short supply (they had used it all up on the Underground) they decided to use gunpowder, which is still a pretty powerful explosive.

They filled a beer-barrel with gunpowder, set it against that part of the prison wall behind which they knew their comrades to be, and retiring prudently to a safe distance, waited for the bang.

It came. The gunpowder exploded. The wall collapsed. Windows for hundreds of yards around were shattered. Passers-by, including the blind match-seller, were injured, many gravely. And a prison officer was killed.

Next May, there was a hanging outside Newgate: Michael Barrett, the Fenian responsible for the death of the prison officer, stood on the drop. All the panoply of a judicial killing in the antique mode was there: the hangman in black, the chaplain in black-and-white, the condemned in his own shabby pepper-and-salt, with a white dunce's cap pulled over a whiter face. There was the chief warder with his huge keys—his badge of office—on a huge steel ring glistening with the use of years. There were subordinate prison officers drawn up behind him in military precision, the military aspect of the men being heightened by the French-type shakoes that they wore. Their silver buttons shone in the golden light of that May morning.

And the crowd. . . ! Sixty years before, on 27th February, 1807, thirty persons had been crushed to death in the rush to see a felon dancing on air; but this mob of 1868 did its best to live up to the famous old traditions—no fewer than nineteen persons were suffocated or trampled to death as Michael Barrett paid his debt.

Now, whether or not it was a good thing to hang a murderer must remain a matter of individual opinion; but this hanging had an effect quite unsought-for by the man who placed the barrel of gunpowder against the wall of Clerkenwell Prison.

The opponents of 'mediaevalism' had long been agitating for the abolition of public hangings; and the scandalous scenes at Barrett's execution gave them their long-awaited opportunity. Whilst the public was still shocked and guilt-stricken, the Abolitionists forced through an amendment to existing judicial procedure, and Barrett enjoys the dubious fame of being the last man in Britain to be hanged in public.

My Uncle Harry 'just happened to be passing by', when he saw the crowd which was filling Old Bailey from Newgate-street to Ludgate-hill. He knew that he couldn't force his way through the crowd, but, so he said, he knew of a back way, through Sea Coal-lane, and then through some alleys at the back of the shops and pubs lining the west side of Old Bailey.

'Saw it all,' he said. 'Tipped a cad half-a-sovereign to get me up to a window in the attic.'

'Well,' said I, fascinated by my own horror, 'what ... what was it like, Uncle? Was it ... terrible?'

'Nothing to it,' said Uncle, reaching for the Latakia with one shaky hand, and the whisky-decanter with the other. 'Nothing to it. All over in a minute. Never felt a thing. Merciful release.' He added, with the air of an after-thought: 'They don't have 'em any more. Crowd got out of hand.'

'I know,' I said.

'The year Napier put that blackamoor in his place,' said Uncle.

Only long afterwards did I realize that Uncle was talking of General Lord Napier of Magdala, and Theodore, King of Kings and Lion of Judah. . . .

Gaslight. . . .

Never was there illumination which had the power to cast shadows so dense.

Perhaps it is the gaslight which makes the Victorian scene so starkly a matter of contrasting, of irreconcilable, opposites.

Zenana and other Missions competing with the War Office to 'convert' the Black Man in their individual and highly characteristic ways: the War Office with the Lebel or the Martini-Henry rifle and the Gatling semi-automatic quick-firer, and the Missions with those machine-printed Bibles and Testaments that all the self-sacrificing, undemanding scholarship of the 19th century had translated into every tongue within or without the Empire. Yet both converging upon the same aim: to get the benighted Black to cover his nakedness with Manchester cotton, and so get back into work some or even all of those 3,000,000 cotton-operatives whom the American Civil War had thrown into the ranks of the hopelessly unemployed.

In Queen Anne's reign London had a population of six hundred thousand; by 1870, that figure had risen to over two million—and much of the rapid increase between 1830 and 1870 was due, in large measure, to the influx of men and women seeking the work which had been denied them or taken away from them in the provinces.

Not even Mayhew, that indefatigable and unsnubbable and infinitely courageous hunter of facts among London's depressed classes, can quite explain how the majority of London's slum-dwellers lived.

In the west, in Belgravia and Pimlico and Paddington and Hammersmith; in the north, in Islington and what we now call Holloway; in the south and south-east, in Dulwich and Norbury and Streatham and Brixton, a new London was arising—a London of semi-classical, stuccoed orderliness, in which the future Middle-Class domination was being incubated.

But there were parts of London which seemed to have the power to resist the compelling changes of that most innovating of all historical periods. There were pockets of slums at the backs of all the older fashionable areas: at the back of St James's-square, Grosvenor-square, Hanover-square, Queen-square, Covent Garden, and those City and East End squares, such as Loutherburg-square, which had not yet lost the respectability which went with their Queen Anne houses.

Especially did the City proper defy change: as late as 1910 there were mediaeval buildings to be found in such 'hubs of commerce' as Bishopsgate, St Mary Axe, Fenchurch-street and many other of the principal thoroughfares of the City. It was as late as 1910 that the late mediaeval mansion of Sir Richard Crosby, by that time a Lyons tea-shop, was taken, stone by stone (how narrowly it escaped the fate of other mediaeval relics!) and re-erected on Chelsea Embankment.

And just beyond the City's western boundary was one of the most extensive survivals of mediaeval and late mediaeval domestic architecture ever to have been found in a modern capital city.

Half a square mile of tiered, lath-and-plaster houses lay within an irregular rectangle, bounded on the south by the Strand, on the north by Holborn, on the west by Drury-lane and on the east by Chancery-lane, with, of course, penetrations through all these boundaries. At the back of Fleet-street, itself with hardly a modern building, there were no modern buildings save those which had been built in the Inner and Middle Temples at the beginning of the 19th century.

From Ludgate-circus to Charing Cross, over ninety-nine per cent of the houses, up to the last quarter of the 19th century, had been built before 1700; and it was not until 1907 that the proportion of old houses to new dropped below the fifty-per-cent figure, in the district of which we are talking.

It was not, indeed, until the coming of the big hotels to the Strand that it became, in any sense of the word, modernized, and even as I write there are still nearly two dozen Strand houses which were built before 1700—three of them retaining their original 17th-century plaster façades (you may see them in the Strand, just opposite The Royal Courts of Justice).

There is no doubt that this persistent dwelling in the shadow of late mediaeval London exercised a curiously retarding effect upon the minds of those who habitually passed their time among the decaying relics of a shuttered past. And since all around them Change was vigorously, imperiously demanding to alter everything, this obstinate hanging on to outworn physical conditions, and the outworn modes of thought and sentiment that living in such places induced, bred in the die-hard conservative elements of London's population an active, conscious, aggressive resistance to the liberal, innovating tendencies of the age.

So it was that, within this citadel of decaying lath-and-plaster, and hardly less decaying red-brick—equally delightful to the artists who sketched the exteriors, and to the bugs and cockroaches which infested the interiors—an open defiance of the developing Victorian convention was the certain dynamic of the vigorous, seedy life within this modern Alsatia.

Its most famous street (as well as its most picturesque) was Holywell-street, known to its more regular frequenters as 'French Letter-row'.

It was to this narrow street of lath-and-plaster houses, with its small, secret shops dealing in every sort of dubious goods, from literary and pictorial pornography to unlicensed firearms, aphrodisiacs and unexcised booze, that Dante Gabriel Rossetti came, to hunt up some recherché smut for Monckton Milnes's great pornographic library, 'Aphrodisiopolis', at his great country mansion, Fryston Hall, Yorkshire.

Here again is the strange dichotomy of the Dwellers by Gaslight: the ethereal author of *The Blessed Damozel*, looking like something out of a picture by Fabrizio da Gentile, poking about in the penny-boxes of French Letter-row, trying to find something filthy to send to his grand friend, Milnes.

And on one historic occasion, when he found something far different from the object of his search, his delight was such—again the contrast of gaslit glare and gas-born shadow—that he hurried home, to share his wonderful discovery with Swinburne—another 'collector' for Milnes's library.

What Rossetti, hunting for smut, had found was the remaindered first edition of *The Rubaiyát of Omar Khayyam*—price one penny.

Never can a penny have been better spent; never can a penny have bought so much!

I like to think of Dante Gabriel, standing outside the shop with the small, secret window, through whose dirty panes the dim light of a fishtail gas-flame hardly illuminates the penny-boxes on the pavement, straining his eyes to read the magic verses—all thought of more dubious writings swept happily away in the joy of discovering the authentic Vision—here, in this nasty little street, in the chill darkness of a London twilight, in the misty wind which pipes up from the oily, shadowed Thames.

That gaslit London—the London which has created the world in which we live to-day—was like a wedge, driving deep into a resistant mass of darker ways. As the new, brighter London pushed the older London away, that older London clung to the edges of the new—and in places escaped the general clearing-out. One of the most notorious streets of seedy booksellers was Hemming's-row, which ran behind the National Portrait Gallery, and was swept away only when Charing Cross-road was built at the end of the eighties.

Looking for a single cause of the liberalizing tendencies of the 19th century—there was no one cause, I realize; but seeking a single cause, all the same—it seems to me that it might be possible to claim that all the 'progress' that the 19th century made in matters of social legislation, in modifying the harshness of the penal code, and (most of all) in hiding unpleasant things from the sight, had its origin in a spontaneously developed, near-general horror of *blood*.

This is no place for deep or superficial psycho-analytic examination of the stresses behind the Victorian tendency to revolt from 'unpleasant' sights (and 'unpleasant' ideas, too). But it is certainly worth the while of a student of such things to consider the fact that, in the year that public hanging was abolished, the Meat Market at Smithfield, against whose bloody scenes Charles Dickens had inveighed, was taken—'out of sight, out of mind', one might say—to distant Caledonian-road. (Yet it was that same Dickens who, in Rome, got up one morning bright and early, to see a felon clubbed to death by the Papal executioner.)

To this sudden and nigh-universal revolt against blood may well be attributed the public welcome given to the newer weapons, which killed— or were reported to kill—without an excess of bloodshed. 'They kill cleanly' was the general and highly significant phrase. The new rifles, firing a projectile with a muzzle-velocity of 1,200 feet a second, seemed ideally 'civilized' to a culture which had turned against the sword. Only in the pages of the boys' novels and magazines was the cult of the more primitive weapons still observed: hence the fact that the damning phrase used for such literature was 'blood and thunder'—soon shortened to mere 'blood', or 'penny blood'.

We shall see later that the series of 'Jack the Ripper' killings accounted for only a handful of series-murders contemporary with 'Jack's'. The so-called 'East End' disappearances, which took off middle-aged men, elderly women, teen-age girls and schoolboys, and extended over a period of nearly ten years, never aroused the fear (because they did not arouse the horror) that 'Jack the Ripper's' handful of murders did. But the maniac 'Ripper' murders had this in common: each was marked with a profuse letting of blood, even though it was clearly demonstrated that the savagely mutilated victims were all dead before 'Jack' started his insane butcher's work on their bodies.

But by one of those paradoxes common enough in the history of social advancement, this deliberate hiding-away of 'unpleasant' truths had the effect of calling public attention to them.

Just as Bluebeard had to make regular visits to his secret chamber, so the Victorians could not resist paying more and more attention to what they had hidden away. They became obsessed with the horror of that submerged life which formed a part of their own comfortable everyday; and, in the end, they did the sensible thing—they resolved no longer merely to hide it, to ignore it.

They resolved to legislate it out of existence.

How this was done we shall see in a later chapter.

But the process of destroying the dark substructure of Victorian existence was far advanced long before the Sixties came to an end.

We may sneer at the 'philanthropists' of a century ago: condemn their tireless nosey-parkerdom as the product of an energetic idleness. These pamphleteering, lecturing crusaders may well have been inspired to their crusades only by vanity, by publicity-seeking; but in spite of themselves they did good.

Someone said to me the other day: 'You wouldn't have liked Plimsoll, Lubbock, Monty Rowton or Shaftesbury—especially Shaftesbury. No wonder his son shot himself in a hansom-cab the year after he came into the old man's title!'

I don't suppose I should have liked them: any more than I like the people who organize those Do-Gooders' Sabbaths in Caxton Hall.

But all who have ever taken ship have cause to bless the name of that persistent brewers' manager, Plimsoll of the 'Plimsoll Line'; the factory-girls and shop-assistants and office-clerks did well to call the man who had given them their Bank Holidays 'St John Lubbock'; and any trade union leader of the last hundred years who could claim that he had done as much for the down-and-outs as Rowton, or as much for the down-trodden workers as Shaftesbury, would have something to boast about. It need hardly be said that the history of trade unionism reveals no leader with a record comparable to that of any of these amateur philanthropists.

The unification of the diverse patterns of that gaslit world was—and is—achieved in the enigmatic personality of the Queen.

It is often said (and Samuel Beeton's new 'Lady's Newspaper', *The Queen*, commented acidly upon it) that with the death of the Prince Consort the Queen went into an unpatriotic seclusion from which she never really emerged.

This remark, true enough in essence, needs some explanation.

First of all it must be said that if the Queen cut herself off from physical contact with her people she broke off contact in no other way. (She even wrote a letter to the Home Secretary, at the time of the Ripper murders, suggesting ways in which he might be caught. Her letter reveals the fact that she had carefully read the entire *Times* account of the killings.)

And it must be said, too, that so far as her 'seclusion' was concerned, intimate physical contact with her people had been broken off, not when the Prince died, but when the Queen married him.

Few of her subjects, save those in her immediate Court circle, had seen the Queen after her marriage. In 1861, the year of the Prince Consort's death, Victoria was forty-two: the portraits of her on the coins and stamps of the day were taken from the medal that William Wyon had engraved for her visit to the Guildhall in 1838, the year after her accession—when Victoria was only nineteen. Not, indeed, until the year of the Diamond Jubilee, when the Queen was seventy-eight, did that young girl's head disappear from the coins.

With an image so far removed from reality, is it any wonder that the Queen became, in the public mind, something not quite human?

Age could not wither her, so, obviously, the years could not condemn.

But the reality—which even to-day we cannot quite persuade ourselves to see—was far removed from the general concept.

Broken-hearted the Queen may have been. She was. She had lost not only a husband, but a lover who could offer her a complete physical and emotional fulfilment.

But she was a Hanoverian, and she was tough.

We forget that she was a Hanoverian. We should remember this, and remember that two of the outstanding qualities of the Hanoverians were their complete absence of snobbishness and their kindness of heart.

One should remember, too, their sense of humour, based upon a clear perception of fact.

Let me give one example of the Queen's mental attitude, where it seems to differ so strikingly from what people believed that attitude to be.

In 1858, when, the mutiny in India now put into cold storage for the better part of a century, and the Queen assumed sovereignty over the vast Indian sub-continent, an eccentric laid his 'Humble Petition' before her.

The petitioner, Marshal-general George Henry Neville Strabolgie Plantagenet-Harrison (the rank was a Chilean one) pointed out in his petition that as he was the rightful Duke of Lancaster, Earl of Warwick and Earl of Northumberland, he was claiming these titles, now held by 'usurpers'.

He went on to demand that he be summoned to the 'House of Peers' to take his seat there as Duke of Lancaster, and he further asked that all the rich revenues of the Duchy—soon to be settled on the Prince of Wales—be turned over to the Marshal-general.

Any other sovereign, receiving this impudent petition—especially any of Victoria's German princeling cousins—would either have clapped the Marshal-general into a fortress or (more likely) into a lunatic asylum.

But the Queen *was* amused. She had the Marshal-general's very long pedigree checked, and found that though the blood had come down by a *very* circuitous route, there was still Plantagenet blood in his veins.

And the Queen respected blood, however watered down. She did not restore the Marshal-general to the rank and usufruct of Lancaster: but she did find the old snob a cozy little billet in the Tower of London, a comfortable sinecure that he enjoyed until his death in 1873.

In a sense not comprehended today, the Queen ran the country. She was, for all the show of Parliamentary rule in the 19th century, the last of the Absolute Monarchs. The prefix 'Royal' to so many of the titles of our older-established charities and benevolent institutions was granted by the Queen. Through the efforts of the powerful body of amateur philanthropists, Queen Victoria saw to it that the un-selfseeking socialism of Albert was fostered, strengthened, developed—its aims brought within the compass of inevitability and practicality.

It has often been charged against her that when flogging was abolished in the Army and Navy in 1859, she protested.

First of all, what was abolished was flogging *without trial;* and what the Queen protested against was not the abolition of flogging, but the weakening of discipline.

Those who recall her protest should recall, too, what was vividly in the Queen's mind as she made her protest: that a slackening of discipline among the troops in India had brought about one, *only two years before,* of the bloodiest mutinies in history.

The sixties had begun with a civil war in the United States of America: the decade ended with a bloodless but perhaps even more fundamental revolution in London.

While Bismarck and King William I were destroying the ramshackle empire of Napoleon III, the Queen and her legislature were hard at work abolishing such of the older England as had survived into the 'Sixties.

We think of our own as an innovating age: nothing that we have done in the course of this present century can compare in fundamental importance with what was undertaken and achieved, in social change, during the ten years of the 'Sixties.

The franchise was extended, until all but the hopelessly unsettled could vote. The purchase of commissions was abolished in the Army. Free education was established as a national principle.

The last vestiges of ecclesiastical power, where that power intruded upon the prerogatives of the Civil Law, were swept away. And though the overhauling of the whole legal system was to be carried out in the succeeding decade, the plans for that overhauling were drawn up before the end of this most fateful decade.

London itself was surveyed and found wanting; and plans for its modernizing and development began to be carried out before the sixties ended. Most of the Embankment had been finished by 1870, and many new streets, including Queen Victoria-street, had been opened.

The next decade was to see such an expansion of London as to establish that pattern that it still preserves: the London not only of the Ruling Centre—of Westminster and the City, of Mayfair and Park-lane and Belgravia and Lancaster Gate—but of the tributary and teeming suburbs.

Suburban London is a Victorian creation. The Victorians built the houses and supplied the public transport by which the suburbs were linked with the capital.

P·A·R·T T·W·O

The Second Decade

Revolution—counting big and small, it's the seventh—breaks out in Paris. To Britain, traditionally a sanctuary of both Royalty and Revolutionaries on the run (both the French Imperial Family and Karl Marx were enjoying the peace and security of Britain at the same time), came all those French princes and nobles who thought the climate of Britain healthier than that of France. They moved into magnificent English country-houses and were much sought after by the British aristocracy. The Imperial Heir was entered a cadet at the Royal Military Academy ("The Shop") at Woolwich to learn to be a Royal Engineer. Before the decade was out, he would be dead at Isandlwana: a British officer, abandoned to the assegais of the Zulus.

France, chastened by her thrashing at Sedan, rebuilt Paris, and welcomed the pleasure-loving Prince of Wales, who found the Grandes Horizontales of the Third Republic—indeed, French life generally—much to his taste. Later, he was to pretend that his insatiable hunger for loose women was a "cover" for political negotiations designed to form an Entente Cordiale. Nobody, not even in England, believed this fable; half-way through the decade, he was packed off to India, taking with him the more disreputable of his companions, and leaving behind material for a scandal which was felt to be first-class (even for Victorian times) when it surfaced.

More and more social freedom was granted to what had been the Underprivileged. Almost everyone above the status of homeless pauper now had the vote. Disabilities under which Jews and Nonconformists had laboured were removed; and the new German

Empire shewing unmistakable signs of Anti-Semitism, Jews both poor and wealthy began to emigrate to England—the latter class moving straightaway, not only into the West-end mansions and huge country house, but also, by marriage, into the British Aristocracy, and, through the traditional Liberal preference for the Foreigner, into Parliament, and even into the Cabinet. At the very end of the decade, Riel, a French-Canadian half-breed rebelled against British rule in Canada; he was put down by General Garnet Wolseley, whose voice, at home, was raised successfully against the Channel Tunnel.

In 1873, the Department of Military Intelligence was founded; the uniforms of the British officers suffered some—but not much—simplification. Between 1870 and 1900, Britain fought no fewer than one hundred and thirty wars—all small. The decade from 1871 to 1881 had its full share of these small campaigns; not until the very end of the century did British troops know more than one major defeat—this was to come during the next decade.

At home, social improvements, under the unflagging drive of the by-now-professional Reformers: Plimsoll (the 'Plimsoll Line' to prevent the overloading of the "coffin-ships"), Sir John Lubbock (Bank Holidays for the masses), Montague Rowton (beds for the down-and-outs), Lord Shaftesbury (improved working-conditions everywhere, from the shops to the Factories to the mines) were unmistakable. The decade ended with more for everyone—including, of course, the Rich. But the most important single event of the decade—an event which meant a great stride forward in the Emancipation of Woman—was the introduction of the typewriter, providing a career for the educated but penniless woman, formerly condemned to the fearful drudgery of the Governess, the horrors of which life the Victorian novelists described so well. A great Decade indeed. . . .

HAD YOU asked any reasonably well-informed Englishman, in 1871, which had been the two most important happenings of the previous year, he would undoubtedly have replied: 'The death of Charles Dickens and the Franco-Prussian War.' And it is beyond question that he would have put the two events in that order of importance.

No death of recent times had stirred the British public so profoundly as had the sudden passing of Dickens. It had stirred them as the death of the French Empire certainly had not done—yet, had they known it, there was a curious connection between the death of the great novelist and the ending of the Napoleonic dream. When the defeated Napoleon III, dismissing his aides, walked alone to surrender his sword and his empire to Bismarck, the Iron Chancellor was sitting in the small house which served as his temporary headquarters, reading.

As the despairing and dying Emperor of the French entered, Bismarck laid down the book that he was reading: it was Dickens's *Little Dorrit*: a book which expresses the 'Little Man's' hopeless hatred of the Juggernaut of Bureaucracy and the blind malice of entrenched Privilege in symbols darker than the despair which filled the Emperor's heart.

How prematurely Dickens had died was what added sadness to sadness. Only fifty-eight! they said. A good twenty years of valuable work before him—and he had to be taken in his prime.

But there were not any more years of work before Dickens; he had come to the end of his resources. He was fortunate in that the stroke of 9th June, 1870, had killed him; had he survived, only bodily life would have remained—the mind would have been destroyed beyond recovery.

Indeed, for one whose heart was rather in the theatre than in the novel, great and successful novelist though he had made himself, his death could not have been more beautifully timed.

He died at Gad's Hill Place, in his own house, in the presence of his two daughters. His wife, from whom he had been separated for some years, was not there; but the passing, even though without Mrs Dickens's proper presence, conformed fully to Victorian ideas of what was 'right and proper' and nothing in that death sullied the image of the Great Novelist, as it existed in the minds of millions of his readers.

But had that death been postponed for only a day, Dickens would have died, not at Gad's Hill Place, in his own home, in the presence of his children and their aunt, Georgina, but at Windsor Lodge, Lindengrove, Peckham, where, for five years, he had been passing half of every week with his mistress, Ellen Ternan. Had he died in that prim yellow-brick villa (double-fronted, with a pillared portico: just the sort of house that the reputed City man, 'Charles Tringham', might have been expected to rent) the secret that all London knew would have been the property of the world, as well.

'Charles Tringham', the tenant of Windsor Lodge, would have been revealed as Charles Dickens, creator of Sam Weller, Oliver Twist, Mr Micawber and Little Nell; and 'Mrs Tringham' would have been revealed as Miss Ellen Ternan, a beautiful small-part actress whose early retirement from the stage had coincided with her going under Mr Dickens's protection.

The liaison, which began in 1856, had cost Dickens his otherwise inevitable knighthood; but all London-in-the-know had conspired to keep the secret from the public—and by dying as he did, and when he did, Dickens ensured that that secret remained unpublished until its publication no longer had power to affect his reputation.

When the autobiography of the best-selling and greatly-respected novelist, Anthony Trollope, was published after his death, it put an end to his books' success—at least, for a period of years—by giving a detailed account of the financial profit of his writing, and by admitting that he had been 'hopelessly' in love with a married woman. Trollope had made it clear that he had never so much as kissed the lady; but though it was all right for Tennyson to mention imagined kisses as—

> '. . . sweet as those by hopeless fancy feigned,
> On lips that are for others . . .'

it was certainly not all right for one who had done the imagining to disclose the fact. Trollope was 'finished' with his generation: one may imagine how 'finished' Dickens would have been had he died with his mistress instead of with his children and their Aunt.

He would have fallen as Lucifer fell, never to rise again—not, that is, while Victoria was still on the throne.

As it was, all was well. Ellen Ternan was sent for by Georgina Hogarth (who many said was another of Dickens's mistresses), but she came to Gad's Hill 'privately', and in the capacity of Friend of the Family, and not as a mistress already wearied of her equivocal position.

Dickens died, indeed, as a Victorian should have died: discreetly. And the Society of which he was a notable part played up to sustain the image that he had created. There was the Abbey funeral with the national mourning as its fitting accompaniment.

And the steel engraving by the young artist, Luke Fildes, who had been chosen by Dickens himself to illustrate the last (and unfinished) novel, *Edwin Drood*, became a best-seller among pictures-for-the-home, as successful as Dickens's novels were best-sellers among books-for-the-home.

This engraving, entitled *The Empty Chair*, shewed the study at Gad's Hill: the manuscript and ink-wells on the plain table; the plain wooden chair before the table empty of the occupant who would never finish the novel.

In its success that picture had few rivals—and such rivals as it had were to be counted on the fingers of one hand: Lady Butler's *The Roll-call*, Landseer's *Dignity and Impudence* and *The Stag at Bay*, Wilkie's *The Death of Nelson* and *Grace Darling* and Holman Hunt's *The Light of the World*. (And those seven pictorial best-sellers sum up, pretty completely, the emotional content of the Victorian public.)

But because the death of Dickens was felt as a national tragedy by the Victorians of 1870, that does not mean that even the man-in-the-street regarded what was happening in France as of no importance. The defeat of the French by the Germans made the British the more uneasy as they were puzzled to know how they should respond to the fact that one great European power had been eclipsed (few realized how momentarily—certainly not the French or the Germans), only to have another Great Power take its place.

It was France who had been represented, by nationalistic propaganda, as The Enemy. True, 'we' had fought side-by-side with France against the Russians, and many a serving soldier and sailor wore medals which had been bestowed by the French Emperor as well as by the British Queen.

Before the Crimean War, the Queen, the Prince Consort and the royal children had paid a state visit to the French Emperor and Empress; but the rapprochement between (to use Chatham's phrase) 'the ancient, inveterate enemies' had hardly survived the peace celebrations.

No one quite knew what the war had effected. Admiral Nachimov, coming silently out of the dawn, had blown the Turkish Black Sea Fleet out of the water, as it lay at anchor in Sinope. Britain, France, Turkey, Sardinia and Piedmont had allied themselves to fight Russia—and Russia had lost. Not 'General Winter' but the Emperor Napoleon III's 'secret weapon' had beaten the Russians. His armoured monitors, designed under his personal guidance, paid for out of his private resources, and towed, by his express command, from Brest to Sebastopol, had not only silenced the Russian forts, but in a few hours of firing had completely altered the pattern of naval warfare.

The war of 1854 had begun, so far as the naval part of it went, with techniques not very much advanced over those with which Blake and Van Tromp had fought it out two centuries earlier. The Allies had taken their 'wooden walls' from the Atlantic to the Black Sea to match the gun-fire from Todleben's stone casemates at Sebastopol. The British had sought to anticipate 1915 by endeavouring to smoke the Russians out of their stronghold with poison-gas—in this case, sulphur dioxide—but the wind blew the gas back towards the British lines, and common-sense prevailed where common humanity would not have done.

It was the Age of the Amateur still. It was from the imaginative non-professional that the ideas were coming which would create those scientific techniques later to be developed by the professional scientists. But the ideas had to come from the amateurs.

Samuel Morse, who made the electric telegraph practical, was a not unsuccessful painter of portraits; the first practical advances in aeronautics were made by a landed baronet, George Cayley; a great pioneer of photography, Fox Talbot, was also a landed proprietor—and so it went. The man who brought the new pattern into naval warfare was not an admiral or even a naval engineer, but Emperor of the French.

Long and secret experiments with armour plate had given Napoleon III a shot-proof covering for a naval vessel. He took three small ships, stripped them down to the water-line, covered them with armour, decks as well as sides, and fitted them with engines.

Heavy breech-loading guns were housed in revolving casemates, and thus armed, the three ships were towed out to Sebastopol.

Arrived at the Black Sea, the tow was slipped from the three heavily-armoured monitors. The Allied fleet had been drawn up in a vast semi-circle, facing the Russian forts, but out of reach of the Russian guns.

The monitors' engines turned over, and, at a speed of little more than two knots, the three strange vessels began to creep towards the forts which had defied assault for weeks.

The Russian guns opened fire. Still the monitors moved forward, in line-abreast. They took their time. Heedless of the Russian guns, though the monitors were hit again and again, the ships' captains chose their positions with precise—one might almost say, self-indulgent—care.

Nothing could stop them. A mile to their rear lay the entire Allied fleet—a fleet 'powerful' only on paper; for not one of those ships dared approach within firing-range of the Russian guns.

Then, as at a pre-arranged signal, the three armoured ships stopped. The black smoke died away from their concealed smoke-stacks. On their stubby masts, the battle-ensigns fluttered up to the truck. There was a moment of deathly, of unearthly, silence. Then, from each armoured casemate the 6-inch naval guns poured their murderous fire into the Russian forts.

First the Russian guns were silenced, then the steel casemates shattered, then the stone and concrete emplacements began to crumble. From gun-site to gun-site the three armoured ships, the water pouring over their low decks, moved in a deliberate and sinister orderliness.

At last, after six hours, all Russian resistance ceased. The white flag fluttered from a broken masthead. The 'impregnable' sea-fortress of the master military engineer, Todleben—the Vauban of the 19th century—lay in ruins; its guns a mass of tangled metal; its ammunition exhausted or exploded; its shattered casemates filled with dead and dying men.

In six hours, the Crimean War had been ended; in six hours, the entire navies of the entire world had been rendered obsolete, and a pattern of naval warfare which had been old at Actium had been put by for ever; in six hours, the world, in one important aspect, had been changed from the Old to the New.

On the French monitors, there was only one casualty: a rating had been wounded by flying shrapnel. The victory had been, literally, complete. Here was a turning-point in history, as fundamental and decisive as that made when the first atomic bomb dropped on Japan.

The British Admiralty had reluctantly agreed to 'go shares' in Napoleon III's 'secret weapon'; but only the French monitors were ready to make the long tow to the Black Sea. It had been a French venture, and in its success the British had had no part.

The die-hard admirals of Britain wanted no part in changing; they feared the challenge that change might bring. They felt that, if they took no part in changing established patterns, everything 'would blow over.' It didn't, of course; it just blew up.

As contracts had been given, our naval dockyards went on building 'wooden walls', a slight concession to progress being made by covering the sides of an old wooden warship, which had fought at Navarino, with armour. For economy's sake, only the sides and not the hull, had iron-plating affixed. The French, on the other hand, went straight ahead with the construction of a completely armoured battleship, the *Gloire*. It was not a very pleasant lesson for the British—'masters of the sea'.

But then, as everyone explained to everyone else, it was only in such 'undemocratic' states as France that changes could be made so quickly.

Funds, in Britain, had to be voted by Parliament; and the whole matter debated before the Treasury would release needed money to the Admiralty. . . .

France, it was obvious, was intent upon building up a navy based upon the new principles. Why. . . ? She had no vast overseas empire, such as Britain had.

But France, in doing something else, seemed to hint at the direction in which her ambitions were running. At immense cost, the old harbours of Cherbourg and Brest were coverted to powerful naval arsenals, equipped with the most powerful long-range guns in existence. And—said the alarmists—those guns pointed in only one direction: towards Britain.

With *Punch*—how typical of the Victorian pattern!—beating the alarm, the Volunteer Movement came into being. Public meetings were called by 'influential' persons; recruiting began in earnest; a natty uniform was devised for the 'week-end soldiers', and—how typical of the Victorian pattern!—the movement that it had helped to call into being provided *Punch*, week after week, with its chief source of humorous comment.

Still, there it was: France was the Enemy . . . and now, as the seventh decade of the 19th century opened, the Enemy lay stricken; a menace to none, save to herself.

Her armies had been beaten, her Emperor overthrown. It did not make the French defeat less shocking that mismanagement and treachery, more than actual military incompetence, had given the victory to the Germans.

Now the conquerors were on the soil of France; Paris was in the hands of the Communards, and before the National Army of Liberation was to free the capital, one-quarter of its buildings were to lie in smoking ruins. It would have been a bold historian of the future who would have dared to prophesy *any* future for France, let alone affirm that, within a decade, France would have restored herself to her old greatness—and something more.

But that was still in the future; and now the British hardly knew whether to be relieved or not that the menace of French ambitions had been removed by the Bismarckian *Blitzkrieg*—the phrase had not yet been invented, but the idea had been realized.

The French Empress, whom upper-crust rumour credited with being a daughter of Lord Clarendon (thus, as her mother was Scottish, making her 'one hundred per cent British'), came to England; on his release from captivity at Hohenlohe, her dying husband followed. They settled down at Camden House, Chislehurst, a Georgian mansion which had once belonged to a lady who had helped—as so many ladies had helped—the young Prince Louis Napoleon, when he was nursing his ambitions to make himself Emperor.

Now that Napoleon was no longer Emperor, the British had no hard feelings towards him; but when it was announced that his only son, the Prince Imperial, was to enter the Royal Military Academy, Woolwich—'The Shop'—as an officer-cadet, all animosity was dead. The Heir to the Imperial Throne a British Officer. . . .

Well, *that* wiped out the past.

Three years after coming to Camden House, the Emperor, stricken with the hereditary Bonaparte disease, cancer of the lower bowel, died. No one was more solicitous in comforting the Empress than Queen Victoria.

When the practice of embalming the dead was honoured amongst the ancient Jews, there was a ritual prohibition against making an incision in a dead human body. To overcome the difficulty of embalming without cutting, the Jews invited a man to perform the forbidden task. He was well paid; and with his money clutched firmly in his hand, he stuck the knife in the body—and ran, as fast as he could. For his 'offence' merited his being stoned to death.

Someone, of course, had had to perform the necessary job of making the first cut in a dead body. The Jews were prepared to pay someone to do it. But having done it, the performer had to be execrated, while the embalmers got on with their business—no longer forbidden, now that the dirty work had been done.

A lot of cleaning-up had to be done in the Britain of the late sixties, and the job was felt to be most properly done by the least popular of Britain's politicians.

Fortunately, just as there was always someone willing to make the first incision in an ancient Jewish cadaver, so there has always been a politician willing to accept responsibility for initiating unpopular but (as he sees it) necessary reform.

It was not only in the Black Sea that the changes from the Old to the New were taking place. Institutions as 'traditional' and as honoured as wooden battleships were being blown away by the wind of change; but so far as Britain was concerned, most of the institutions affected were in other departments than those administered by the Commander-in-Chief or the Lords of the Admiralty; though in their departments, too, changes occurred.

The Church, the Law, the Universities, the Civil Service, the Public Schools, as well as the Army and the Navy, were all affected—and most of the legislation concerned was carried through by Gladstone, a former High Tory who had been converted to Liberalism by forces which are still obscure.

Gladstone was a distinctly unlikeable man ('He addresses me as though I were a public meeting', Queen Victoria succinctly and wittily complained) but of his power there can be no doubt.

His power was such that, even when he was out of office, his political rivals hastened to carry out his measures, so as to anticipate what they knew to be inevitable.

In the third Derby ministry, which came into office in 1866, Disraeli, who was the dominating spirit, adopted Gladstone's policy of electoral reform, and though the Abyssinian campaign of 1868 was a distinctly Tory measure, the whole conduct of the ministry was unabashedly Liberal.

Gladstone returned to power in 1868, in December, and followed up those Liberal measures that his Tory rivals had already initiated.

A realization that the scientific and technical trend of industry and commerce was outdating traditional methods of education and the recruitment of staff (particularly in Government departments) had already become a talking-point by the mid-century. A curious object lesson regarding the effects of 'science' on industry had come with Perkin's extracting a dye—'mauveine'—from coal-tar; the first 'aniline' dye in the world's history.

Perkin was only eighteen when he made this revolutionary experiment; but overnight, as one might say, the young chemist had seriously affected French economy, by producing a synthetic substitute for the indigo of which the French had a virtual monopoly.

Perkin had not pursued his experiments in the low-temperature distillation of coal-tar: perhaps being elected a F.R.S. at nineteen had turned his head. But the Germans took up where Perkin had left off; and in Germany the farseeing Kings and Grand Dukes—or, may be, it was only their far-seeing Ministers—encouraged the New Men with orders and title. Prussia even established a new order of chivalry, the Red Eagle, so as to be able to reward chemists and Jews.

The New Men did not go entirely unhonoured in Britain; but here the policy adopted seemed to be rather one of ensuring a supply of New Men in the future than of developing 'New Thought' in the present.

The fact that there were a lot of business-men in politics—Gladstone was one—made interference with established educational practices possible; indeed, easy.

That it was a Tory government which introduced the Public Schools Bill of February 1868 should not obscure the truth that this was a typically Gladstonian measure, only brought in by the Tories to 'steal a march' on the Liberals.

By this Bill, which had passed both Houses by the end of July, the government of the great public schools was modified—brought up to date.

Eton, Winchester, Harrow, Westminster, Charterhouse, Rugby and Shrewsbury were issued with new statutes; and for good measure, an entirely new public school, organized on the principles incorporated in the Public Schools Act, was founded in the City of London. From the beginning it thrived.

Public Elementary Education was tackled next. As usual in Victorian days, an outside pressure-group was founded to coerce the Government into taking the necessary measures: in the case of Public Elementary Education, there were two groups—the National Education League, with a policy of compulsory education by the state, and the National Educational Union, which hoped to supplement the existing denominational system.

Both groups were founded in Birmingham within weeks of each other in 1869; and in 1870 a conference was called by the Society of Arts, to find some means of reconciling League and Union.

They were, as it happened, never to be reconciled: the Government, in legislation extending from 1870 onwards, solved their mutual differences by establishing state-run schools and by making grants-in-aid to those denominational schools which agreed to be supervised by Government inspectors.

The first Elementary Education Bill was introduced by W. E. Foster in the Gladstone parliament of 1870. It passed without serious opposition, received the Royal Assent, and led to the election of the first Metropolitan School Board, under the chairmanship of Lord Lawrence, before the end of the year.

This was, indeed, the decade of educational revolution—not merely educational reform.

Girton College, 'for the higher education of women', was opened in July 1873; it had been authorized four years earlier; and in 1875 another women's college at Cambridge (Newnham) opened its doors, its establishment having been authorized in 1871.

Amendments to the Public Schools Act came in 1869, 1870 and 1871. The first school built by the London School Board opened, in Whitechapel, in July 1873.

In the following October, a change of immense importance in the history of modern British education took place: the Universities appointed a board to examine public-school-boys; the results, covering pupils from two hundred and twenty-one schools, were published in the following September.

One after the other, the London School Boards were brought into being; and there was need for haste. Nearly half of the 4,000,000 British children of school-age were unprovided for; 1,000,000 were receiving elementary education in government-supported Church of England schools; another 1,000,000 were being instructed in the 'three Rs' in unsupported—and therefore uninspected—schools.

These great plans were carried through without obstruction, but not without opposition. Argument raged about two 'basic' points: should the schools be denominational or undenominational? And should education, if compulsory, not be free as well?

At first, the idea of compulsory attendance was unpopular, even with the most ardent supporters of the new educational policies: Mr Dixon's Compulsory Attendance Bill was rejected by a decisive majority in the Commons—320 to 156.

However, once the step to provide a truly national educational system had been taken by the Legislature, important changes in sentiment were noticeable. With the election of the second London School Board, under the chairmanship of Mr (later Sir) Charles Reed, it was seen that the 'prodenominational' members were in the majority; but the election of the third School Board, only three years later (1876) showed that the 'nondenominational' members were in the majority, and as the decade passed the idea gained force that the State was somehow divorced from the Established Church, in that not all the Queen's loyal subjects were members of that Church, and that to force them to swallow the tenets of one religion with their State-provided education was unjust—and possibly dangerous to the ideals that the Education Acts had set out to serve.

When a further Elementary Education Act was introduced by Lord Sandon in 1876, a clause, introduced by Mr Pell, giving the Educational authorities power to suppress unnecessary school-boards, was considered reactionary. The Bill was passed, but only after Gladstone, who was once again out of office, had hinted that were any such Bill of his to be obstructed by the Lords, he would ask the Queen to make sufficient titles to ensure its passage through the Upper House.

The Lords had been warned. . . .

'Lighthouses of the future', Sherlock Holmes enthusiastically called the new board-schools—and so they were.

Well designed, well built, they stand, many of them to this day: tributes to Victorian enterprise, planning and conscientious workmanship. They taught many, perhaps most, of the children who came to them the virtues, as well as promising them the accessibility, of physical cleanliness. The educators were not to be put off their plans, either, by the legitimate complaint of some parents that their children ought not to be asked to mingle with children of the Dead End. In 1872 the first London School

Board announced that it was determined to open schools for dirty or unruly children—everybody was first to be given the chance of education, and then to be forced, by legislation, to take that chance.

On 14th January, 1876, the first conference of teachers took place.

The Army, as well as the schools and universities, needed Reform—and it got it.

In 1870 the total number of men in the Army was 178,000. To this could be added the 63,000 men stationed in India. The figure for the Home Forces was to rise steeply at the beginning of the 1870s, until in the year 1875-6 it reached 226,000, the figure for the Indian troops remaining constant at 63,000.

After 1876 the figure declined, until in the year 1880-1 it stood at only 136,000, the Indian figure remaining as before.

It was not, as certain reverses on foreign soil gave its critics the opportunity to complain, an untrained army. For one thing, of the 175,460 effective troops under arms in June 1871, only 33,797 were under twenty years of age, and of that 33,797, only 18,614 were under nineteen.

So that over 80 per cent of the men serving in the Army were above twenty years of age: the balance, then, was towards maturity. The stories that one hears about the ragged-tailed street-arabs, choosing the Queen's shilling as an only slightly better alternative to workhouse or gaol, are obviously without foundation. It is no credit to Victorian society that, even as late as the time of the Boer War, half the men presenting themselves for enlistment were rejected on medical grounds; one can imagine how great the proportion would have been had they all been conscripts. But the rejection of half does show that standards of eligibility were high. Men marched in those days—and (as the men who had just conquered Theodore of Abyssinia could testify) they marched over mountains, under a tropical sun, in thick scarlet cloth, with leather equipment, including two full bandoliers and a very full pack.

The mules that they had with them—and they did not always have mules—were needed to transport stores, ammunition, tools; they were not there to carry men. The officers certainly set out with horses, but in many cases the horses ended in the cook-pots, and officers and men ended the long trek, to victory or defeat, on foot.

The principal hardship of the British Army, as Sir John Fortescue has pointed out, was boredom. At least, this was so at home, where, summer and winter, two dishes appeared in the men's mess—and two only: beef stew and plum-duff. Abroad, when Tommy had to 'live off the country', he had a change of diet: he could taste mango and paw-paw, guava and lychee, melon and shaddock. But at home, all he was offered to eat was beef and suet-pudding. His meals, too, were timed to suit the convenience of the cooks, rather than of Tommy. 'Dinner' (which was also 'supper') was served not later than five o'clock; sometimes it was much earlier. This meant that the men were given nothing to eat between tea-time of one day and breakfast-time on the following day—a gap of up to fourteen hours.

Pay had not gone up since the end of the Napoleonic Wars, when it had been reduced to a shilling a day. But this sum was liable to numerous 'stoppages', so that, for the recruit at least, it averaged rather fourpence a day than a shilling.

Experience in the ways of the Army showed the earnest student of How to Stay Sane Though a Solider that *a*) the 'stoppages' went on as long as the sufferer did not protest, and that *b*) the official stoppages were far less and far less prolonged than the unofficial ones. To submit to pay 'stoppages' was how one paid one's footing, and when one had learnt wisdom, and refused to pay more, one had qualified as an 'old soldier', worthy to share in the profit to be made in rooking the rawer squaddies.

Beer was a penny a pint, and three ha'porth of fish-and-chips or pease-pudden-and-faggots made a meal. But even when beer's a penny a pint, one can't have an evening out on fourpence—and not much of an evening on a bob, for all that one has heard differently.

'Blimey, boy, I used to do better on a bob, 'n *them* days, then on a nicker today. Two pints o' beer, seat in the musichall, packet o' fags, plate o' fish 'n' taters—yus, *and* take home some change.'

I've heard the story often enough. The element of the dubious about it I find in the assumed self-denial of the teller. *How* did he get through the evening on only two pints—and *why* did he take some change home with him?

Hanging around London or any of the barrack-towns must have been hell for the single soldier in those days. There was no Naffy; and though Naffy takes an unconscionable profit (so that all who work for it, even as clerks, have to sign along the Official Secrets Act's dotted line, to keep their mouths sealed) Naffy does at least provide Tommy with somewhere to go: to play cards, to read tattered ten-year-old women's magazines, to smoke, to talk, to drink an occasional cup of Naffy 'char'.

In the seventies there was nothing of the sort: only the pothouses, the parks, the street-corners.

Yet Tommy's welfare was still the concern of his superiors.

They were not concerned with his boredom, but they were concerned with his health. They did not know that between 1870 and 1900 Great Britain was to find herself involved in no fewer than *one hundred and thirty wars*— yes, believe it or not, but that was the Price of Empire—but they did assume that the men would be reasonably busy with fighting, and it was the job of those in charge to see that the men were reasonably fit to do the fighting.

Medical services and sanitary arrangements improved. Between the end of the Crimean War and 1871, deaths in the Army had been reduced from 17 per 1,000 to 9.5 per 1,000, and in 1869 a startling innovation had come with the establishment of the Army Service Corps by Royal Warrant—this body, new to British tradition, was to be composed of volunteers, commanded by regular army officers. It had been created to serve as a sort of liaison corps, to link the abject Tommy with the Olympian toff who commanded him.

Flogging, in both the Services, had been restricted to insubordination (with violence) and indecency, by an ordinance of March 1867. By an 1868 amendment in the Mutiny Act, flogging in time of peace was abolished altogether.

The War Office were out to get a better type of man. The time had passed when it was expected that men would respond the more readily to brutality or the threat of brutality.

Flogging had been abolished so that an approach to educating Tommy might the more easily be made: and this remark deserves some explanation.

The Army rankers had always included a number of educated men, if only for the reason that sanctuary had been offered by the Army long after the Church and even Alsatia had had to abandon the custom. It was a Scots sergeant of the Royal Engineers who proposed, in 1848, that a Great Exhibition should be held in London. He submitted his idea to his commanding officer as something by way of an antidote to the Chartism which was demanding Reform in an uncomfortably threatening manner.

The commanding officer passed on the sergeant's idea; it came to the notice of the Prince Consort, who liked it; a committee was formed; the Duke of Devonshire's head gardener adapted one of His Grace's greenhouses to the uses of a 'Crystal Palace'—and the most successful exhibition in the world was under way.[1]

I had the curiosity to turn up the sergeant's record when I, too, was a Sapper. I found that he had been a Master of Arts of Glasgow University. Cobbett had risen to higher rank: he was a sergeant-major, while Poe had

---

[1] So successful, in fact, that the Trustees are still administering the profits made from the 6,000,000 tickets of admission. It is odd, indeed, to see that the London Telephone Directory carries the number of 'The Great Exhibition, 1851'. It need hardly be said that the Labour-organized 'Festival of Britain' of 1951 landed both London and the Kingdom heavily in debt, and made over Battersea Park (deeded as a gift to Londoners by a Victorian philanthropist) to the base uses of a nasty hot-dog and candy-floss rip-off. The one small product of any importance was the reproduction, as a show-piece, of the Holmes-Watson sitting-room at No. 221B, Baker-street.

done even better as a non-commissioned officer, rising to be regimental-sergeant-major.

Indeed, apart from the men who had turned to the Army because they had failed in more honoured professions, there was a large element of the educated in the British Army at any time, and mostly this element came from Scotland, where education, for centuries past, had always been cheap, sound and available to all. Scotsmen, too, had no prejudice against appearing educated.

With a sound basic education, any Scotsman could adapt himself to promotion if it came his way: Hector Macdonald, the plough-boy, rose to be a Major-general Sir Hector MacDonald, K.C.B. at the end of the 19th century. 'Fighting Mac' did not need to be 'groomed for stardom': as an ordinary Scots lad, with an ordinary Scots education, he was the educational equal of his betters.

The trouble, though, was that where 'criming' was an Army tradition, it was too easy to 'crime' the educated men into an inescapable alliance with the rawest elements. Once the educated were—literally—'blood-brothers' of the uneducated through the common ownership of a dirty conduct-sheet, such men were lost to the Army in any capacity higher than that of a sergeant. It was impossible to promote a man to commissioned or even warrant-rank who could not produce a clean conduct-sheet; and once the conduct-sheet was dirtied, men of ambition despaired, to become elements more subversive of discipline than the scouring of Ratcliffe Highway or St Giles's.

The first step, then, to be taken if the Army was to take advantage of education was to abolish 'criming' as a respected Army tradition. The most debasing of the punishments went first—flogging—and though Number One Field Punishment (twenty-four hours, tied to a gun-wheel, under fire) remains, so I am told, On the Books, only Legend affirms that it was given as late as the early part of World War I.

Of course, the civilians cried out against this 'weakening of discipline'; Queen Victoria merely voiced an extremely common opinion when she expressed herself as against the abolition of flogging. But then, the civilians have always known better than the generals what's good for the Army—and the Nation.

> For it's 'Tommy here!' and 'Tommy there!'
> And 'Please to stand aside!'—
> But it's 'Saviour of his Country'
> When the troop-ship's on the tide. . . .

as Kipling so bitterly pointed out.

Still, though the civilians have their say, and though their say often has the effect of slowing down commonsense progress, quite often things get done despite the omniscience of the civilians.

So with the revolution which took place in the Army after the Crimean War. The Government was going to spend a lot of tax-payers' money in giving education to the masses; the generals did not see why they should not profit by the education which was coming. The job, then, was to 'respectabilize' the Army—Top and Bottom. Make it a profession for others than Lord Dundrearys, Old Lags and Ploughboys-out-of-a-Job.

The Army was conscious that it had had a bad Press. When Lord Lucan, a 'hero' of the Crimea, had been called an incompetent, and worse, by some cad of a journalist in the *Daily News*, his elegant lordship promptly sued the proprietors of the *Daily News* for libel. The case was heard before an average jury, which might have been supposed to be more impressed by an earl with a distinguished war-record than by a journalist.

However, the earl lost.[2] The jury agreed with the *Daily News*.

That was just one of the bits of bad publicity that the Army was getting. Those who had the welfare of the Army at heart determined (in the modern phrase) to brighten up the Image.

Education was despised in the Army, by both Officers and Other Ranks. When Palmerston said, 'Things have come to a pretty pass when religion thinks it has the right to invade one's private life!' any average Army man might have echoed: 'And things have come to a pretty pass when education thinks it has the right to have anything to do with us!'

In only one corps was the tradition of education respected: the Corps of Royal Engineers. But here, remarkably high intelligence was so often allied with something very near crankery that something was to be said for the suspicion in which the R.E.'s 'learning' was held by the rest of the Army. Attempting to decypher Hittite (Captain Conder, R.E.), discovering the inscription of King Mesha in the Pool of Siloam (Colonel Wilson), getting offered the Imperial Throne of China (General Gordon)—these were only a few of the unmilitary bizarreries associated with the Royal Engineers.

What the Army wanted was a sort of educational standard which would not—once they had got used to the idea—put the average men off.

The way, it was obvious, was to make entry into the Army, at all levels, possible only through passing an educational test. In this way

---

[2] A most unfortunate family, with the present Earl's whereabouts unknown, as the police try to serve him with an arrest-warrant on the charge of having murdered his children's 'Nanny'.

men would respect education, since without it they could not become soldiers.

Seeing, in the proposed changes, a 'democratic' move, the Liberals on both sides of the House welcomed the revolution.

The report of the Royal Commission on Military Education gave the reformers all the authority that they needed to make changes—and the changes soon followed.

In August 1870 it was announced that the Report of the Royal Commission recognized that 'over-regulation-payments' for commissions had been ignored by Authority—in other words, that there had long existed a 'black market' in commission-purchase.

In the following year the Army Regulation Bill, to abolish the purchase-system and to replace it with entrance by competitive examination (such as, in the previous year, had been foisted on the Civil Service—only the Foreign Office managing to escape), was passed by the Commons but rejected by the Lords.

Now a curious and significant thing happened. In the Lords, the Bill had been argued ably by the Duke of Cambridge, cousin of the Queen and Commander-in-Chief, for life, of the British Army. He, who might have been thought to represent all that was reactionary-aristocratic, pleaded for the Bill. At 2 a.m. on the morning of 18th July, after the Bill had been debated for no fewer than three days, the jumped-up Peers of Commerce and Trade rejected it by a majority of twenty-five.

Cambridge went to the Queen. As a young man, the Duke had eloped with, and married, a most respectable actress; and this morganatic union, in willful defiance of the Royal Marriages Act, had never been 'recognized' by the Queen, who, it was said, had wished to marry George, Duke of Cambridge herself.

The Duke's wife had no title; she was addressed always as 'Mrs FitzGeorge'; and plain 'Mr FitzGeorge' was the style of the Duke's sons.

Nevertheless, this—in the Queen's eyes—unfortunate marriage (it was one of the happiest on record) was not held by Her Majesty to be any bar to the Duke's own advancement.

Field-marshal and Commander-in-Chief, Knight of the Garter and of all the other principal orders of British chivalry, George, Duke of Cambridge represented, in the eyes both of his Queen and of her subjects, all that was endearingly obtuse and charmingly innocent in the aristocratic tradition. Until his death in 1904, George always wore the blue riband of the Garter with his day clothes—and no one thought it eccentric. Deaf as a post, he used to ramble on at dinner-parties, so the tale went, with accounts of his military exploits, for he had come, as his kingly uncle George IV had come, to believe that he had been present—and actively present—at every notable battle, from Agincourt to Alma.

But behind the rather stupid-looking Hanoverian exterior, blue bull's eyes and a red face as paunchy as his stomach, the Duke had the shrewdly commonsensical Hanoverian mind. Especially had he the wonderful adaptability of the Hanoverian: that inability to be abashed or frightened by the prospect of Change which is the secret of the Hanoverians' matchless survival-quality—and why Great Britain is still a Monarchy to-day.

Of all the defenders of the Bill to turn the Army system upside-down, no-one would have picked out the Duke. Yet it was the Duke who argued most passionately for it—and, when the New Men chucked out the chance of ridding Britain of its last traces of feudal stick-in-the-muddery, the Duke showed that he could be cunning as well as courageous; autocratic as well as democratic.

What they had forgotten about the Duke was this: he did not 'automatically' feel himself in alliance with Gentlemen.

He did not, in fact, consider that Gentlemen had more in common with him than people who were not Gentlemen. It was a pity that the Gentlemen forgot this—they might have played their cards differently. If there was one sure way of angering the Queen, it was to suggest that she was Queen of some particular section of her people more than of some other: that she was more the Queen, say, of the members of the Church of England than of members of the Roman Church; more the Queen of the English than of the Irish.

Time and again, she intervened personally to make it clear that all minorities among her subjects—Roman Catholics, Jews, Quakers, Salvationists, striking dock-workers—were the special subjects of her regard.

George thought in the same way.

He went to the Queen and told her that a measure of the utmost importance was being held up by a lot of reactionary parvenus in the Lords. It was true that they were opposing what, in effect, was revolutionary. But that it was revolutionary showed how necessary it had become.

So the Queen did something almost as revolutionary—since Britain had come to believe that her autocratic powers had been stifled by the concept of Constitutional Monarchy.

She called in her private advisers, and they found her the precedent she required. They had to go back quite a way—to the fifth and sixth years of Edward VI's reign. But had it been necessary they would have gone back to the reign of Alfred.

They found that this particular precedent had been used, in similar circumstances, in the forty-ninth year of George III's reign. That had been only sixty years earlier, so that no one could complain that it had been unknown since post-mediaeval times.

The Acts relied upon made it clear that, in the matter of the Armed Forces of the Crown, the Sovereign, at his or her discretion, may act without the advice of Ministers or the consent of Parliament.

While the reactionaries were congratulating themselves on having thrown out the offensive attack on Caste and Privilege, the Queen abolished the purchase-system by Royal Warrant—and that was that.

One would have to go back more than a century—merely reading the contemporary accounts would not be enough—to realize the profound shock with which this action of the Queen's was received.

Here, when all had thought it decently buried, was Autocracy—that everyone had thought legislated out of existence.

But no. And, what was more, it was perfectly legal Autocracy.

If the House of Lords did not know what was good for the country, the Queen had the power to shew them.

And shewn them she had. After that, a new vested interest arose: the Army crammer. But it was examination-marks, not pounds-shillings-and-pence which, in future, were to make a man an Officer and a Gentleman.

Then, before the opposition had time to go into hiding and plot an overthrow of the new order, the reformers brought the Army out into the open. For the first time, army manoeuvres on the titanic German scale were organized, and the Press sent its 'war correspondents' to cover the mock-battle being fought out by 50,000 men, equipped with the most modern arms, over an area which stretched from the Severn to the Solent.

When the manoeuvres were finished, and certain lessons had been learnt in the actual campaigning, a complete set of new drill movements and tactics was introduced.

Then, in the following year (1873), the Department of Military Intelligence was established; and, to make the break with the days of purchased-commissions and entry-by-favour complete, radical alterations in the dress of officers were ordered in 1880.

One improvement did not come: the scarlet tunic was retained.

No one, apparently, had impressed upon the kinder-hearted of the reformers that blindness among tailors sewing the scarlet tunics in the ill-lit sweat-shops of the East End was an occupational disease only the less terrifying because it had come to be accepted as inevitable—sooner or later.

Those who cry out against the factory-system of employment must realize that the work of such reformers as Lord Shaftesbury was made possible only by the concentration of labour that the factory-system provided. The betterment of working conditions could not have been attempted had the factory-system not been introduced, and had industry continued to be tied to the cottage and the sweat-shop. By concentrating the workers in one place, the employers rendered themselves vulnerable to the reformers—it was the owner of sweat-shops and the employers of those who 'took work home' who longest stood out, successfully, against reform.

By one of those curious socio-economic paradoxes, the factories of which the development gave the reformers of working conditions their excuse and their opportunity to agitate for improvement were never, even at their terrifying worst, as bad as the noisome dens of Whitechapel and St. Giles, of Southwark and Burdett-road, and Bethnal Green.

Mayhew has described some of the conditions in which the sweaters' wretched slaves worked: but where were the powers to create, out of the taxpayers' money, an army of inspectors large enough to enter and correct every sweat-shop known to exist; to invade the rooms of tenements in Battersea and the Borough, to see that women did not hand-colour the plates in such a book as, say, Charles Dickens's *Christmas Carol* for twopence, or cover and trim a parasol for one penny three-farthings or finish a pair of trousers—button-holes, buttons and all—for twopence?

It is no condemnation of the Victorians that they were the more moved by what they could see than by what they could not; and their objections to reform argued less their want of heart than their conscious possession of principle. They felt that charity can harm as much as hurt—it took the 20th century to see that high wages and good working conditions are sound economics, though there was a book published in Victorian times— Eugène Sue's *Mysteries of Paris*—where, most improbably, is to be found the full though fictional anticipatory description of Cadbury's 'garden factory' at Bournville, and the new economic principles which inspired that type of factory development.

The sweat-shops stuck it out, indeed, far into this century, and even to-day they exist. But so far as they could, the Victorians attacked the principle of sweating. It was in this seventh decade of the 19th century that one of the greatest advances in the liberation of the worker from complete subservience to his employment took place: the establishing of the August Bank Holiday, through the efforts of Sir John Lubbock, the banker. Here was one day, stated by law to be a day on which no employer had the right to call upon an employee to work.

Protestant England had gained much from the Reformation, but it had lost its Saints' Days, and such national holidays as had survived the Commonwealth—'Queen Elizabeth's Birthday' for instance—had been put down by Authority on the grounds that holidays gave rein to license. Merry England came into the 19th century without one holiday it could call its own.

It took some powerful lobbying on Sir John Lubbock's part, and a deal of rhetoric and patience, to persuade the Government to grant the people one free day per annum.

Those who objected to the proposed Bank Holiday prophesied that the inch would make an ell; that other days would be appropriated to holidays, and that before we knew where we were factory-workers would be expecting the annual week's holiday that clerks were given.

Fortunately, the prophets were right. That one holiday did lead to others. And the attack on the actual working hours formed part of the larger scheme of liberation from round-the-clock labour.

The Shop Assistants' Acts, the Early Closing Acts and others of the sort, though they came later, sprang from the idea that man is not born into this world to work as long as others can get him to work. But of that more later.

Let us return for a little to the Army of the Queen.

The year 1870, which saw the abolition of the old system by which British armies were officered, saw the making of a great military reputation.

In that year, the French-Canadian half-breed, Riel, led the Red River rising against a Canada now predominantly British, in authority if not in population.

The man sent to smash Riel was General Garnet Wolseley—bearer of a name which, in all its slightly differing forms (Wolsey, Wesley, Wellesley), has meant much in our island history.

Fair of hair, palest blue of eye, chinless, small, slim and almost half-witted in appearance, Wolseley's character was everything that his appearance denied. He was tough, intelligent, brave, imaginative, far-seeing, electrically adaptable, patient, ruthless, tolerant and merciful. He was loved by the Very Highest and all below the Top. It was those just above the middle who feared the brilliance of this consistently brilliant man.

What was more, he could teach his brilliance to others; and if Herbert Kitchener was his star-pupil, every other British general worth his salt owed such success as he had to the closest imitation of Garnet Wolseley's methods.

Because he seems to me to be the most representative of the 'newer' Victorian generals, I have selected him here to represent, as it were, the Victorian military mind—at its best.

For over thirty years Wolseley directed the military operations of an empire which, even by 1870, ruled nearly 500,000,000 human beings.

First as fighting general, then as acting commander-in-chief, Wolseley won by his superb 'appreciation' (to use the military expression) of any problem in tactics or strategy the near-delirious admiration of the public and the more restrained but no less complete acclaim of his peers.

Since 1807, when the Ashanti, 'warlike Negroes of West Africa', had, by conquering Fanti, a country containing the British settlement of Cape Coast Castle, come into uneasy proximity to the Raj, British-Ashanti relations had been of the 'armed truce' type.

A showdown had been decided upon in 1863, but the military operation of May 1864 had had to be called off because 'General Malaria' had put the majority of our troops *hors de combat*. King Coffee Calcalli had reluctantly to be left to tyrannize the Fanti, 'allies' of Britain.

Ten years later, though quinine had not yet been promoted from aphrodisiac to malaria-preventive, the British Government decided that King Coffee Calcalli was threatening its prestige, and General Sir Garnet Wolseley was ordered off to the West Coast to put Her Majesty in his place.

Sir Garnet received his appointment as 'Governor of the Colonies on the West Coast of Africa' in September 1873. Six months later, after the palace and city of King Coffee had been burnt, and a treaty of 'perpetual peace' and an indemnity of 50,000 ounces of gold[3] had been exacted, Sir Garnet returned in triumph to Portsmouth, to be received a few days later by the Queen.

The cost of the expedition had been £900,000, rather a lot for those days, and though Coffee's successor, Mensah, sent the Queen a golden axe, as a symbol of his total submission; Coffee, though defeated, had not been dismissed. But his later 'rebellion' was dealt with by generals other than Wolseley, who had more important tasks to carry through.

In their method of using Wolseley's talents may be seen a revival, on the part of the British military authorities (working very closely with a strictly commercially-minded Government) of a system that Rome had used in developing and maintaining her empire. (If we less educated British wonder that even the Radical-manufacturer-M.P.s of Victoria's day understood the classical quotations in the original tongues—though not the original pronunciations—with which speeches were tricked out, we must remember that the 'classical education' that our Progressives despise also included a deep study of Roman history.)

Rome's system—and it was Britain's system at the end of the 19th century—was to use generalship of two complementary types.

---

[3]Then worth between £175,000 and £180,000 ($875–190,000).

To one general was allotted the task of invading and taking over a new province. He was the Imperial Legate, and he was expected to remain in residence. The other general acted as a sort of one-man 'shock troop', of the kind that the Americans call a 'trouble-shooter'. He came, he saw, he put things right—and was summoned back to the capital to be assigned a fresh task, as and when his peculiar talents were needed. Wolseley was a general of the second type. Kitchener, his most brilliant pupil, was a general of the first type (or at any rate he was cast for the first-type rôle).

In the case of Wolseley, as of any other 'trouble-shooting' general, he could think only 'critically'. Immediate solution of pressing problems was his forte; and his opinion on matters involving long-term policies was, at the best, useless and, at the worst, contemptible.

As, for instance, his opinion on the Channel Tunnel.

By 1873, the Balance of Power had undergone one of its periodic swings. Prussia had established herself as a Great Power, organizing the weaker German states into a confederation over which Prussia had unchallenged hegemony: the German Empire.

Opposition to the formation of this empire had been ruthlessly crushed by Prussia, who had not hesitated to embark upon a civil war to establish 'federal rights' over 'states' rights', the war breaking out in the year after the end of the American Civil War had successfully established the same principle.

More, Prussia had not hesitated to abolish certain states which had incautiously backed the wrong side; and Hanover had been converted from an independent kingdom into a mere province of Prussia, even though the reigning monarch, George V, was a Prince of the Blood Royal of Great Britain and Ireland.

The lesson was not entirely lost upon Britain, as it had not been lost upon either the friends or the enemies of Prussia.

Napoleon III had left France: he was dying of cancer at Chislehurst. Both Communism and Royalism had been faced and overcome in France; France was now a 'respectable democracy', strictly middle-class in make-up and sentiment, under the benign rule of a Marshal of Scottish descent. The theory of the Balance of Power demanded that Britain ally herself with France, as the only stable power in Europe with sufficient resources to make her, as an ally, partner in a combination adequately powerful to challenge Prussian ambitions. Italy was just recovering from the long struggle for unification; Spain was uneasily experimenting with a Republican form of government.

France was now 'democratic'; she had paid off the indemnity of 2,000,000,000 gold francs that Bismarck had demanded ('If I'd known how quickly they would have paid up, I'd have asked them for ten times that,' the Iron Chancellor remarked); she had rebuilt Paris; she had, despite the Franco-Prussian War, got herself a first-class navy of the most modern type; and her interest lay in an alliance with Great Britain.

Now was the time, the backers of the Channel Tunnel decided, to press their claims.

Everything was in their favour. The political atmosphere was favourable; the money (it was Rothschild money) was available; the practical difficulties had been swept away by the invention of a tunnelling-machine by the ingenious Colonel Beaumont, R.E. Here was one case in which the characteristic imaginativeness of the Royal Engineers ran on fairly practical lines.

Using Beaumont's 'mole', two pilot tunnels were driven out from Dover and Cape Gris Nez. The tunnel itself had been a practical possibility since the French engineer, Albert, had suggested it in the short Peace of Amiens, in 1802; but with Beaumont's tunnelling device it became instantly realizable, at reasonable cost, as well as within reasonable time.

This cost was estimated at £5,000,000; the time, about two years. A Parliamentary majority in favour of the tunnel had already been secured, by skilful lobbying and by the creation of a 'favourable attitude.' It is not realized, now that we are almost two centuries from the first proposal, and we are still awaiting our tunnel, that the Channel Tunnel *was* sanctioned by a parliament in the seventh decade of the 19th century, and that a treaty between France and England, setting out the terms on which the countries would collaborate, was actually signed.

(A curious result of this treaty remains with us, for all that the tunnel still lies in the future: since the tunnel would unite, physically, France and England, the border between the two countries was fixed at a point midway between the two ends of the tunnel.)

The pilot tunnels had been driven out through the chalk and greensand: something near two miles on the English side, a little less from Cape Gris Nez. And there they stopped. Mushrooms have been grown in the English pilot-tunnel ever since; France has managed to find not even that trivial use for her section.

For Wolseley stepped in, and said No, just as seventy years later Montgomery stepped in and said No.

Risking reprimand—and worse—for daring, as a mere colonel, to oppose the views of a General Officer, Beaumont pointed out the foolishness of supposing that the French, or anyone else, could use the tunnel for invasion. Wolseley even said that French soldiers might infiltrate 'disguised as civilians'.

Beaumont, using *The Times*, the *Daily Telegraph* and the *Morning Post* as his platform, argued that a couple of platoons could guard the entrance (or exit, if you prefer). What was more, Beaumont urged, he was prepared to arrange for poison-gas (what diabolical ideas our Victorians gave the next-generation Germans!) to be introduced into the air-circulating system: *that* would put paid to any invading Frenchmen carrying Lebel repeating rifles disguised as umbrellas!

Wolseley, through the correspondence-columns of newspapers having far more effect upon public opinion than is the case today, 'went to the country.' Playing upon the traditional ignorant fear of French animosity, and the traditional ignorant hatred of the French capacity of getting more out of life, Wolseley made the public's flesh creep; and as he didn't care a damn about the Rothschilds' or anyone else's money, Wolseley won, where even the power of Banker-backed Politics failed.

It might be easy to argue, as indeed I myself have argued elsewhere, that these dedicated killers, left to their own devices, could not invent anything half as technologically complex as a stone axe; but it would be far too narrow a judgement to condemn Wolseley's intelligence because he argued against the tunnel unintelligently. He was, in fact, 'arguing down to his audience.' He knew perfectly well that the French couldn't invade England through the tunnel—just as, I imagine, Bernard Montgomery knew it.

But that wasn't the sort of invasion that Wolseley feared: he was afraid of the invasioin of ideas; frightened of a too-close linking of French with British interests. And there is no doubt that the coming of the tunnel would have linked the two 'ancient inveterate enemies' in a bond too tight to be broken.

For Wolseley was an Empire man, and he saw that, as France and Britain were both after Empire, a union of interests at home would mean either the prospect of Condominium—an unlikely prospect, indeed!—or the abandonment, by both countries, of their expansionist policies; for to Wolseley, Empire by negotiation was not Empire at all. You went after colonies, not for glory, but for—well, you can call it 'loot' if you like. But whatever you call it, behind the Flag march, not the soldiers nor even the proconsuls, but the traders.

Wolseley—and his masters—found themselves far more interested in learning the lessons of the Alabama business than in speculating on the possible advantages of a Channel Tunnel.

Few British Governments have had to carry through a measure as unpopular as that by which the 'Alabama Claim' was settled.

In the earlier part of 1872, a sop to the Mob was given by the passing of the Ballot Act, by which, for the first time, voting at Parliamentary elections was made secret. Now any man with a vote could register it, knowing that his choice of candidate might not involve him in dispute with the Vested Interests of his borough.

It was a good measure, even though we may suspect that the timing of the Act was not without ulterior motive.

In the latter part of the year, Gladstone's government had to announce that they were prepared to accept the award of the Committee of Arbitration sitting on the Alabama Claim, and that Her Britannic Majesty's Government were sending off a cheque for £3,000,000 of the taxpayers' money to the Treasury of the United States of America.

The Civil War had ended in 1865 with the complete defeat of the South. For five years the victorious, 'humanitarian' North were too busy ravaging the conquered states of their fellow-Americans, paying off old scores, feathering their nests, destroying the means of possible revival on the South's part, to bother about exacting revenge from those who had assisted the South during the war.

But by 1870 the North, gorged with revenge, could take a breather, and cast its cold eye abroad, looking for enemies not so near home. Lincoln had gone, but his carpet-bagging spirit still went marching on. . . .

Alabama, a fast cruiser, had been built in a Birkenhead yard to the orders of agents for the Confederate States. She was only one of many ships built in Britain for the South, but unlike some others, she dodged the blockade that the British Government was putting on such ships and their captains (not a few, caught, were fined and imprisoned, under the Foreign Recruitment Act).

Alabama got safely away, hoisted the Confederate ensign, and sank or captured several Northern ships before being captured and sunk herself. Before she went to her end, she had accounted for, the North said, many millions of pounds' worth of Abolitionist shipping. This was the basis of the famous Alabama Claim against the British Government. It did not matter that Britain had prevented many of her nationals from taking their ships to blockade the North; it mattered not that many a Briton had taken his pay from the North to blockade the South; *Alabama* had been permitted to slip the leash, and the United States wanted compensation.

We are still two chapters off Pan-American imperialism, but coming events, as they say, cast their shadows before; and now Washington was as uppish as though Pan-Americanism was already a plank in American foreign policy.

Most people know that immediately after the end of the Civil War, the U.S. Government helped the Mexican 'patriot', Juarez, to overthrow and murder the French-backed Austrian Archduke, Maximilian, who had been made, by the bayonets of the Foreign Legion, Emperor of Mexico.

What most people have forgotten is that before abandoning Mexico to the United States, Europe, in the shape of a combined British-French-Spanish force, landed troops in Mexico. It was not Juarez who ordered them out, but Washington.

When they went, Washington had the satisfaction of knowing that it had secured a bloodless but none the less complete victory over Austria, France, Spain and Britain: not bad going for a Union only a year old!

Convinced, by the evidence, that Britain would not fight except where nothing vaguely resembling an international principle was concerned (she had not even fought over the Slidell and Mason affair, when the North was in the thick of the Civil War) the United States pressed the Alabama Claim hard.

Bluffed into acquiescence in Washington's demands, Britain agreed to submit the claim to international arbitration; and it is an historical fact that 'arbitration', where Britain is concerned, *always* means that the verdict goes against Britain.

This is a rule to which, so far, there has been no exception.

Arbitration conformed to rule: Britain was ordered to pay the United States Government compensation for the damage wreaked by *Alabama*. The damages were assessed at £3,000,000, about 5 per cent of the total of the loans on which various American states had defaulted since the beginning of the century.

Gladstone paid up: it did nothing to enhance his waning popularity. . . .

Alabama was built, with the enthusiastic approval of the people not only of Birkenhead, but of all Lancashire. As she was launched, all who saw her slide down the slips hoped that she would tip the balance against the North; not because they hated Negroes or loved President Davis, but because by blockading Southern cotton the North had thrown three million Lancashire cotton-operatives out of work.

There was no alternative employment, save for a few; there was no unemployment pay or national relief. Only Charity—and though Victorian charity was the object of all classes, to feed and house three million people for eight years would tax the charity even of this provident age. Lancashire Nonconformism was not socialist until the 'Hungry Sixties'; it is still deeply anti-American—a matter of the heart rather than of the head, which is why the prejudice will outlive your lifetime and mine.

One thing was clear to the British Government: an alternative source of raw cotton must be found, so that never again would trouble in America threaten the livelihood of millions of the British, and even the survival of Britain herself.

Our classically-educated rulers of a century ago recalled that togas of Egyptian cotton were a 'luxury item' in ancient Rome; and the President of the Board of Trade doubtless reminded them that cotton had been introduced into America from Egypt.

The cotton that Egypt still produced was the finest in the world, but Egyptian internal economy was not of such a nature as to guarantee a regular supply of cotton in the quantities that Lancashire industry would need.

Still . . . if Egypt were to be 'taken in hand'. Yes. . . .

Now the trouble was that France had already established more than a mere foothold in Egypt; she had re-cut the canal that the Romans had re-cut, and if the phrase 'sphere of influence' meant anything at all, then Egypt was surely within the French 'sphere of influence.' To become more closely united to France by means of a tunnel was surely not to be thought of when plans to rehabilitate Lancashire seemed all to be pointing towards trouble with France. . . .

Egypt, in 1870, was nominally part of the Turkish Empire. In its collapse, the Turkish Empire greatly resembled the Roman and the British in that it included 'dependencies' which were, in fact, nothing less than sovereign independent states. Such a state was Egypt, whose rulers, though enjoying only the title of 'Viceroy' ('Khedive'), were, in all other respects, independent autocratic monarchs. They did not even pay the customary annual tribute as from a 'vassal' to a 'sovereign lord'. Yet it was not until 1922 that the fiction that Egypt was part of the Turkish state was finally admitted.

The French engineer, De Lesseps, had finished cutting the Suez Canal in 1869. The French Emperor and Empress (it was the last time they would ever go abroad together, save into exile) ceremonially opened the canal with all the pomp and circumstance of French stage-management inspired to dazzle a Levantine audience.

The Empress's confessor, Monsignor Baur, a converted Jew who was to return to the faith of his fathers, blessed the enterprise; and the canal opened to business with the Khedive a 44-per-cent shareholder in the Suez Canal Company.

Now Khedive Ismail admired the French; even more he admired those gallant pleasures with which the French can put a rosy-tint into the drab prospect of earthly existence. Ismail loved Women (which is allowed by the Prophet) and Wine (which is not).

But most of all he loved gambling; and it was not long before, broke, he let it be known that he was thinking of borrowing on his Suez Canal holdings in Paris, a city which saw much of him.

In the meantime, following his settlement of the Alabama Claim, Gladstone had been defeated.

To quote a contemporary:

> The prestige of the Gladstone Ministry rapidly declined; the Education Act alienated non-conformists and Churchmen alike; reduction in the number of dockyard workers caused dissatisfaction; elimination of the purchase of Army commissions irritated the officer classes; when Gladstone introduced his Bill to unite Irish colleges in a single University open to Catholics and non-Catholics alike, he was defeated and resigned.'

However, there were still some necessary (and necessarily unpopular) measures to get on the Statute Book; and Disraeli had no intention of risking his popularity with Queen and Country by undertaking to push them through.

Gladstone, who only sighed after popularity, but never expected it, knowing that Popularity and Principle don't mix, took up the burden that he had just laid down, and jumped straight into the fray with the highly contentious Judicature Act.

Gladstone has deserved better of posterity: had he lived in the days before the camera, he might have enjoyed the sort of honour that he surely deserved. But he was such a dismal-looking old codger that only earnest humbugs respected him—or paid him respect, which is not the same thing, I know.

If we are to judge by such a portrait as the pencil-drawing that Richmond has left us, Gladstone was a quite remarkably good-looking young man. He had a gentleman's education, even if he was not a gentleman by birth; and had he stuck to a gentleman's politics, he would have been accepted as a gentleman by all who had preceded him, been contemporary with him, or followed him at Eton and Christ Church. Then his face wouldn't have mattered so much: indeed, I doubt very much that it would have been the same face.

But the pursuit of Principle, in the face of Unpopularity, played such havoc, not only with Gladstone's good looks, but with all that was human in his appearance, that much may be forgiven those who cannot be just to Gladstone.

Yet think of the courage of a man who would dare to reform the Judicature! To tackle such Vested Interests as the Army, the Civil Service, the Universities, the Public Schools and the Church calls for courage bordering on the selflessness of monomania; but to tackle the Judicature. . . .

Yet he did it. And just as he had taken away ancient privilege from those other powerful Vested Interests, so now he took it away from the most Vested Interest of them all.

The Judicature Act, along with several supplementary Acts, consolidated the three Common Law Courts, the Chancery and other tribunals, into one Supreme Court of Judicature, to consist of two principal divisions: the High Court of Justice, comprising the Queen's Bench, Chancery and the Probate, Divorce and Admiralty Divisions, and the Court of Appeal, from which appellate jurisdiction lay to the House of Lords. The Court of Appeal Gladstone strengthened by the addition of three (afterwards four) Law Lords of life tenure.

It is an ill-wind that blows nobody good, and in abolishing the ancient Order of the Coif, Gladstone provided the existing Serjeants-at-Law with a unique opportunity of feathering their nest.

Now that no more serjeants were to be appointed in England (the legal rank was retained in Ireland until the passing of the Free State Act in 1922), the Gentlemen of the Coif decided that they had no longer any use for their ancient Serjeants' Inn, which had stood at the corner of Chancery-lane since 1415.

No one knew quite to whom this valuable tenure belonged, but if it did not belong to the Serjeants-at-Law, to whom did it belong? Whatever a lawyer hates, it isn't money; and public disapproval of a quick profit may always be interpreted as common jealousy—and despised accordingly.

The serjeants, having been voted out of existence by Gladstone, voted their Inn out of existence, and sold it to a speculative builder for £73,000—a sum that they divided up among themselves.

Many a colourful old office was swept away by this modernizing of the Law, to the great distress of the Betjemans of the day; but in a period when the Law found itself concerned quite as much with contracts as with crime, it was obvious that only a streamlined justiciary could cope with the legalities of a Joint-Stock Era.

Disraeli had returned before the final changes had been effected in the Judicature: Gladstone had been exactly one year in office when his ministry was once again overthrown, and this time Disraeli was ready to take over.

The Khedive's shares were on the market, and Disraeli, not Gladstone, was the man to handle the job of getting them into British Government control, as the first step towards making Egypt the desired alternative source of raw cotton.

As the contemporary quoted above put it: 'Disraeli's mission was to give the country a rest at home, and pursue a foreign policy more in accord with the demands of British prestige and interests.'

Not everything was neglected at home: there were three Acts which are worthy of the best traditions of enlightened government at any period. The Public Health Act of 1875 was a codification of earlier legislation which, even today, remains the backbone of British sanitary law. The Artisans' Dwelling Act of the same year was the first serious attempt to grapple with the problem of housing the poor. The Merchant Shipping Act, on the Statute Books only through the persistent campaigning of the brewers' manager, Samuel Plimsoll, is one of those Acts which seem to be legislated, not for one country, but for all the world.

By this Act, 'coffin ships'—at least those flying the Red Duster—had their long history terminated. The Act laid down strict rules to prevent the use of unseaworthy ships or the overloading of seaworthy ones. In honour of the man who had fought, despite the sneers and worse that a 'fanatic' always earns, for the lives of seamen, the loading line on ships has been called a 'Plimsoll' mark ever since.

But sound and needed as these domestic measures were, it was in his acts of foreign policy that Disraeli showed his quality and gained his notable fame.

The story of how he bought the shares of the Suez Canal is too well known to be more than summarized here.

Learning, through the connections that his early conversion to Christianity had not lost him, that the Khedive was planning to sell his shares in Paris (it was the end of November 1875, and Parliament was in recess) Disraeli got the Rothschilds to step in quickly, and buy the shares—price £4,000,000.

The deal was made before Parliament had time to debate and ratify the purchase, and in a number of history-books, one or two novels and a couple of dreary films, the 'dramatic' quality of that quick decision to buy has been plugged with more false emphasis than was ever used to sell a detergent on T.V.

The critical point of the 'drama', is always the question: what would have happened had Parliament refused to back Disraeli after he had bought the Suez Canal shares? Suppose that Parliament had refused to sanction the deal? had refused to cough up the four millions to 'pay back' the Rothschilds?

That such questions could be asked shows how distorted fact may become after little more than a century, and fact, too, involving so important and widely-discussed an event as Britain's acquiring a major—but not *the* major—holding in the Suez Canal. (Until Nasser's expropriation, control of the canal always remained in French hands, as the control of the still-existing and still immensely powerful Suez Canal Company still does.)

If Parliament had refused to ratify Disraeli's private arrangement with the Rothschilds, Britain would have been the loser of the shares, but the House of Rothschild would hardly 'have been left with the shares on their hands'. Other people were just as interested in acquiring the Khedive's shares as Disraeli was. What he did, and what the Rothschilds helped him to do, was to secure an option on those shares, on behalf of Britain, without putting down a penny of option-money.

The Rothschilds trusted to Disraeli to find the money; and Disraeli trusted himself to produce it. It seems to me that there is far more 'drama' in the plain, unvarnished facts of this wonderful transaction than in the hopped-up versions of novelists, playwrights and 'historians' who know as little of the simple rules of commerce as they do of parliamentary procedure.

Well, Disraeli got the shares; and as far as the Khedive was concerned, he had, by selling the shares to Britain, got himself something more than a mere awkward neighbour: he had got himself what at best was a strict trustee, and at worst might turn out to be a rapacious and ruthless taskmaster.

For the moment, French and British interests coincided, so far as putting the Khedive's kingdom in order was concerned. The French were not particularly interested in Egypt's cotton-potential, but they were interested in protecting the large French investments in Egypt and, as a much longer-term policy, in extending the French hold on the southern Mediterranean sea-board. Algiers had now been French for forty years; the French had their eye on Tunis: Algiers had once been part of the Turkish Empire, Tunis was still nominally so. Between Tunis and Egypt lay another part of overseas Turkey, Tripoli: on that, too, the French had designs. Nor were they reconciled to giving up Egypt to the British—but for the moment, they were prepared to work with the British against the hereditary Macedonian dynasty which now ruled Egypt in the name of the Sultan.

If Britain and France mistrusted and feared each other, they both mistrusted and feared more that Russia which was 'steam-rollering' her way towards the Adriatic and the Atlantic.

Disraeli has often been called a 'popular' premier. So he was, compared with Gladstone. But his 'popularity' must be reckoned as he stood in the Queen's estimation. So far as the public was concerned, Gladstone was by far the more 'popular'.

Indeed, many of the acts which increased the Queen's regard for Disraeli incensed politicians of both parties. But backed by the Queen's admiring approval, 'Dizzy' could afford to ignore the general opinion of both Houses of Parliament. It was so with his Royal Titles Bill of 1876, a beautifully timed piece of entirely private legislation (for no one but 'Dizzy' was its inventor or sponsor).

By this bill, the Queen assumed the additional title of 'Empress of India', an 'un-English' style which shocked even the most loyal—one may say particularly the most loyal—of her subjects. The Queen, indeed, to pacify widespread objections, voiced most indignantly in both Houses, let it be known that she would never use it in Britain.

But it pleased the Queen mightily; and by timing it to be introduced just after the return of the Prince of Wales from his tour of India, Disraeli made it appear as though, in some fashion, the Prince had made the step up from Queen to Queen-Empress proper and inevitable. It gave the Prince his first taste of responsibility for important changes; and though the Queen did not relish the idea that 'Bertie' should have anything to do with affairs of state, she was pleased enough in this case to think that her son and heir had produced some beneficial result from what (to judge by the confidential reports which had reached her) had been one long junket.

―――――

The Prince had been shipped off to India following a scandal with which his name had inevitably been linked.

It was in 1875 that his former colonel, Valentine Baker, had been charged with having committed an 'indecent assault' upon a young lady, Miss Emily Dickenson, in a railway-carriage, between Woking and London.

The colonel had got into a compartment containing only Miss Dickenson, had passed the time of day with her, had sought to hold her hand, had pressed his odious attentions upon her, and had so terrified Emily that she had opened the door, and was hanging above the railway-track when a clergyman in a neighbouring compartment had seen her, and had pulled the alarm-chain.

Colonel Valentine Baker, Officer Commanding the crack and fashionable Tenth Hussars, had stood his trial at Croydon Assizes, had refused to allow Miss Dickenson to be called for examination, but had failed to impress Mr Justice Brett, by this gentlemanly conduct, into persuading his lordship to mitigate the sentence.

The colonel got one year's hard labour, and was fined £500.

Released from prison, the ex-colonel made his way to Turkey, where the Sultan received him courteously, doubtless thinking that any man who had been badly treated by the British deserved his friendship, and made him a colonel again: of Turkish Gendarmerie.

When the Turks beat back the Russians at Plevna, Baker Pasha was one of those whose generalship gained victory for the Turks.

Promoted to Inspector-general of Gendarmerie in Egypt, Baker came into contact with British troops during the Egyptian campaigns of the next decade, and it was he who made possible the decisive victory of Tel-el-Kebir.

Baker's story is mentioned here solely to point out that the Prince was held to be unfortunate in his choice of friends, not all of whom found themselves in the dock, but of whom many were to be found cited as co-respondents.

Queen Victoria objected to Bertie's companions on the Indian tour—in particular to 'Sporting Joe', the Earl of Aylesford, whose wife, pursued earnestly by the Prince and by the Marquess of Blandford, had a son by the latter, with whom she lived, in open sin, in Paris.

The public, however, did not know much about the companions; and the Press-relations, under the charge of Herbert Russell, the war-correspondent who had exposed the scandals of the Crimean administration, did a good job of whitewashing.

But if the Queen and her advisers thought that the Prince had had a change of heart as he had viewed the glories of his mother's eastern empire, they soon found that they were mistaken. In March 1875 the first of the cases that Sir Charles Mordaunt brought against his wife had been heard before Lord Penzance. Lady Mordaunt had accused herself of infidelity with a number of titled or otherwise 'smart' co-respondents, including the Prince of Wales, Lord Cole, Lord Newton, Sir Frederick Johnstone and Captain Farquhar, and Sir Charles had taken the confession to court. He was not to get his divorce until three trials and five years later; but in the first trial the Prince was called, and gave evidence that there had never been 'any improper familiarity' between Lady Mordaunt and himself. Nobody believed him, but all were impressed by the gentlemanly—one might almost say sporting—gesture of consenting to enter the witness-box to defend a lady's honour.

Five months later Colonel Baker was sentenced to a year's imprisonment; and though the Queen opposed the suggestion of an Indian tour for the Prince, she was overruled, and in the autumn of 1875 he sailed on a P. & O. liner, from Brindisi for Bombay, pressing through the newly opened Suez Canal.

The liveliest members of the Marlborough House set accompanied the pleasure-loving Prince: Lord Charles Beresford, the Duke of Sutherland (one of the finest guns of all time), Lord Carrington, Lord Suffolk and Lord Aylesford ('Sporting Joe').

It was not so much that this lively set returned to fresh mischief: fresh mischief had already brewed on the trip.

Blandford had stayed behind. As soon as Aylesford had left with the Prince, Blandford moved down to a country inn near to the house in which Edith Aylesford was living in grass-widowhood.

A friend now wrote to 'Sporting Joe' telling him what was happening between his wife and Blandford. Aylesford, despite the Prince's expostulations, took leave of hs royal host, and caught the next steamer back. He did not arrive in time to prevent his wife's going off to Paris, to live in open sin with Blandford.

The Prince returned very angry with Blandford; not only for having broken up the party, by making it necessary for Aylesford to cut short his trip, but for having made off with a lady on whom the Prince had cast loving eyes.

He began to speak harshly against Blandford, when opposition showed in quite the most unexpected quarter: Lord Randolph Churchill, Blandford's younger and more than somewhat unbalanced brother, took up the challenge, and on Blandford's behalf, loudly threatened the Prince.

If the Prince, Randolph said, did not 'lay off' Blandford, then Randolph would publish the love-letters that the Prince himself had written to Edith Aylesford.

The Prince was so indignant at having his love-letters used against him in this way that he sent Randolph a challenge through Francis Knollys. 'Randy' kept his royal challenger waiting for his answer; but finally sent this, through Lord Falmouth:

> 'Lord Randolph Churchill requests me to present his loyal, humble and dutiful respects to His Royal Highness the Prince of Wales, and to state that though he is willing to meet any gentleman that His Royal Highness may care to nominate, he cannot lift his sword against his future Sovereign.'

Thus—social banishment for Randolph; a throne-rocking scandal avoided for the Prince.

But it was not easy for the Prince to avoid, if not scandal itself, then the appearance of scandal. It was not only the 'Yellow Press'—they did not call it that, of course, in those days—which reported and mis-reported every piece of gossip concerning the Prince and his friends; a senior Civil Servant, Mr A. A. Dowty, of the Paymaster-General's Office, published, at each Christmas beginning with Christmas 1870, a skilful but libellous 'exposure' of the Prince.

The first of these attacks, entitled, *The Coming K——* was a clever parody of the then immensely popular *Idylls of the King*. 'The brochure,' says Sidney Lee, 'purported boldly to draw the veil from the private life of the Prince and his comrades, and to suggest his unfitness for the succession to the throne.'

Though these attacks were anonymous (respected Mr Dowty did not wish to risk promotion and pension, for the sake of avowing his republican principles) they were not published anonymously. Five were issued, under the general title of *Beeton's Christmas Annual*, before Beeton, the royalty-hating widower of the famous Mrs Beeton, died in 1876.

Mr Dowty could not find another publisher as sympathetic as Beeton had been, and not caring to entrust his secret to an untested publisher, he gave up lampooning the Prince—at least in writing.

But there were always others to take up the burden of the attack; though only one of the slanderers need detain us here.

In 1879, Adolphus Rosenberg, owner and editor of a grisly little scandal-sheet, *Town Talk*, was charged at the Guildhall with having uttered a defamatory libel of and concerning Mrs Mary Cornwallis West. When they got Adolphus to court, a further charge was joined to the original indictment: that he had libelled Mr and Mrs Edward Langtry.

Of course, the interest in both Mrs Cornwallis West and Mrs 'Lillie' Langtry was that each was supposed, by the majority of people who read of them in the newspapers, to be a mistress of the Prince.

The libels differed greatly in gravity. Of the Cornwallis Wests—he was Lord Lieutenant of Denbighshire—Rosenberg had merely said that he and his wife, whose photographs appeared in many shop-windows, took commission from the sale of the picture-postcards. It was a contemptible libel, and the Cornwallis Wests were ill-advised to have taken any notice of it.

The other libel was far more dangerous. Rosenberg announced that the Prince was to be cited as co-respondent by Mr Langtry. When other London journals, of a more responsible nature, pointed out that no such case appeared in the calendar, Rosenberg affirmed boldly that Langtry had been induced to drop it, on the promise of being appointed to a colonial governorship.

Langtry, in court, stated that there was not a word of truth in the story. He and his wife were not parted; they were not contemplating parting; he had not cited the Prince or Lord Londesborough or anyone else; and he had not been offered a colonial governorship.

Rosenberg got twelve months—for having dragged the Prince's name into the columns of his seedy journal. For it would have been hard to have libelled Langtry: he had no money, yet he and his wife had been able, with no apparent source of income, to live in a style matching that of the great folk who knew his wife, even if they did not quite 'know' Edward Langtry.

'The Jersey Lily', indeed, was not a flower born to blush unseen—or undiscussed. Nor had her friendship with the Prince resembled that which ripened, in a moment, between King Cophetua and the Beggar Maid. 'Lillie'—'a most beautiful creature, quite unknown, very poor, and they say has but one black dress', Lord Randolph Churchill wrote to his wife—got to the Prince after having passed through the hands (or should one say, 'through the beds'?) of Whistler and Millais, before proceeding to the American Morton Frewen, Lady Randolph's brother-in-law, the Duke of Albany, Queen Victoria's son, the King of the Belgians, Prince Louis of Battenberg (by whom she had a daughter, whom we all knew before World War II), and the Crown Prince of Austria—later to die so tragically at Mayerling.

La fin couronne l'oeuvre—and 'Lillie' finally added the Prince to the already dazzling list of her lovers.

It was curious that the Prince should have chosen the Tite-street studio of Mr Oscar Wilde, the 'aesthete', for his first assignations with the Lily.

What harm, in truth, did this do to the Crown?

The brilliant Parliamentary careers of two Republicans—Dilke and Parnell—were ruined because public opinion would not show the same tolerance towards their sexual indulgences as was shown towards those of the Prince.

The truth is that all these attacks on the Prince of Wales, whether coming from the worldly or the 'good', did neither the Prince nor the Throne the least harm.

When, at a reception, the Prince of Wales gave precedence to the King of the Sandwich Isles, and heard later that Prince Frederick of Prussia had been affronted by the 'snub', Edward's comment, in its robust common-sense, was worthy of the great Dr Johnson himself.

'Well,' said Edward, 'either the man is a king or he's just a buck nigger. If he's a king, then he takes precedence of mere princes—and if he's only a buck nigger, then he has no business here.'

The British people thought along similar lines: Either, they said, the Prince is a prince, and is thus entitled not to to be judged as ordinary folk, or he's to be judged like you and me—in which case, what's he pretending to be Heir to the Throne for?

Though the evening papers gave a stick of copy to reporting that the one-hundred-and-fiftieth Atlas rocket had been fired from Cape Canaveral, and though monstrous births may now be safely credited to a 'tranquillizer', and not to the appearance of a comet, the last half of the Victorian reign was a much more 'scientific' epoch than ours. People then were busy finding out, where, today, they are idly just taking marvels for granted.

Even the *Boys' Own Paper* ran science-fiction stories—all the Jules Verne novels appeared in its pages—and articles which dealt with the wonders of the new scientific age.

Johann Philipp Reis, the Gelnhausen schoolmaster, had first demonstrated his electro-magnetic telephone, before the Hanover Philosophical Society, in 1861—the year in which Swan, at Newcastle-on-Tyne, had demonstrated the first incandescent electric lamp.

In 1879 both those world-changing inventions were to achieve practical form: the lamp with Edison's improvments, and the telephone, brought to near-perfection by Edison, Bell, and Gray.

In 1879 the first telephone exchange was opened in London, with ten subscribers. The old Gaiety Theatre had been illuminated with 'the Electric Light' (arc-lamp) in 1877; and in 1880 arc-lamps were installed to illuminate the crossroads at the Mansion House. By 1879 the incandescent lamp was on the market; and by 1882, following the great Electrical Exhibition at the Crystal Palace, the first power-station in Britain (at Brighton) had been set up.

Within ten years, the Age of Electricity would have been firmly ushered in: already patents for radio and television had been applied for.

Indeed, it was in the period immediately following the death of the Prince Consort in 1861 that our modern world was given its blue-print, and not only in the realm of strict 'science.' In 1871 the change-over to the Decimal System, in currency as well as in weights and measures, was defeated by only one vote in the House of Commons. The Linotype and other mechanical systems of type-setting were introduced in the seventies—Mackie's steam type-composing machine 'is ruled by a perforated thick paper in a continuous strip about 2 ins. wide. It permits compositors to set up about 12,000 types per hour, as against the earlier average of 2,000.'

Wood-pulp paper—a product of the 1840s—and the mechanical setting-up of type made for cheaper printing and publishing, and enabled enterprising business-men to supply the needs of a reading-market created by the new Education Acts, as well as by the insatiable interest in the contemporary world which is the outstanding characteristic of the Victorian, no matter what his or her class.

The typewriter, in its practical form, had been first marketed by the Remington Rifle Company, in 1873. This already well-established company, whose firearm had helped to Win the West for the White American, understood the technique of Public Relations well. Its first advertisements carried the story—with picture—of how the daughter of Count Leo Tolstoy, the Distinguished Russian Novelist, had taught herself to be a 'typewriter', so as to act as her Distinguished Papa's amanuensis.

Snobbery apart, the typewriter gave the unendowed 'female' a new livelihood; got her away from the factory, the nursery-governess's soul-killing existence, and the incredible sweating of work 'done at home'. Moralists might like to reflect on the number of women saved from prostitution or suicide (or both) by the typewriter's having given them a new and 'respectable' occupation; one which could use the hitherto least-valued talent of the Victorian woman: education without money.

That was the decade of the Phonograph—crowds packed the Royal Institute to hear Professor Tyndall show how the phonograph, given the line, 'Come into the garden, Maud', would answer it back—tinnily, it is true, but accurately, none the less.

How they loved inventing, those Victorians! In the Midlands in 1878, Mr George William Garrett, curate of Holy Cross, Manchester, put his steam-driven submarine, thirteen feet long, through her paces in the calm water of Liverpool bay.

Four years later, the Prince of Wales was to journey to Landskrona, in Sweden, to see the launching of the submarine that the Reverend Mr Garrett had built in partnership with Nordenfeldt, the famous Swedish designer of the machine-gun which bears his name. An English parson found the secret of underwater navigation in 1878—and the 'waters beneath the earth' were no longer safe, even for fish.

In that year, Cleopatra's Needle, a 'gift' from the Khedive to Great Britain, was towed into London, after having been lost at sea for a year—the tow broke as the 'needle' was being brought from Egypt.

With much ceremony, it was set up on Bazalgette's new Embankment, for this decade had seen not only the opening of new roads through London's tight-packed and narrow-streeted City part, but the channelling of the Thames between two granite embankments, which stretched from Chelsea to Blackfriars, and might have gone on to the Tower, had not the 'City Fathers' put personal profit above the public good.

Beneath the roads which traversed these two Embankments, Bazalgette had arranged that sewers, gas-mains and underground railways should run; all neatly boxed and yet instantly accessible—the pattern that the subterranean 'services' of all great cities was to follow in the future.

Automobilism should have been a product of this decade, at the latest, seeing that automobilism, already well-established by the mid-1830s, when steam omnibuses were running on schedule from London to Birmingham, had been halted—driven off the roads—by Act of Parliament, only so as to give the over-capitalized railways that monopoly which alone could spare the shareholders total ruin.

A steam omnibus took to the road in Glasgow, carrying sixty-five passengers; but horses did not like the clanking, smoky road-engines, said those who did not like the clanking, smoky road-engines—and what automobilism needed to bring it back from the legalized illegality of outlawry was the internal-combustion engine.

Robert Boyle had experimented with the i/c engine as far back as the reign of Charles II. A working gas-engine was installed outside Paris in 1827, but it was so noisy that the neighbours complained, and got an injunction against the user. Edison turned his attention to the internal-combustion engine, taking up where Boyle had left off. Boyle had used gunpowder as his 'fuel'; Edison experimented with nitro-glycerine, in the form of an explosive paper-strip. The ingenious American met one of his few failures here; nearly blew his hand off; and wisely left the perfecting of the *practical* internal-combustion engine to others.

It was in 1879—truly an *annus mirabilis* in the history of invention—that Gottlieb Daimler put the first 'horseless carriage', powered by an internal-combustion engine, on the road.

What made the world give it a better reception than had been accorded to Cugnot's steam-waggon of 1769 was that right from the beginning Daimler's motor-car could beat the horse—where Cugnot's could not. Neither the seventies or the eighties were ready for the change from Horse to Internal-combustion Engine—but we note that it was in the seventies that it arrived.

It was the internal-combustion engine which was to make mechanical heavier-than-air flight possible; for in the history of aerial navigation the petrol-driven propeller (or 'aerofoil') type of aeroplane had to proceed from the engineless glider, and precede the 'jet-plane.'

But the seventies had already come to examine the possibilities of 'jet-propulsion', as it was called even then. The reaction-motor, in which a jet of high-pressure steam is expelled with considerable force, is attributed to Heron of Alexandria (flourished *circa* A.D. 100), and had been successfully adapted to the Philips model helicopter in 1847. The metal-clad, rigid airship, for which Richard Boyman obtained a patent (British, No. 3262) in 1866, was designed to be jet-propelled; and in the following year Butler and Edwards obtained another patent for a steam jet-propelled aircraft, whose design was clearly based upon that of the paper 'darts' that children use.

But in the seventies, all the experimentation with jet-propulsion was in connection with ships, light surface-craft of shallow draught. Some impressive advances were made.

The old order changed, giving place rapidly to the new: the toll gates which, taking the place of the ancient City gates, had curiously retained an antique 'privacy' for London, were all being swept away: on 3rd October, 1878, Waterloo-bridge was declared free of toll, to open the way more conveniently to the hansoms and growlers bringing the travellers from Waterloo Station to the splendid new hotels which were about to arise in Northumberland-avenue.

London, indeed, had already embarked upon that widening—that rippling outwards in concentric circles—which was, at no very distant date, to link central London with the towns and villages of Essex, Kent, Middlesex and Surrey, and by dense suburban building to make one huge city, fifty miles across.

P·A·R·T T·H·R·E·E

The Third Decade

We are still, and shall so remain for several decades, in the Age of Gaslight—and Gas-cooking as well (though that came in forty years earlier, as did the domestic hot-water "geyser"). But the third decade of this survey—that from 1881 to 1891—saw the entry, not hesitant, but a truly triumphant entry, of the Age of Electricity. The previous decade had seen the introduction of the now-perfected incandescent electric lamp: the joint effort of Joseph Swan and Thomas Alva Edison. Bell, Gray, and Edison had perfected the Reis telephone of 1861, and now, in 1879, London had its first telephone-exchange. The Savoy Theatre advertised that it was fitted-up with "the electric light", and Lady Randolph Churchill, American daughter of a millionaire and Mother of Winston, had her house in Connaught-place also fitted with "the electric light"—the first private house in London to enjoy this luxury.

The Paris Electrical Exhibition of 1881 had been followed by the equally successful Crystal Palace Electrical Exhibition of the following year: Electricity was to provide, not only illumination, but traction also; London's first electric-powered 'Underground' railway coming in 1890; a true "Underground", built with the Greathead Shield, and made possible by electric elevators and electrically-illuminated stations and carriages.

Before the decade was out, the world would have had its first intimation of the phenomenon of Radiation, as, by accident, Becquerel detected the ability of radium-containing pitchblende to fog unexposed photographic plates. In 1882, the Prince of Wales and many other European and Asian and American notables, went to Landskrona, in Sweden, to see the launching of the Nordenfeldt II, the submarine perfected by the Swedish machine-gun inventor from the original design by a British clergyman, the Reverend Mr. William George Garrett, of Manchester. There were still plenty of scandals in the highest places, with divorces and non-divorces (the Judge refused a decree to the cross-petitioning Lord and Lady Aylesford, on the grounds that the behaviour of both was execrable). Lady Colin Campbell and Lord Euston (refused) and the Earl of Durham (refused) were others who obliged the newspapers with very readable matter. The Prince of Wales, staying at Tranby Croft, was involved in a gambling scandal, in which the baronet, Sir William Gordon-Cumming, was accused of cheating. The baronet lost his libel action, but the crowd hissed the Prince as he left the Law Courts, after having testified against his old friend. A worse scandal involved the Heir Presumptive, the effeminate Duke of Clarence, when a homosexual brothel was raided, and Lord Arthur Somerset ("Podge", as the Prince of Wales called his Superintendent of the Royal Stables) left in a great hurry, on the boat-train for Dover— he was not alone. But perhaps the greatest scandal, involving Great Names only by scandalous rumour, were the Ripper killings of 1888; somehow (and perhaps not wrongly) associated in the public mind with the strange disappearances which covered the entire decade: men, women, boys, and girls.

At the beginning of the decade, the beaten British troops were staggering back from the defeat of Maiwand; Dr. Watson among them. At the end of the decade, Sherlock Holmes, the most popular character in all fiction, made his quiet First Bow in the pages of Beeton's Christmas Annual for 1887, the year of the Queen's Golden Jubilee, and that of "Black Sunday", when the Horse Guards and Foot Guards were called out to subdue the rampaging mob. Things were going badly in South Africa, but the flare-up was to wait until the end of the next decade. Organized Labour was flexing its muscles.

WHAT CERTAINLY struck the Londoner as the first most important happening of the 'Eighties was the revolt of the Transvaal Boers, five days after Christmas 1880. The choice of timing gave every patriotic Briton his opportunity to express his contempt for the 'hypocrisy' of the Bible-punching Boers, who couldn't even respect the Nativity of that Christ Whose name was—so report said—never off the bearded lips of Ole Kroojer and his pals. If any proof were needed to confirm what the average Briton had long suspected, that the Boers were Christian only in name, this was it.

In the previous September, the great Sir Garnet Wolseley, Britain's military panacea, had forced submission on the Zulu chiefs, which settlement left the British free to turn a belatedly trained, but now sufficiently experienced, army on to the Boers.

Military historians have had much to say about the tactical and strategical advantages that the Boers enjoyed—their freedom from restricting traditions, their knowledge of the country, their ability to dispense with basic military training (seeing that every man among the Boers could ride a horse and handle a rifle). To assess what the Boers did in 1880, one must bear in mind, not that the British were not aware that the 'farmers' possessed these undeniable military advantages, but that the Boers themselves were. They—as well as the British—thought that they were opposing untrained civilian personnel against trained regular soldiers. And so they were. They thought that they had but one advantage—that of surprise. (And so they had: it had never occurred, even to the militarily-intelligent Wolseley, that the defeat of the Zulus would provoke the Boers to attack: he thought that the 'lesson' of Cetewayo's defeat would keep the Boers quiet.)

Almost a month after Kruger proclaimed the Boer Republic, and Joubert and Pretorius, with their commandos, took to the veldt, the main 'rebel' armies came up with Sir George Colley at Laing's Nek, and Britain suffered the sort of humiliating defeat that she had not known since the American Revolutionary War—a sound trouncing at the hands of farmers.

Sir George rallied his forces, while, of course, the Boers were rallying theirs, and a month later a second battle was fought at Majuba Hill, the

British being again defeated, and Sir George killed. It was a black day for British military prestige—and the lesson was not lost in Egypt.

On 5th April, 1881, Great Britain 'recognized' the independence of the new Boer Republic; Kruger and his colleagues 'recognizing' the suzerainty of Great Britain. Honour wasn't quite satisfied on either side, but, as they say, a *modus operandi* had been devised sufficiently satisfactory to both sides. Each side knew that the arrangement was, by its nature, only temporary: the decisive struggle, the showdown, was to come.

A much more important happening was the opening of the first Electrical Exhibition at the Crystal Palace, in 1882.

The Electrical Exhibition held in Paris in the previous year had not only been widely reported in the British Press, it had drawn many visitors from Britain (return fare, 1st-class rail and steamer: £2 16s.).[1] What had astonished even the exhibitors was the conclusive proof that a fully-developed electrical industry was already in being—all that was now needed was the mechanism of 'marketing'; the means to persuade the public to ask, so that a widespread demand could develop the supply, and so bring down the prices from 'experimental' to 'practical' level.

The new decade began with Disraeli's going to the country in a general election. His party was defeated at the polls, Disraeli resigned, and Gladstone was once again in power. The pattern broadly was a turning away from imperial problems, and a concentration on home affairs. Though Montenegro was being 'awkward', and the Turks were anything but contented with the settlement of the Berlin Congress of 1878, it might fairly be said that Disraeli had smoothed over the Balkan and Middle Eastern troubles: there would be no war for a little. Gladstone the Peace-handler was due back for his accustomed rôle.

Much of the parliamentary session of 1880 was taken up with the seemingly ludicrous but in fact immensely important 'Bradlaugh Case', in which Bradlaugh, a professional atheist, refused to take the oath customarily administered to new Members of Parliament on taking their seat in the House. The phrase 'So help me, God!' stuck in this honest republican's throat; and as there was no parliamentary power (if, indeed, there had been parliamentary will) to accept Mr Bradlaugh without his oath, he was declared unfit to sit in the Commons.

It was not a new situation; only an old situation in a new aspect. Grudgingly, Parliament had admitted Roman Catholics, Anabaptists, Quak-

---

[1] Then $13.44.

ers, Irvingites, Countess of Huntingdon-ites, Jews—all who worshipped (or said that they worshipped) God in a manner differing from that laid down in the Thirty-nine Articles. But the House had never before had to deal with a professed atheist. The pliant Disraeli would have found a formula; the die-hard Christian, Gladstone, did not seek a formula.

All the same, Parliament, though much taken up with the case of Mr Bradlaugh, found time to enact one of those 'brakes-on-progress' Acts which, unlike so many other Acts, do what they set out to do: in these cases, hold things up.

The Electric Lighting Act of 1882 may well be admired as a classic of the Put-Back-The-Clock school of legislative thought. It says much for the faith of those behind the new electrical industry that they pushed on with their plans as though the Act had never been passed, and even as the dreary platitudes of the ignorant parliamentary parasites were talking the fatuous Act into being, Colonel Crompton, the 'Grand Old Man' of Electricity, was fitting up the new Law Courts with 'the electric light'. The Law Courts were opened and the Act made law in the same year—1882.

To use a modern phrase, the work of these pioneer 'electricians' (the 'grander' title, 'electrical engineers', was introduced only some twenty years later) was very much of an 'off-the-cuff' nature.

Writing as a very old man, nearly forty years later, Crompton recalled both the difficulties and excitement of those pioneering days:

> Referring to the ordinary familiar forms of electrical apparatus, that is, switchboards, fuse boards, ceiling roses, pendants, portable fittings, with which we are all now so familiar—you can hardly believe how many of these were thought out and developed by Harold Thomson and Lundberg, and how much of the theory of the magnetic field and of the armature and magnetic winding of modern dynamos was developed by the Crompton staff of the early days.
> The success of the large generating-station at Vienna led us to start the Kensington Court Company in London on similar lines—i.e. direct currents generated in parallel, with accumulators as a reserve, the current being generated by dynamos coupled to Willans engines. About the same time, Ferranti started the Grosvenor Gallery Station to distribute electrical energy for lighting by high-pressure alternating current transmitted through overhead wires, and transformed on the consumer's premises to a pressure usable on the [Joseph] Swan lamps by Goulard and Gibbs' development of induction coils, which began to be called transformers.

If these pioneers needed an incentive to stand fast in their endeavour, and to get on with their work, they had it not only in the dead-hand lumpishness of the Parliamentary 'legislators', but as well in the blind prejudice of those actuarial 'geniuses', the insurance 'experts', who, to give Electricity its proper handicap, proposed to raise the already high insurance-rate of £3 13s. 6d. per £100 for the Crystal Palace, 'on account of the introduction of electric light'.

It is obvious that no one around Cornhill had bothered to find out anything about electric light—not even by reading the excellent description of the exhibition in the *Illustrated London News* ('These lights can be turned on and off as easily as gas'). No—Electricity was new, and must therefore, by Monopoly, be penalized.

With no one bothering to know what Electricity had already accomplished, it is not astonishing that no one dared predict what it would do—in the fields of transport, communication, medicine and surgery. Yet before the decade was out, our modern Electrical world had come into being, despite the 'Government', despite that other Backbone of Britain, the Insurance Company, despite, even, the honest competition of the gas industry, which received a 'shot-in-the-arm' late in the decade, when Baron Auer von Welsbach invented his 'gas-mantle' of cerium-impregnated cotton.

What prevented Governmental opposition to electricity being more fierce than it was, was the fact that it had helped politicians to indulge more freely in their favourite occupation, and only talent: Talk. They were not attracted to electricity because it promised practical submarine navigation or even safe home-lighting; or fast suburban travel or private carriages which did not leave a trail of horse-droppings behind them.

But electricity had brought the Telephone—and anything which made it easier to talk, which brought a larger audience of willing or unwilling listeners within the deadly range of their voices, was, as they used to say, 'meat and drink' to the politicians and civil servants.

Another aspect of the Telephone did not hold any interest for the Rulers, though it was none the less important for that: the fact that in the telephone-exchanges which were opening all over Britain there was one more 'respectable employment' for women.

Women were already employed in large numbers by the General Post Office, especially on the master telegraphic-exchange at St Martin-le-Grand. Those who opened the new telephone-exchanges turned inevitably to women to staff them; here was one field in which women did not need to 'break through'.

> 'The system whereby two persons at a distance are enabled to talk together, is operated from switch-boards in so-called "Exchanges". Women are mostly employed to operate these "slipper-board" or "peg-board" exchanges, and have proved themselves capable of as high a degree of accuracy and conscientiousness as men.'

This was written in 1883. Within the decade, most of the great trunk lines were to be opened, while through the Channel cable direct telephonic communication would be established between London, Manchester, Birmingham, and the principal of the other British cities, with all the capitals of Europe.

The 'Hello Girl' was a product of the eighties from whose established position later decades were not to shift her; though with the invention of the Apostoloff automatic dialling-system in 1892 the eventual 'redundancy' of all human telephone-operators was pronounced.

The trouble, politicians have often found, in labelling themselves, is that the uninformed Public will insist on taking the labels seriously—taking them as some indication of what the politicians wearing them ought to do.

Gladstone was a declared 'Liberal', and so was supposed to be, by the ignorant Mob, a Friend of the Working Man and an Enemy of the Bosses. The Irish, who have the realism which belongs only to the impractical, never thought of Gladstone save as a bitter reactionary—and, of course, the Irish were right.

The British working man and small shopkeeper insisted on believing that the Eton-and-Christ-Church-High-Church Gladstone was, because of his connections with Trade, a sort of radical who would upset Thrones and Constitutions to get justice for the Common Man. Gladstone was prepared right enough to challenge established authority and powerful tradition, but not to help the working man—only because Gladstone disliked almost every human being who wasn't a practising prostitute.

The fact that he hated Tories—especially Tory aristocrats—royalty (especially royalty which had a good time), generals, admirals, foreigners (especially highly-polished Russian, Austrian, French and Italian royalty and diplomacy), non-Christians (especially Turks), gave far too many people of the lower rank the idea that he loved *them*.

When Gladstone seemed to hold back in the matter of social reform, his 'supporters' in the Mob grew restive, and the same sort of industrial discontent which had followed the Napoleonic Wars came to trouble the Britain of the eighties. The workers 'combined' and struck; though, often, they struck before they 'combined', unity being a product of the first bold defiances of the few.

The great Dock Strike of 1889 was the orderly culmination of a disorderly growth of resentment against the 'casual' element in employer-employee relationships. When John Burns called out the casual dockyard workers, to strike for a minimum of sixpence an hour, and Ben Tillett took his own Stevedores' Union of non-casual labour out, in support of the casuals, the nation realized, not so much that power had shifted from the

Bosses to the Workers—it had not—but that the Workers, through their politically-active and class-conscious leaders, had acquired a power that they had never had before.

Much of this power was to be taken away by 'respectabilizing' the leaders: John Burns, first as Member of the London County Council, then as Member of Parliament, and then as Cabinet Minister, showed, in his own successful history, how easily a 'man of the people' could be made to switch loyalties. But not all the power was taken from the workers themselves; not all the power could be taken.

When Bryant & May's match-girls struck, skilful publicity by sympathizers, not all of whom had an axe to grind, brought the whole nation out on the side of the girls, whose health was daily threatened by a disease—'phossy jaw'—which, to the 'Eighties, had the same power to terrify that lung-cancer has for this generation.

Working men such as John Burns, Ben Tillett and Will Crooks rode to power on the upthrust of the movement that they soon learnt to control and 'milk', even if they did not actually originate it.

But the encouragement to the more downtrodden workers to realize their abject and unjust condition, and then to rebel against it, came not from the working-class trade-unions organizers, but from the upper classes—mostly those members of it with very little to do. Lord Shaftesbury, of course, had been championing the workers, in and out of Parliament, for forty years and more when he died in 1883. (In the following year, his heir shot himself in a hansom, while passing through the 'Avenue' named after his illustrious father.) But there were many others to take up Shaftesbury's work of 'Christian socialism'; to denounce sweated labour, to demand humane working hours and conditions of labour.

The universities poured earnest young graduates into the East End, to start missions, and to help the workers by adopting their way of life. Later, Clement Attlee was to be one of these young graduates, though not all those who went from Oxford to Whitechapel went as far as he.

But before the great dock strike broke out, with Cardinal Manning and the Lord Mayor of London on the side of the dockers, and half the bourgeoisie of Britain subscribing to the relief of the strikers' families, the trade-unions had taken to the streets. In 1885 and 1886, the mob went rampaging along Piccadilly, Regent-street, St James's-street, breaking the windows of clubs and tearing down the iron shutters from the big shops.

On Bloody Sunday, 1887—the year of the Queen's Golden Jubilee—the organized unemployed marched, against the orders of the Commissioners of Police, to Trafalgar-square. The police halted them, and fierce battles broke out, in which the police, both foot and mounted, were losing, despite the lavish use of truncheons.

Behind the police were the Foot Guards with fixed bayonets and loaded rifles, and as the police struggled with the savage mob at the corner of the Strand, two squadrons of Life Guards came up from Whitehall, and bore down with bared sabres on the rioting unemployed.

Many were wounded, one out-of-work was so seriously injured that he afterwards died, and Burns and Cunningham Grahame—the typical 'Eighties alliance of the would-be gentleman with the nearly-a-gentleman— were arrested, tried for having incited the mob to disorder, and given six weeks.

The lesson was not lost on Burns. He had had all the martyrdom that he felt he needed to 'put him right with' the workers; now he saw the advantages of seeming to control the violence of which the bosses had seen a striking example.

Disraeli, the Arch-Tory, had been the one who had legalized trade-unionism in 1871, in return for the unions' bitter and successful attack on Gladstone, who had backed the clauses in the Criminal Law Amendment Act, penalizing various union activities.

One would have thought that the Tory strain would have been strong in primitive trade-unionism; but not even gratitude to Disraeli and anger against Gladstone could wean trade-unionism from its traditional non-conformist, republican, anti-booze bias. Besides, how was a trade- unionist to know who, exactly, was backing him—Dilke, Balfour, Harcourt?: they all had a shot at offering themselves to the working man as the Socialist Saviour.

Yet it was the aristocracy, and those who hoped that they might be taken for aristocrats, who protected Labour in the formative years, when it was groping for self-realization—just as had been the case in France before 1789.

With this difference, that the 'working man' who began to feel his feet and try out his strength in the 'Seventies and 'Eighties represented the 'aristocracy' of Labour. It was not the working men who were organizing in the second half of Victoria's reign, it was the *skilled* working men. The very name, 'trade-unionism', reveals the nature of Labour's origins—no aristocrat of fiction treated an honest workman with more contempt and hatred than the skilled workmen of fact treated 'unskilled labour'.

What has been forgotten in our backward glance at the 'humble' origins of a party which throws up its Gaitskells, its Crossmans, its Dribergs and its Jays, is, first of all, the immense influence of pre-Raphaelitism far beyond the literary and artistic coteries of the Rossettis, the Burne-Joneses and the Ruskins, and, second, the fact that pre-Raphaelitism went far beyond the mere painting of 'pre-Raphaelite' pictures or the composing of 'pre-Raphaelite' verse.

It is astonishing how serious historians have forgotten (if, indeed, they have not completely ignored) the fact that a sentimental love of the Working Man was a Victorian addiction, affecting all classes not actually to be classed as 'working'.

The Prince Consort was outstanding as one most seriously affected by this romantic love of Toil and the Toiler. Outraged by the time that it was taking for the Meek to inherit the Earth, Albert the Good attacked 'underprivilege' in his characteristic way. The working man was being diddled in the matter of house-accommodation? Right! Let's provide him with homes. The builders said that homes with 'all mod. cons.' couldn't be provided for the working man—at an economic cost? Right—let's show them that they can be built—and at an economic rate!

Designed and built by the Prince, the twin houses, of two separate dwellings, each with eight rooms, kitchen, bathroom, w.c., stand, a monument to his creative energy, and a reproach to ours, in the park at Camberwell.

Under the spur of the Consort's nagging drive, his friends and toadies stirred themselves to get things done, and the Society for the Improvement of Dwellings for the Working Classes was only one of the schemes which owed its origin to the Prince's half-guilty love of the working man. The American millionaire, Peabody, looking around for the most popular way in which to exercise his philanthropy, found it in the building of huge tenements throughout London—spending, they said, near half a million in giving the London working man a decent home.

There was, indeed, something of Mussolini's fabled 'March on Rome' (he stormed the Eternal City, you may recall, by riding there in a first-class railway compartment) in the collapse of the citadel of Privilege before the Socialist leaders of the 'Seventies and 'Eighties.

The victory, in truth, was theirs before they had even begun to fight. They no more had to fight for 'recognition' than, eighty years later, the blacks of Nigeria, Sierra Leone, Uganda, Kenya and Tanganyika had to fight for their 'independence'.

They weren't all sentimentalists in the days of Victoria, and some clear-sighted men, hidden away in those quiet, secret places where all the plans are made, and all the really essential work of government is done, saw that it was not poverty which was threatening the stability of the state, but the Charity which was coming to have a vested interest in Want.

It takes a clear eye, as well as a hard heart, to realize that it is more often the case that Charity creates Poverty than that Poverty calls forth Charity.

The highly organized machinery of Victorian charity was not only creating a nation with more paupers than the Britain of 1930 had unemployed; it was laying an unfair burden upon the wealth-creating capacity of the workers—for the charitable gifts of the rich no more came out of some purse of Fortunatus than did the money paid by the Government for guns and ships.

The corrective to this absurd and dangerous situation lay, the practical economists saw, in, first, raising the standard of *responsibility* of the workers: give them votes, give them money (by higher wages), give them property, give them a share of the taxation formerly levied only on the well-to-do. (And if the reader thinks that I am exaggerating what the economists planned, let him see what the economists have achieved: income tax down to the level of the officeboy.)

Of course, very few people indeed were aware of what was happening. The rich continued to be moved by poverty, and Labour organized itself to fight for concession after concession, not knowing that it was due to get them anyway—in good time.

And there was nothing unreal about some of the poverty which moved so many hearts: as late as 1930, I saw the conditions in which some of our people were living, and I was shocked. Fifty years earlier, I might have seen conditions a hundred times worse.

On the other hand, prices of the basic foods were so cheap that it was almost impossible for anyone to know actual starvation.

The deficiency diseases were rampant—as they would be today if most people ate only the food they 'liked'.

Even buying one's food in a cook-shop, one could survive, in London, on twopence or threepence a day[2]: a ha'porth of broken biscuits, half a stale loaf, a pennorth of pease-pudd'n-an'-faggots and a couple of saveloys. It was not princely fare, but you weren't going to die of starvation.

And if you hadn't a bed, and the 'spike' was too far off or too crowded, you could kip down where you liked: as in present-day Paris, where even a German occupation and the post-war rule of the Communists has not entirely dehumanized the city, the police, if they found you sitting on an Embankment bench or huddled under the Adelphi Arches, wouldn't arrest you for vagrancy.

There was something in British life that the 1939 war ended: an economic system which geared itself to every possible economic standard. No matter how little you had to spend, the minimum was always below

---

[2] As the very factual Edwardian novel, *No 5, John Street*, makes clear. The author, Richard Whiteing, allows his 'Idle Rich' hero, determined to live among the London poor, just three pence (6 cents) a day for food. No-one, since the novel's publication, has challenged the facts on which Whiteing based his 'socially conscious' book.

your means. To-day, there is a minimum which is above far too many people's means.

Well, that was the way of it: the menace of poverty, the more dangerous because the Victorian vice of charity threatened it with perpetuity, had to be met and conquered. The people had to be enriched, so that they might be taxed—for paupers can't pay taxes.

It was no good looking to the sentimentalists and the sweaters to help in altering the system: each group had their own reasons for preferring things as they were. There was only one type of man capable of carrying through the Great Change: the politically-conscious, ambitious man of the working class, with just enough of education to make him feel superior to the rabble that he was rousing, and with not enough brain to see the catspaw rôle for which he had been cast.

Not even the brainiest of them (such men as Shaw and Wells, for example) could realize that they were bringing up battering-rams to knock down an open door.

And what of the City itself? What changes there were were visible mostly east of Temple Bar, which had been removed from Fleet-street to Cheshun in 1878; so costly a move that half the City Council had had to resign, as a more pleasant alternative to a prosecution for embezzlement.

In the West End, Grosvenor-square and Mayfair showed hardly any changes: the Queen Anne and Georgian houses served the Late Victorians as adequately as they had served the Early Georgians; few of the 'Great Houses' were rebuilt—one or two in Grosvenor-square—hardly any were even altered. Though the stage-coach had survived the coming of the railways only by a couple of decades, the horse-drawn vehicle still held the monopoly of the London streets, and perhaps it was because the horse linked the present so closely with the past that the Victorians, for all their love of novelty, were content to live in the houses that their grandfathers and great-grandfathers had built.

The Great still lived very grandly indeed; and though the footman, attending his mistress whilst she shopped in Bond-street and Regent-street, was on the way out, he was by no means gone.

Household servants in the grander houses were always in livery, and the family carriage, with bewigged coachman sitting over heraldically emblazoned hammer-cloth, was no perquisite only of the Lord Mayor.

Everyone, of course, had a servant—you had to be really on the breadline if you could not afford to have at least some child, at a shilling a week, running your errands and washing up.

There were still one million domestic servants in employment as late as 1900.

All the same, the 'Eighties saw the beginnings of a fundamental change in social behaviour: people began to dine out, even though homes—what with the electric light and central heating—were never more comfortable, and servants were still plentiful.

But the great hotels had come to London, and it became a fashion to dine in their 'saloons'.

It was not the older hotels—the 'Family' and 'Family & Commercial' Hotels—which got this new fad-trade. It was the new, big hotels, built on the Austrian model: the Buckingham Palace Hotel, the Westminster Palace, the Langham, and the new railway hotels, at Paddington, King's Cross, Euston, St Pancras, Cannon Street and Charing Cross. The newer they were, the more splendid they became; with the new hotels in Northumberland-avenue, the Grand, the Metropole and the Victoria, out-shining even the swagger Inns of Court.

Home life, at the very top of Victorian society, began to be boring; people liked to get out a bit, and the new hotels gave them something to go out for: plenty of marble, good orchestras, first-class chefs, perfect service and a management sworn to preserve the privacy of the guest inviolate from brash 'friendliness', even though dining in a public room. (The 'brochures' of these hotels laid great stress upon the fact that one was always safe from 'undesirable acquaintance' in these places.)

For those who were so captivated by the food and the service in the restaurants of the new hotels that they felt they would like to adopt hotel life altogether, there were 'hotels' such as the Belgravia, in Grosvenor-gardens—then a very select residential district—which catered for permanents only. Here one lived in a fine suite of rooms, with private bathrooms attached, and had one's meals served in one's own dining-room.

It was getting very 'middle-class' to want to spend much time at home. . . .

Even those who could not adopt the new 'fad' of dining-out, either from lack of money or lack of enterprise, found the domestic scene growing tedious. For those who didn't care to read, night after night, there was only sewing—and not everyone could sew. It is true that the theatre and music-hall were in their vigorous prime, but the middle class, from the centre downwards, did not go to either. It was not until that shrewd British Israelite, Sir Augustus Harris, had the bright idea of grafting music-hall 'turns' on to the Pantomime that Rich had invented in Queen Anne's time, that the middle classes felt free to attend the music-hall. They happily went, with the children, to see Dan Leno and Herbert Campbell, at Drury

Lane, in 'Pantomime', where they would never have gone to see these two drolls go through their antics at Collins's, the Old Mo or the Sods' Opera.

The tedium of home life weighed on all classes in a manner which was never permitted to be described in a novel. We call the Victorians hypocritical, 'because they never mentioned sex'. Such a charge could only have been levelled by people who have never read a word of what was published in Victoria's reign. I suppose the most torridly sexual scene in all literature—not excluding *Fanny Hill* and *Lady Chatterley's Lover*—is that in which Helen seduces Sir Richard Calmady, in *The History of Sir Richard Calmady*. Of course, 'Lucas Malet', the author, knew her job a good deal better than D. H. Lawrence: she could write the hottest of hot stuff without being forced to adopt urinal-wall terminology.

But the charge which might be fairly levelled against the Victorians, if one wished to charge them with hypocrisy, is that they suppressed, not the mention of sex, but the mention of the appalling tedium of 'home'. Rarely indeed does this tedium find actual expression in print; but the whole attitude of the Victorians speaks a fretting, a chafing, under the social behaviour which called for the pretence that 'east, west, home's best'.

This tedium led, at times, to some very odd happenings, the least difficult to understand being the frequent cases of extreme cruelty to servants. (As Arnold Bennett was later to say of bigamy, ill-treatment of domestics was the most respectable of all crimes.)

When Mrs Camilla Nicholls, after a five days' trial in 1898, was given seven years' penal servitude for having ill-treated and starved to death her servant, Jane Popejoy, the cause lay probably less with either Jane or her mistress than with the boredom that Mrs Nicholls suffered.

Where boredom does not find its relief in brutality, it will certainly find it in garrulousness, and to talk oneself indiscreetly into a slander action seems to have been the favourite occupational (is that the word for a product of idleness?) disease of the 'Eighties.

I turn up the Calendar for the decade, and all sorts of well-known names leap to the eye.

Mrs Weldon sues Sir Henry de Bathe for slander: awarded £1,000 damages. Ernest Parke gets a year for a gross libel on the Earl of Euston. Sir Albert Lawson-Levy (later Lord Burnham) owner of the *Daily Telegraph*, sues Henry Labouchere, M. P., owner of *Truth*, for slander and libel—Sir Albert has also to face a counter-charge that he has beaten Labby over the head with a stick, outside the Devonshire Club. Major Burrowes is fined £400 and costs for having assaulted his brother-in-law, Lord Howard de Walden—who had been 'talking'.

Her Majesty Queen Victoria at her Golden Jubilee, 1887.

Trial-trip of the world's first Underground Railway, the Metropolitan, 1862. The line was opened to the public in the following year.

What the British, up to 1869, turned out in their tens of thousands to see and enjoy. One of the last murderers to be hanged in public, John Wiggins, fought fiercely on the scaffold outside Newgate Prison, while loudly protesting his innocence.

Catherine Walters, the notorious and eminently successful self-proclaimed 'Queen of London's Whoredom'.

Agnes Willoughby, ruin of the ancient estate of Felbrigg.

The demure and religious-minded strumpet, Laura Bell, who 'took' the brother of the King of Nepal for £250,000 for one night's 'hospitality'.

'Lillie' Langtry, the most successful of all the high-class harlots of Victorian Britain; the original of the 'Irene Adler' of Conan Doyle's *A Scandal in Bohemia*, she dispensed her expensively-purchased favours among most of the male members of the Royal Family, not excluding the Prince of Wales.

President Abraham Lincoln, whose face the dying Prince Consort saved—thereby saving the Union as well.

Lord Lytton, son of the famous Victorian novelist. This second Earl was Viceroy of India and (like his father) a dedicated and credulous dabbler in the Psychic.

Louis Pasteur (1822–95), the great French bacteriologist, called in as consultant by a Manchester brewer to discover the cause of the brewer's sour beer, contributed to the fortunes of brewers, winemakers, and milk-producers, and, beyond that, to the general health of mankind.

Lord Randolph Churchill, brother of the Marquess of Blandford, rival of the Prince of Wales for the irregular favours of Lady Aylesford. His mind already unbalanced by the illness that was to kill him, Lord Randolph still had enough sense to decline the Prince's challenge to a duel.

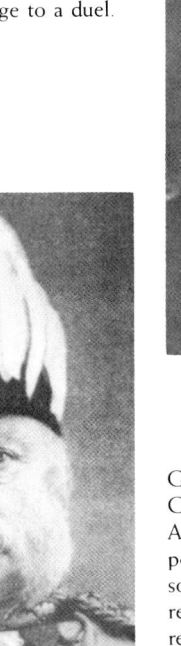

George, Duke of Cambridge, KG, Commander-in-Chief of the British Army. The Queen's cousin, she is supposed to have wished to marry him, and so never forgave his marrying a most respectable actress, to whom Victoria refused any rank higher than that of 'Mrs' Fitzgeorge.

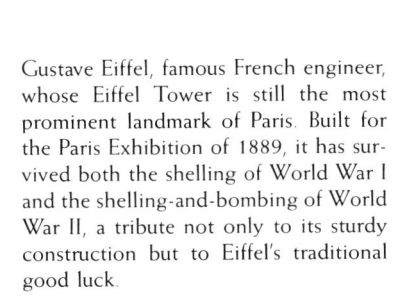

Gustave Eiffel, famous French engineer, whose Eiffel Tower is still the most prominent landmark of Paris. Built for the Paris Exhibition of 1889, it has survived both the shelling of World War I and the shelling-and-bombing of World War II, a tribute not only to its sturdy construction but to Eiffel's traditional good luck.

Colonel Valentine Baker, of the crack Tenth Hussars—the Prince of Wales being its Colonel-in-Chief. Convicted of an 'assault' on a young lady in a railway-carriage, the Colonel served a term of imprisonment before leaving England for service with the Sultan of Turkey. He did *not* lose friendship of any of his British friends.

Eugen Sandow, the Swedish Physical-culture professor and practitioner, in an age as addicted to Health-faddery as is the present. Musichall 'turn' as well as the author of the Sandow System of Swedish Drill, Sandow overtaxed his vauted strength when he killed himself in trying to lift an overturned motor-car from a ditch.

Cecil Rhodes, the imaginative, ambitious, hard-working, infinitely resourceful Empire-builder; the instigator of that raid by his lieutenant, Dr. Starr Jameson, into the Transvaal, which led, three years later, to the disastrous Boer War, and—eventually—to the collapse of all Rhodes's achievements and the end of British rule in Africa.

His Royal Highness Albert Edward ('Bertie'), Prince of Wales, as he was during the deplorable Blandford-Aylesford affair. Completely dedicated to a life of pleasure, his many sexual adventures made him more, rather than less, popular with the rank-and-file of his Mother's subjects.

Stripped now of all political power by the Radicals (including a Duke's grandson, Winston Churchill), the peers of Britain are left only with their titles, their coronets, their robes, and membership in the House of Lords, of 'the finest Club in Europe'. Here a Duke, Marquess, Earl, Viscount, and Baron await their carriages.

A Victorian tea-shop of the more ambitious kind: The Royal Victoria Coffee Palace—soft drinks only for all the family.

London's first telephone-exchange, opened in 1879, was staffed entirely by women—yet one more important step in the progressive Emancipation of Woman from Factory, Domestic Service, or the Death-in-Life of employment as Governess.

Thanks to the unremitting agitation of Sir John Lubbock (later Lord Avebury), banker, etymologist, paleontologist, and philanthropist, the Bank Holiday Act was passed into law, and workers were assured of one free day a year at least. Here Londoners celebrate their freedom on Hampstead Heath.

The Great Western Royal Hotel, at the Paddington, London, terminus of the railway. Built in 1852, 'in the Francis the First style', the hotel was then regarded as the most luxurious in Europe. It was from Paddington Station that Sherlock Holmes and Dr. Watson left for King's Pyland, in the affair of *Silver Blaze*.

The Apogee of Empire: the Diamond Jubilee, 1897. In this symbolic painting by A. Forestier, the aged Queen-Empress is receiving the acclamation of her subjects of every race, colour, and creed—none aware that, within two years, the might of Empire was to be tested and found grievously wanting.

Both as Prince of Wales and as King, Edward's success as the owner of winning racehorses made him popular with the masses. His first Derby win was with *Persimmon*, in 1896; he was to win another Derby as King, with his horse, *Minoru*. Here he is shown leading in *Persimmon*.

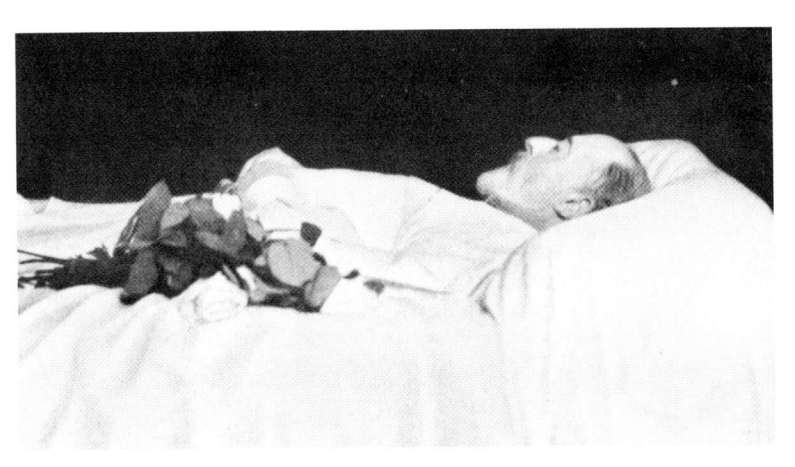

The Dead King lies in state in Westminster Hall: 7th May, 1910. With the passing of Edward the Seventh, not merely one man's life had come to an end. His death marked the end of an Age, the end of a Civilisation, and the end of—as men were soon to see—an Empire. After him was to come the Deluge.

'Sweated Labour'—greatest blot on Victorian society. In a Bethnal Green slum of 1863, a military tailor and his entire family make the glittering uniforms then *de rigueur*.

Slum-clearance on a vast scale, and noble efforts to abolish poverty notwithstanding, Victorian Distress still continued to shame Victorian Prosperity. Philanthropists of all classes, from the Prince Consort, Lord Shaftesbury, and Lord Rowton downwards did what they could for the down-and-outs—here is one of the Salvation Army's efforts at a solution.

The Cycling Craze of the late 'Nineties: 'They look very odd to our eyes, these London shopgirls, dressed-up in men's tweed golfing-suits, with feather-trimmed Homburgs and starched linen collars, to go cycling'. Here are three typical women-cyclists, obviously enjoying themselves.

'Mary' Cornwallis West, another of the Prince of Wales's mistresses, and co-plaintiff, with Mrs. Langtry, in the libel action against Rosenberg. Not at all as promiscuous as 'Lillie' Langtry, her daughter by the Prince married well into the German nobility.

An elderly Suffragette (they were mostly younger women) is hustled off by two not over-harsh London bobbies. The 'revolutionary' Commons-Lords battle, the threat of civil war in Ireland, and the (too often exceedingly violent) activities of the Suffragettes provided the most important domestic news as the Edwardian reign drew to a close.

Police-response to the first of the 'Jack the Ripper' killings in Whitechapel, London—seven more were to take place before 'Jack' was returned to the lunatic-asylum in which he was to die, four years after this ineffectual notice was posted up by the Metropolitan Police chief, Sir Charles Warren.

POLICE NOTICE.

TO THE OCCUPIER.

On the mornings of Friday, 31st August, Saturday 8th, and Sunday, 30th September, 1888, Women were murdered in or near Whitechapel, supposed by some one residing in the immediate neighbourhood. Should you know of any person to whom suspicion is attached, you are earnestly requested to communicate at once with the nearest Police Station.

Metropolitan Police Office,
30th September, 1888.

The first notice circularised to householders in the East End during the hunt for the Ripper

Crosby Hall, a late Mediaeval mansion that lasted in London until 1910, when it was removed to a Thames-side site in Chelsea. It survived the bombing of World War II.

1897: More Progress, as the crowds turn out to see the Thames Embankment lit, for the first time, by electricity. The Embankment, supreme engineering achievement of Sir Joseph Bazalgette, still remains one of the more notable triumphs of Victorian technology: a road above, contained by a riverwall; below: sewers, gas- and electricity-mains, and an Underground Railway.

Nocturne in Gaslight—the old Empire Music-hall in Leichester-square, London—prime target of the 'reforming' Do-gooder, Mrs. Ormiston Chant and her attendant harpies. Young Winston Churchill was the leader of those defending the Empire promenade and bar against Mrs. Chant's 'moral' onslaught.

We can go farther, and say that the several pressures upon the Victorians to 'get away from home' took them into the open in a remarkable and unprecedented way. The fashionable solicitor was Sir George Lewis, whose oriental pliancy, it was said, enabled him to prevent most of the great scandals from ever reaching the Courts. In that case, the number must have been very great, since never was there a time such as the 'Eighties, when so much coroneted dirty linen was washed before the Court of Queen's Bench.

The Earl of Aylesford—the Prince of Wales's friend, 'Sporting Joe'—sought to divorce his wife, Edith, who was living in sin in Paris with the Duke of Marlborough, and had had a child by the Duke (then only the Marquess of Blandford). Case dismissed, on the grounds that 'Sporting Joe's' own immoral conduct put him outside the Law's protection.

The Earl of Durham, a short while after, entered *his* plea for divorce, on the grounds that his wife was insane at the time of her marriage. A curious plea. After an eight days' hearing before Sir James Hannen, the case was dismissed.

That made two earls asking for release from matrimony—and being refused. There was to be a third: the Earl of Euston, son and heir of the Duke of Grafton, a descendant, albeit on the wrong side of the blanket, of Charles II.

Lord Euston, when a subaltern in the 10th Hussars, had first lived in concubinage with, and then married, a woman who called herself Kate Cook, a slattern strumpet from the slums of Glasgow. On his marriage, which was 'celebrated' at an obscure country church in Warwickshire, Lord Euston came into £10,000. He handed this to his wife; she handed it to a shady solicitor who had arranged the marriage; and the shady solicitor had the lot.

Married in haste, and repenting almost as quickly, Lord Euston emigrated to Australia, to 'redeem himself'. He 'obtained a post under Government', and went quietly about his Australian duties while his father's private enquiry agents cast about for evidence on which a plea for annulment of the marriage might be based.

The case was heard. Lord Euston asked that the marriage be declared null and void on the grounds that, at the time of her marriage to Lord Euston, the respondent had a husband living.

Unlike so many other of the late Victorian *causes célèbres*, the Euston case lasted only a day. The evidence was truly remarkable, even for a period of remarkable evidence: Kate, when marrying Euston, had described herself as a 'spinster'.

It was true that she had been married, and that the man whom she had married was alive at the time of her marriage to Euston.

But as Kate's adroit counsel showed, the previous 'husband' himself had a wife living at the time that he 'married' Kate.

So that Kate's first marriage was a bigamous one; she was, for all that she had believed otherwise, a single woman when she went through a ceremony of marriage with Lord Euston, and she was the legal wife of the heir to the Dukedom of Grafton. Whom God had joined together, the Law was unable to put apart.

Seekers after divorce were, on the whole, unlucky. Their legal advisers encouraged them to pour out their troubles to the Court—and to the singularly unreticent Victorian newspapers—only so that the judge could moralize . . . and order both parties to remain married.

This is what happened to Lord and Lady Colin Campbell; he petitioning for divorce, on the grounds of his wife's alleged adultery; she counter-charging 'cruelty' (because, Lady Colin alleged, her husband was suffering from a venereal disease when he married her) as well as adultery with his private nurse.

None of the charges on either side was proved—though the parties separated after their unsuccessful attempt to be legally free of each other. Lady Colin, who had already begun to earn her living by writing, developed into a 'Society journalist', telling ambitious shop-girls and sempstresses how to leave calling-cards or how to give an At Home.

But even where these court-cases were not made interesting by the presence of Great Names, many were quite as interesting because of the curious—one might almost say bizarre—nature of charge and evidence.

For instance, though it was at Edinburgh, in 1882, that Charles Soutar was arraigned for having stolen the cadaver of the Right Honourable the Earl of Crawford and Balcarres, lately deceased, it was in London that the singular disappearance of the German baker, Urban Napoleon Stanger, set the whole town talking.

The disappearance centred about Baker-street, Clerkenwell (now renamed Baker-row) and before the police were called in, a friend of Stanger's had commissioned a private detective to find the missing man. The detective failed, but his momentary appearance at the preliminary hearings, when the missing baker's manager, Stumm, was charged with his murder, caught the attention of a struggling young Irish doctor named Arthur Conan Doyle.

Using a different plot, but setting the action in Baker-street, and echoing some of the names of actual persons ("Stanger'—'Stangerson'), the young doctor wrote a story, *A Study in Scarlet*, about a detective named Sherlock Holmes. Sold for £25 to Ward, Lock & Co., the publishers, for inclusion in their *Beeton's Annual* of 1887, the story brought eventual fame and riches, not only to the young doctor, but to his children.

But we shall see later how writers fared in the 'Eighties—the beginning of the brief Golden Age of Authorship.

In spite of opposition, the City Council had adopted arc-lamps to light the busy intersection at the Mansion House; and shops and theatres all over London were calling attention to themselves by hanging the fizzing, clicking blue-white brilliance of the arcs outside their premises. Against the shy, sad, muted golden glow of the gas-lamps came the sharp white stridency of the electric light. And . . . something very odd, and something very disturbing happened. It was as though the dim gaslight, shocked and driven back by the harsh brilliance of the new illumination, made friends with the darkness, which had grown stronger by contrast with the brighter light without.

Over London came, not so much a general moral corruption, as the frightening evidence that old evils had roused themselves; had grown stronger . . . and bolder.

It is not easy to explain why this should be so, though in a novel of mine, *Higher Things*,[3] I have talked of the strong psychic link between Light and Sanity, and between Darkness and the release of Evil.

But, as I say, it is not easy to explain the terrifying manifestations of evil which set London trembling in the 'Eighties.

It wasn't hashish, as it had been with the Mohocks of Queen Anne's day. It wasn't Drink—for Gladstone had let the brewers 'adulterate' their liquor with invert sugar, and the Victorians of the 'Eighties had already begun to drink less. It certainly wasn't the Telly—Friese-Green and Lumière were only just about to begin work on the Cinematograph. It's hard to say what caused the strange things which happened in London then; all that we know is this, they happened—and they scared the living daylights out of everyone.

The disappearance of Stanger, the baker, was but one among the many disappearances which have been so carefully listed by that strange American historian of the Inexplicable, Charles Fort.

The epidemic of the Vanishing Londoners began in 1881, the very year in which the first arc-lights went up in the City.

The strange aspect of the disappearances, which were mostly centred about the London districts of East Ham and West Ham, was the absence

---

[3] London: Macdonald & Co., 1946.

of what we may call an 'age-pattern'. Young girls, young boys, middle-aged men and elderly women—all appeared to be equally acceptable as prey to whoever—*or whatever*—was whipping the victims away. There were, apart from the fact that the persons had disappeared, other factors linking the disappearances.

In many—though not all—cases where children had disappeared, the children had either been seen talking to an old woman (description unsatisfactorily vague in all cases where witnesses swore that they had seen her) or the old woman had been noticed somewhere around the place where the child had last been seen.

Another disturbing oddity about the disappearances was that one or two of the girls seemed to have had some sort of premonition that 'something was going to happen'; but that, asked by their friends why they were hanging around the streets, so near their homes, and didn't go home, they gave evasive answers, and moved off . . . but not to go home.

Take the case of Eliza Carter, for instance. Eliza is important, for she 'vanished', only to be seen again, before she finally went. She had been obviously in a state of terror, but no one could persuade her to go home. She was never seen again, but a blue dress, identified by her mother as having belonged to Eliza, was found on the football field at East Ham. *The buttons had gone as completely as had Eliza.*

A singular comment on this old mystery came to me some two years ago, after I had published an account of Eliza Carter's disappearance in a London evening paper. I had a letter from an old lady, in which she told me that Eliza had been her playmate, and that she had been the last—except the agency of disappearance—to whom Eliza had talked.

But perhaps the disappearance of Charles Wagner, young son of a West Ham butcher, was even more mysterious. No one knows how Charles was lured away from West Ham, but when next he was seen, he was lying dead at the foot of some cliffs at Ramsgate, 74 miles from London.

In this case (one of the very few disappearances to be followed by the finding of the victim's body) the corpse bore no sign of injury, and the autopsy revealed no cause of death.

To the Londoners of that time, Whittier's famous and popular poem must have borne disturbing overtones of terror:

> . . . An' all they ever found
> Wuz jest his pants and roundabout.
> An' the Gobbluns 'll git *you*,
> Ef you don't watch out!

For nine years this pattern of disappearance continued; the last victims being three girls, who were whipped away together.

The date was January 1890. Of those three girls, one—and one only—was to turn up again. Her body was found in an empty house in Portway, facing West Ham Park. Her name was Amelia Jeffs, aged fifteen. Weeks had passed since, with her two companions, she had vanished. She had been strangled, after what had been obviously a desperate fight for life.

What was behind it all. . .? Something more than the public was permitted to know.

Witnesses, searching their collective memory, recalled having seen a woman talking to the three girls who had vanished from Portway; and assuming that this woman was the same as that 'unprepossessing woman with a long ulster and a black frock' who had been seen talking to Eliza Carter, seven years before, the coroner delivered himself of a judgment which, perhaps commonplace to us, must have startled some of the Victorians.

'Women,' said the coroner, 'are as susceptible to the lowest forms of mania as men.'

It rather sounds as though Mr Coroner knew more than he was saying—daring, by 1890 standards, though his statement was.

But what did he know? And what exactly was that 'lowest form of mania' which snatched persons of both sexes and all ages out of this world, over a period of ten years?

The decade, indeed, had begun with Terror—but Terror of a more 'human' sort.

Beginning with the blowing-up of Clerkenwell Prison in 1867, and continuing right through the seventies, dynamite outrages had scared Londoners stiff. The 'Eighties were to see the Dynamiters at their most active, and most terrifying.

On 16 March, 1881, an attempt to blow up the Mansion House nearly succeeded; two years later, to the day, a bomb was exploded close to the Local Government Office, in Whitehall, great damage being done.

An attempt to blow up the offices of *The Times* was a failure; and so were attempts on the House of Commons, the Nelson Monument and London Bridge. The police were particularly vigilant, and managed to detect many of the explosive parcels and bombs, after they had been placed in position, but before they went off.

It was when the Dynamiters, warned off 'public monuments' by the presence of too many too-vigilant policemen, turned their attention to less august landmarks that they began to get their most spectacular results.

They went for the railway-stations, particularly the Underground Railway stations; and their methods were always the same: a brown-paper parcel, 'left behind.'

The parcel which was 'left behind' in a third-class Underground carriage at Praed-street injured sixty-two people when it blew up—and many of them would have been better off dead.

On 27 February, 1884, the cloakroom of the main-line station at Victoria suddenly went up—and the two cloakroom attendants went up with it. On 30th May, in the same year, at 9:30 p.m., a bomb nearly demolished the old Detective Department in the original 'Scotland Yard', and completely destroyed a nearby public-house, injuring many people.

False alarms, explosive packets found before they had a chance to go off (the bomb on the Home Secretary's windowsill did go off; and so did the one outside the Junior Carlton Club) patrols on the houses of important men, day-and-night watches on railways, docks, water-works, and so on, kept every available policeman busy—and crime flourished as never before.

Naturally the public were jittery, and it was in such an atmosphere of terror that the Vanishing Plague struck.

I have read many so-called 'factual' studies of Jack the Ripper (and here I exclude from consideration the two masterly 'fictional' studies by Mrs Belloc Lowndes and Patrick Hamilton) and nowhere have I seen it stated that there was a linking among the Dynamiting, the Vanishing and the Ripper killings. Not, of course, that one person had a hand in all three; no. But it was the excessive calls on the police that the dynamitings involved; the draining away of the police from outlying districts, so as to concentrate them in the most central parts of central London; it was these which gave the Ripper and those responsible for the vanishings an unprecedented and, indeed, ideal opportunity for the practice of their several grisly vices.

It is curious, looking back, to see what terror the Ripper inspired, noting that the one 'fact' deducible from a nation-wide study of his killings was that his victims appeared to be limited to the class of next-to-down-and-out 'unfortunate'. It is not true that Queen Victoria feared for her own skin, although she read every account of the Ripper in the newspapers, and actually wrote to the editor of *Lloyd's Sunday News*—by no means a 'top-drawer' journal—suggesting methods by which the nightmare killer might be trapped.

But hundreds of thousands of respectable people were terrified—one can only assume that they feared that when Jack had tired of gralloching seedy whores, in the dingiest East End streets, he might turn to the female inhabitants of the more respectable quarters, and try his hand at hanging *their* entrails on the gas-brackets.

For a man who was never caught, not even identified[4], it is astonishing how many 'identities' Jack has collected. As a boy, I heard from my mother,

---

[4] For my own proposed identification, see my *Clarence: The Life of the Duke of Clarence & Avondale;* London, W. H. Allen, 1972.

my aunts, and assorted servants, *exactly* who Jack the Ripper was—the most slanderous identification, I remember, being that of the venereally-infected son of a royal surgeon. ('They couldn't hang a man with *those* connections. . . . They had to hush it up. They never brought him to trial. Locked him up in Broadmoor. He's still there, they say. . . .')

The fog was everywhere: it blurs the horror of Doré's engravings; it heightens the horror of the Sherlock Holmes tales, where we seem always to hear the clop-and-jingle of the hansom, shadowy in the brown mists of the 'pea-souper'. Nothing can be seen clearly for that omnipresent fog. The sad lowing of the fog-horns echoes over the London of the 'Eighties; and in that world of half-light, half-darkness, the most grotesque tragedies were played out.

As Someone—or Something—was snatching away the Eliza Carters, and Jack was ripping up the poor tarts near the Ratcliffe Highway (where the evil Williams, immortalized by De Quincey, crimed out *his* dreadful hour), the fleet of troop-ships tardily ordered by Gladstone to proceed to the relief of General Gordon lay fog-bound in the Thames. The fog was so thick that nothing could stir on the river.

Not until six weeks after the troops had marched up the gang-planks were the ships able to weigh anchor, and set out for Egypt—and by that time, the tragedy of Khartoum was over: Gordon's body, hacked to pieces, was crocodile-bait in the Nile; his head, no longer crowned with his famous tarboosh, grinned on a spear-point above the Merchants' Gate.

The psychologists had already begun to hang out their boards; but a saner explanation of all this nightmare is to be found in the first verses of John: there was too much darkness for evil not to have flourished. If it sounds fanciful to see, in Colonel Crompton and his fellow 'electricians', the great sanity which was to end so much of the night-spawned terror of London, consider well what the darkness that they were destroying was bringing forth.

Nature herself seemed to have taken a turn for the worse—Nature herself, not merely men, seemed to be committing crimes.

Take the case of the Elephant Man, for example. . . .

One night, as the icy fog curled around him, Sir Frederick Treves walked along the Whitechapel-road; he had just left the London Hospital, where he was one of the honorary surgeons.

Over the entrance of a 'hole in the wall', a dirty canvas, flapping in the wind, caught his eye. By the dim light of a gas-lamp, Sir Frederick could just make out the words crudely daubed on the canvas.

They invited the passer-by to enter, and see a veritable freak of nature—the Elephant Man. Admission—twopence; children—one penny.

There was no barker at the entrance, no attendant—they had, it turned out, gone to the nearest pub. Impelled by he knew not what impulse, Sir Frederick pulled back the stained canvas flaps, and walked into the darkness: a darkness relieved only by the faintest glimmer of light in the innermost recesses of the 'hole in the wall'—a roofed space between two buildings.

There, sitting huddled over a hot brick, and wrapped in a piece of old tarpaulin, was the Elephant Man. Sir Frederick gently pulled away the tarpaulin from the head of the sitting figure—and what the surgeon saw made even his case-hardened nerve flinch.

The Elephant Man was well named—if one had to name him.

One assumed that he was a human being only because no animal had ever looked like him. There was hardly one feature, distinctly and unmistakably recognizable as 'human', in the face which turned up to meet Sir Frederick's shocked gaze.

Sir Frederick drew out his pocket-flask, and gave it to the Elephant Man: it was, as I have said, a cold, dank night.

Then, drawing up an old packing case, the eminent surgeon sat down to wait for the return of the Elephant Man's keeper—to buy the Elephant Man, and take him back to the London Hospital.

So it had been Treves's intention; but, on this first contact with the Elephant Man and his 'owner' (if one might call him that), the surgeon was to be disappointed: the 'owner' refused to part with the Elephant Man, and Treves had, perforce, to retire baffled—though not before he had managed to slip his visiting-card into the hand of the Elephant Man.

Treves heard no more of the poor creature who had so excited his pity, until news came from Belgium, where the Elephant Man had been abandoned, but, though unable to explain himself, had had the presence-of-mind to produce Treves's card. The Belgian police communicated with Sir Frederick, and arrangements were then made to 'ship' the Elephant Man back to England, where, in the London Hospital, arrangements had already been made by Treves for his reception and care.

The next day, Sir Frederick saw to it that a suite of rooms, cut off from all contact with the general life of the hospital, were put at the disposal of the Elephant Man. Only nurses who had been invited to see him, and who had survived the ordeal, were permitted to tend his wants. No one knew where he had come from—the 'keeper' said that he had found him wandering about, seemingly no one's property, and it had occurred to the finder that the Elephant Man would well earn his keep as a one-man freak-show. Alas, the 'keeper' complained, the Elephant Man was so horrible that even those possessed of the most morbid curiosity shrank from looking on this most terrible of all travesties of humanity.

They did not even know to which sex they should assign the Elephant Man. He could tell them nothing of his origins; he could hardly speak, anyway. All that they knew was that he was about twenty—and God knows how he had passed the years since his monstrous birth.

Between the good and gentle surgeon and the Elephant Man developed a singular and moving rapport; and Sir Frederick testifies to the fact that John Merrick, the Elephant Man, for all that God's hand lay so heavy on him, was good and gentle, too.

In his quiet, closely-guarded world, the Elephant Man found warmth and food, cleanliness and comfort, for the first time in his terrible life. They waited on him, as the saying goes, hand-and-foot—and he responded to the nurses' selfless care with a gratitude which touched all hearts.

The Patron of this hospital, in London's then sadly squalid East End, was Queen Alexandra, then Princess of Wales, and among the pictures that the Elephant Man had cut out of the illustrated magazines was one of the Princess.

She was deeply interested in the Elephant Man, and often asked Sir Frederick to describe what was being done for him. She sent the Elephant Man a photograph of herself, so that he could put it on the mantelpiece of his room—and then, one day, Sir Frederick let drop that of all things the Elephant Man wanted, to see and speak to the Princess was the thing he wanted most.

When the Princess said that she would go, the horrified surgeon protested vigorously—almost violently.

It was impossible; Her Royal Highness did not know—*could* not know—what it was that she was promising. Even nurses, hardened by their profession to shocking sights, had confessed themselves unable to be near the Elephant Man.

'I shall go to see this poor creature,' said Alexandra—and she went.

They could not dissuade her. They showed her into the presence of the Elephant Man, and the noble woman did not flinch; she smiled (for all that there were tears in her eyes) under the monstrous regard of this sad exile from humankind.

And she took the twisted hand in hers, and bent over the ghastly head as the poor creature kissed the lovely hand of the Princess.

They say that she fainted, just as the door closed behind her—and she may well have done. She deserved respite: her nobility had served its purpose.

In all the darkness of that benighted decade, no light shone to match the spendour of that heroic pity.

Half a century later, T. E. Lawrence sneered at Queen Alexandra in her old age, and G. B. Shaw, never regarded as the most kindly of men, rebuked Lawrence in terms which leave no doubt of their burning sincerity. There is a kind of nobility which does not permit itself to be without defenders. . . .

Compared with much of the peace-time, civilian occupations, the various military adventures of the 'Eighties seem as normal and healthy to us as they seemed to the men and women of the time.

They were 'colourful' wars, in a very literal sense—even the warships, though rating 10,000 tons and protected with armour up to four feet thick, were still painted prettily: primrose yellow smoke-stacks, white upper works, lavender hulls, with a scarlet strake meeting at the gilded carving below the bowsprit.

Once out of the Channel and North Sea fogs, the sailors presented as cheerfully spick-and-span an appearance as the bone-white holystoned decks; and the broad-brimmed yellow straw hats, bound with blue, gave the Jack Tars a jolly Mediterranean look, like that of good-natured pirates in a children's story-book.

Though khaki had been used in the 'Seventies, it was not until the very end of the 'Eighties that the soldiers said goodbye to their scarlet and blue.

Most of the wars of the 'Eighties were still fought with the soldiers and their officers in red—the lesson in camouflage that the British sea-rovers of the second century gave, when they not only painted their ships green (decks, masts, rigging, sails and all) but themselves as well, had been lost during the intervening sixteen centuries. Another decade was to pass before the vested interests in brightly coloured uniforms had to give way before the harsh realization that scarlet-clad troops made a wonderful target against the ochre sands of Egypt.

Before we survey the many battlefields of the 'Eighties on which it is hard to know how British troops fought and died, (so standardized, to suit the public taste, were the 'despatches' and 'our artist's impression of the fighting',) we must notice the complete absence of what has come to be a basic constituent of War—Hate.

Arabs and Fuzzy-Wuzzies and Zulus and Ashanti did some curiously horrible things to Our Lads (off-shore sailors, bombarding the forts at Alex and elsewhere, were not exposed to these barbarities) and Kipling, later, summed up peculiarly military danger when he wrote:

> When you're wounded, and left on Afghanistan's plains—
> And the women come out, to cut up what remains—
> Then roll to yer rifle, and blow out yer brains—
> And go to yer God like a *soldier!*

But the Tommy did not hate those of his enemies who wished to castrate and behead him. Tommy regarded this doom as merely one more foreign military custom; not really different, in essence, from the French habit of putting their soldiers in baggy scarlet trousers, or the German habit of providing sausage in the rations.

Tommy, indeed, conceived a great admiration for Fuzzy-Wuzzy—gelding-knife and all. Nor did the civilians, the class which has always taken war far more seriously than the men who fight the battles, develop that hate which now poisons the relations of mankind, whether or not they're actually at war.

I look through the records of a century back, and I seem to see, in the absence of a certain class of inventor, the reason why the 'Eighties were not dominated by hate, and we, alas!, are.

It was a time of great inventive activity. The submarine invented by the young Irish parson, Garrett, had been developed by the machine-gun-inventor, Nordenfeldt, and to the launching of Nordenfeldt II, at Landskrona, in Sweden, went many of the leading personalities of Europe and America, including the Prince of Wales. There were new guns, both heavy and light—Hiram Maxim demonstrated his machine-gun, firing 666 Martini-Henry cartridges (at 1½d. a cartridge) a minute, in 1887—Jubilee Year. Two armament-buyers for the Chinese Government were the first to purchase the new gun—'... a fine weapon ... invaluable for subduing the heathen', said the explorer, Stanley.

There were new explosives—not only Mr Nobel's dynamite, but the British Government's own high-explosives, including the highly powerful Lyddite.

But (and this should be noted with care) there wasn't a 'scientist' among the inventors. Almost all the military inventions came from engineers, whether military ones or not.

Lebel, Minié, Gatling, Lee, Metford, were all soldiers. Armstrong, the heavy-gun and torpedo man, was a Tyneside solicitor—of all things. Hiram Maxim was a French Canadian engineer, self-taught, rather as William Morris, later Lord Nuffield, was self-taught, as, indeed, was Edison. Remington had an already flourishing arms business, and, anyway, turned to making the new typewriter with the same enthusiasm with which he continued to make rifles.

But even where there was an occasional 'scientist' to be found turning his attention to lethal weapons, he was a man with an established position in his community; a man who could look forward to living out his life as he wished: he certainly had no fear of concentration-camp or gas-chamber to turn him into a refugee.

It is not the least horrible of the results of the Hitlerian frenzy—the *furor novus Teutonicus*—that weapon-inventing has passed into the hands of men whom the hate and persecution of other men have turned into exiles, and who, in turn, have sought to 'sublimate' their own hate of their persecutors by inventing weapons for those persecutors' enemies.

The trouble about Hate is that it is non-selective. The Hater may think that his enmity is directed against one person or one class or one people; but Hate itself has its own dynamic. It is the devil unbottled. Hate won't stay concentrated, 'beamed'.

Hate bounces back, gains strength on the rebound, goes out after everyone. To Hate, all Men are Enemies.

The horror of modern war—and the worse horror of the wars to come—are caused by, and are directly proportional to, the Hate which made the Inventors exiles, and the Hate which inspired their own thinking.

The 'Eighties were free from this Hate—or even the fear of this Hate. Anti-Semitism was known in Germany; it was active in the Germany of the 'Eighties. But, in Germany, the Law was not anti-Semitic. The Jew, faced with the animosity of anti-Semitism, could look for refuge higher up: his learning, his achievement, his wealth, would protect him—and his wealth was as inviolate as the wealth of a German Christian.

They didn't like Jews in Germany; and they didn't like Roman Catholics in Britain—especially in London. But the anti-Semitism of Germany was like the anti-Romanism of London: they were private antipathies, and the State—and even rational Society—gave them no patronage.

When Hitler drove out the Jewish scientists, he did not drive them out merely to invent weapons to overcome Nazi Germany—he drove them out, God help us, to invent weapons to overcome Mankind.

Since we are on the subject of the Atomic Ragnarök, let us note that it was in these hate-free 'Eighties that the first intimations of the Great Secret came to set the scientists wondering.

The phenomenon of radiant energy had been detected by Gray as early as 1846; and in 1852 a team of experimenters belonging to the British Association succeeded in sending messages by 'wireless' telegraphy across the River Tweed. It is certain that Johann Philipp Reis, who invented the electro-magnetic telephone in 1861, had already invented a mechanism for radiating electrical energy. He destroyed this mechanism in a fit of pique; but its description leaves no doubt of its capabilities, even if some doubt remains of its purpose.

In the late 'Seventies, following the discoveries of Faraday and Clerk Maxwell of the nature of magnetism, Hertz began those investigations into the nature of electro-magnetism which, through his detection of the so-called 'Hertzian' waves, led directly to the achievements, in wireless telegraphy, of Tesla and Marconi, and, before the century was out, to the wireless telephony of Aubrey Fessenden.

By 1880, electrical experimenters were aware that the generation of an electric current, in certain conditions, could cause the radiation of electrical energy outside the conducting wires.

But by 1890 the fact had become apparent that in matter itself was some principle which caused a radiation of energy. The years until the end of the century were spent, by many scientists, in ascertaining the nature of that principle, and the nature of the energy which was being liberated.

Like many of the fundamental discoveries of mankind, the discovery of 'natural' radiant energy was made by accident.

The physicist, Henri Becquerel, son and grandson of physicists, put some unexposed photographic plates away in a cupboard.

When he got them out for use, he found that they were 'exposed', although the black and red paper wrapping was still intact.

Something in the cupboard was affecting the plates, even through the light-proof wrapping.

What was it?

The only possible source of the 'light' which was affecting the plates was a piece of pitchblende, which had been given to Becquerel, and that he had placed in the cupboard. A few tests clearly showed that it *was* the pitchblende which had the property of affecting the emulsion of photographic plates, even though they were secure within their protective light-proof wrapping.

Something, then, within the pitchblende, had the power to affect photographic emulsion as had light—but with this difference, that the protective wrapping, proof against light, was not proof against the far stronger penetrative power of . . . what?

It was left to the following decade, first, to isolate the 'something' in the pitchblende which could fog photographic plates, and second, to suggest an explanation of this 'something's' strange power.

The explanation, to which a British scientist, J. J. Thomson, was to make the most valuable contribution, led mankind to the contemplation and the eventual understanding of a new world—the world of sub-molecular and sub-atomic pattern. The knowledge to which that chance-seen fogging of the photographic plates was to lead was a knowledge capable of changing, not only man's world, but Man himself.

'Discovery' and 'invention' are the factual proofs of truths first seen by the story-tellers and the poets. It isn't that the poets and the story-tellers 'have strange premonitions', as that the smiths learn, much later, to do what the poets and story-tellers have already sensed is possible to be done.

The second half of the 19th century was a period of tremendous technological advance: it seemed as though the inventors had never invented so much in such a short time—and that every advance in scientific knowledge had been first stated, as 'fiction', by a writer. The writers of that time were never busier. It is an envy-causing fact that at no time in the world's history were writers in Britain more respected, more encouraged to give, if not always of their best, then of their fullest, or more richly rewarded, with money as well as with praise.

When we look back on the success of such 'popular' writers as Rider Haggard, Conan Doyle, Marie Corelli, Jules Verne, Guy Boothby, Mrs Henry Wood, Thomas Hardy, H. G. Wells (and here we have eight writers whose success was established within the last quarter of the century) we are struck by the fact that they all moved easily between 'straight' storytelling and what, to-day, we should call 'science fiction'.

Yet not one of these eight, with the possible exception of Wells, had had a scientific education or technical apprenticeship (Wells got a scraped-through pass-degree in botany).

What is true of this eight is true of almost every other writer of the day: the knowledge that the world was on the verge of a fundamental change, through far-reaching scientific discoveries, so affected the contemporary writer's thinking that he or she could not confine the storytelling to the domestic scene, but must needs go, for subjects, to the fanciful, the bizarre, the 'prophetic'.

The Great Change was so imminent that the Public, as well as the Writers, were uneasy with the intimations of Change.

They turned to the writers as never before—not grumbling if a writer, having charmed them with the tale of a Norfolk parsonage, followed up his best-seller with some eerie tale of vampires or Visitors from Outer Space. That would be a best-seller, too; so great was the authority of the writer that he was free to choose his subject, and the public always applauded his choice. There was not a 'creepy' writer who didn't write equally well (and equally successfully) on simple social themes, and there wasn't a 'romantic' novelist who didn't turn, at least once, to the 'arabesque and the grotesque' (to use Poe's phrase) as the medium of his fancy.

There were several 'confederate circumstances' to give the writer this unprecedented and unrepeated pre-eminence in Britain.

The ten years since the passing of the first Education Act had added millions of literates to the population. Printing was cheap, and the introduction of mechanical methods of type-setting and pictorial reproduction had made the production of books cheaper even than it had been before 1870.

The half-tone process was invented in 1827, but for several reasons, did not 'take on'. However, in the hands of the French—in particular the famous firm of Goupil Frères—this process of engraving had already, by the early 1870s, reached a standard of quality not surpassed to-day.

The mechanical type-setting machines date, as we have seen, from the early 1870s: mechanical type-setting, *plus* mechanical methods of art-reproduction, *plus* the cheap wood-pulp paper introduced in the 1840s, add up to the least costly book and magazine in the history of mankind. The firm of Richard & Edward King Ltd, of Tabernacle-street, City, produced full-length, cloth-covered board-bound novels by Verne, Dumas, Grace Aguilar and other best-sellers, at the incredible (wholesale) price of twopence-farthing (4½ cents).

Much harsh criticism has been levelled at Smith and Mudie ('two hymn-bawling Nonconformists', Mr Cyril Pearl calls them), because of the censorship that they imposed on writers, denying those writers, the critics have complained, distribution through Mudie and Smith libraries if the writer did not toe the strict 'party line' laid down by the two circulating-library dictators.

What the critics mean is that no writer was free to discuss every topic, and that all writers were forbidden to express themselves in terms such as, for instance, D. H. Lawrence uses in *Lady Chatterley's Lover*.

This is foolish criticism, and, if the truth be faced, is not levelled against Smith and Mudie because of their business policy, but because of their religion.

Years ago, when I was discussing the Victorian writers with the late Ralph Straus (himself an unchallenged authority on all aspects of the Victorian literary scene), we agreed that the Victorian writer was far freer to choose his subject than the writer in our 'emancipated' times. (If you would like to test the truth of this remark, just try out any present-day British publisher with a few of your more adventurous themes!)

The critics of Smith and Mudie should remember, not what they 'suppressed', but what they so efficiently backed. For one thing, they kept the price of books up, while still selling them in their hundreds of thousands. The book was *produced* cheaply, but was *not sold* cheaply; and, since the author's royalty is reckoned on the retail price of the book, the author did well.

The author did no less well when it came to selling his short stories and articles to the magazines. Comparing the prices paid for literary work in the 1870s, 1880s and 1890s, we see that the author gained more, not *relatively*, but *absolutely*.

In other words, the author got more gold pounds for his work than his successor of to-day receives paper pounds.

For her first short story, sold to the *Athenaeum* in 1878, Marie Corelli received £18 18s.; for his story, *Habakkuk Jephson's Statement*, sold to the

Cornhill in 1883, Conan Doyle received £30 9s.—and, what was more, he was paid on acceptance. When I sold my first short story to the *English Review*, in 1934, under Douglas Jerrold's editorship, I was paid £5 5s.; the story was published seventeen months after acceptance, and I received my miserable five guineas twenty months after my agent (who took fifteen per cent of the 'fee') advised me, with considerable self-satisfaction, that he had 'got me into the *English Review*'.

Staff-writers, whether on newspapers or magazines, were paid less well, though we should not forget that Dickens, as a twenty-one-year-old reporter on the *Morning Chronicle*, was getting a guinea—£1 1s.—a day.

My old friend, Vaughan Dryden, was employed by the Aldine Press, in the 1890s, to churn out the raw material of boys' magazines at 3s. 6d. (89 cents) a thousand. But he was expected to do—and did—30,000 words a week; so that he never took home less than five guineas a week—'And I lived better, on that five guineas,' said Vaughan, 'than I could on a hundred to-day.'

He said that twenty years ago; to-day, he would have to say, 'better than on three hundred'.

The pages of such journals as *Cassell's Magazine*, the *Graphic*, the *Queen*, the *Quiver*, are instructive on this subject of authors.

Most journals of the gossipy sort ran articles on the homelife of Popular Authors, and my advice to authors of to-day is never to turn up these old journals in the Reading Room of the British Museum. 'A sorrow's crown of sorrow is remembering happier things.'

The rewards came as quickly as fully: within six years, Conan Doyle had moved from a three-pounds-a-week practice in Southsea (young brother, Innes, cleaning the brassplate and doing the household chores because the creator of Sherlock Holmes couldn't afford a servant, even at 1887 wages) to a fine house, complete with stained-glass windows sporting the armorial bearings of the Doyle family, that the successful author had built for himself in the Surrey stockbroker-belt.

It took two books—and two books only—to turn Henry Rider Haggard (we are still in the 'Eighties) from an unemployed ex-colonial to the lord of a splendid Norfolk manor. How clearly I can see in the woodcut reproduction of a photograph, showing Rider Haggard, rich on the profits from *King Solomon's Mines* and *She* (publication in the Jubilee Year of 1887 helped) leaning back in his comfortable desk-chair, in his comfortably furnished study. 'Mr Rider Haggard's study is hung with the sporting mementoes of his active days in South Africa.'

Let there be no misunderstanding: authors were respected because they were successful—because their success could be measured in terms of money; because they could buy or build 'gentlemen's' houses, and employ the statutory number of domestics. They were not respected because of the quality of their writing or the adequacy of their ideas: that would be too much to expect from the British public, even of a century ago.

They were equally respected, provided that they were successful, whether they wrote good sense or rubbish. When Marie Corelli, who built up a tremendous reputation on ungrammatical rubbish, went to Baden-Baden, His Royal Highness the Prince of Wales sent an equerry over to summon her to the royal presence.

H.R.H. shook—some say, even fondled—Marie's tiny hand; and declared himself an admirer of Marie's works; one of the few tastes, then, that H.R.H. had in common with his august Mama—and, by the way, with the Queen's most detested Minister, Gladstone.

Though the public supported authors, and made them rich, the last author who had also been a popular hero died with Dickens. After Dickens, no author—not even Nat Gould—ranked as a hero with the public.

Indeed, not even jockeys and footballers won the popular acclaim; hero-worship was reserved to naval and military leaders. Certain groups had their own heroes, of course; but for the mass of the population only Service leaders roused that uncritical admiration which, when received, makes the object a 'hero'.

And on the whole the objects of the public's admiration were not undeserving of the tribute.

Granted that wars had to be fought, the leaders fought them well. If they failed, it was rarely because of the poor quality of their men (these leaders were of the sort which does not ask for ready-trained men; they could do the training) but for lack of support on the political front manifested in those mysterious hold-ups in supplies which to-day would call forth the word 'sabotage'.

The career of a fighting general or admiral in the latter part of the last century must often have been a frustrating affair. 'The Country' appeared to be dedicated to a policy of imperial expansion; but there was a Prime Minister, in control over long periods, who was set against this policy.

When Gladstone was in, Empire-building was out—it made it hard to pursue a consistent military policy. Its effects may be seen in the fact that the 'pacification' of Egypt and the Sudan, beginning in 1882 with the bombardment of Alexandria, did not end until 1898, with the taking of Khartoum.

If, of course, the military strategists could show that what they were doing, or intended to do, though serving the cause of Empire, was saving Christians, Gladstone could be made to support the campaign.

The Irish Catholics the Grand Old Man did not regard as Christians, within the meaning of the Act, but his Home Rule policy deserved better of both his contemporaries and his successors.

The Irish are not so dissimilar from other peoples in that they find it hard to be persuaded to like something for which they have an instinctive dislike merely because it is presented as for their good. And too many, for different reasons, opposed the Home Rule policy for it ever to have had a chance of passing on to the Statute Book.

Besides, Parnell and the other Irish Nationalists could never forgive Gladstone for having been forced, by public opinion, to clap Irishmen in gaol; and when, as a highlight of the campaign of arson and assassination that Parnell & Co. supported, Lord Frederick Cavendish and Mr Burke were shot and killed in Phoenix Park, Dublin, by a 'patriot', the British public turned away from any proposed Irish 'settlement' save one based on, and carried through by, pure coercion.

There were links between Ireland and England which had nothing to do with Parnell, but which were equally troubling to Gladstone.

For having refused the Prince of Wales's challenge to a duel (the reason being the Prince's jealousy of the Duke of Marlborough, in the matter of Lady Aylesford) Lord Randolph Churchill got the virtual banishment of his brother, the Duke, to Ireland, as Lord-lieutenant of that troublesome kingdom.

Randy, already half-mad with the disease which was eventually to idiotize him and then (mercifully) to kill him, resented this 'persecution' of his brother, and organized a Fourth Party, without any particular policy save that of irritating the Prime Minister by that gross insolence which was Randy's particular gift.

Gladstone was getting old; and the jeers and catcalls of the Irish Nationalists—often carried shrieking from the House—and the only slightly more civilized baiting of Lord Randolph and his crypto-Republicans—would have tried a calmer spirit even than Gladstone's.

In 1880, Egypt was virtually ruled, not by the Khedive, but by a Franco-British commission acting for the bond-holders who had, in Alan Bott's phrase, 'financed (and fleeced)' the Khedive.

Against this humiliating situation, Arabi Pasha roused the nationalist instincts of a sufficient number of Egyptians to back his revolt against the Khedive, ineffectual successor to that Ismail who had sold the Suez Canal shares to Disraeli.

But Arabi was not rebelling against the Khedive, even if he thought that he was. He was rebelling against the Franco-British commission; against the money-markets of Paris and London.

An expedition to Egypt to 'restore order' was proposed as a joint venture; but the French, with Tunis and Indo-China on their own programme, declined to co-operate—and Britain 'went it alone'.

The British Mediterranean Fleet sailed for Alexandria, shelled it, and met so little opposition that our warships then entered the inner harbour, in order to bombard the ancient Greek city more effectually. An expeditionary force was landed, under the command of Sir Garnet Wolseley, and Arabi was soundly beaten. This success of British arms did something to restore the prestige lost when the Boers trounced the British, under Colley, at Majuba and Laing's Nek.

In the ordinary way, Gladstone would then have 'disengaged' himself; even though, 'in a fit of absent-mindedness, Britain had acquired domination in Egypt'.

Indeed, the Grand Old Man made every effort to do so; but another Nationalist leader, the Mahdi, had risen in the Sudan, and he was represented to Gladstone as a slave-trader and an oppressor of Christians. Much against his will, and with disastrous dilatoriness, Gladstone reluctantly authorized an expedition under General Gordon, and sacrificed Gordon later, by even more vacillating methods.

With Gordon's death, and the fall of Khartoum to the Mahdi, Gladstone could plead the necessity of leaving the Sudan to its own devices. Not until fourteen years later was Khartoum to be re-taken, and by that time Gladstone had gone to his rest.

Expeditions to Afghanistan—the march on Kandahar made the reputation of Roberts, afterwards ennobled as Baron Roberts of Kandahar—to Burma (which resulted in the annexation of King Theebaw's kingdom) and to various West African states, served to keep the Russians and the French in check, and to add to our 'spheres of influence' in the Dark Continent—where the Enemy was the Boer republic. Gold and diamonds were not safe in the hands of Bibletoting farmers.

By 1878, France had so far recovered from the Communist burning of Paris and the savage reparations-bill presented by Bismarck, that the rejuvenated nation presented the world with the almost arrogant assurance of her recovery in organizing the Exhibition, in Paris, of 1878. Eleven years later, in 1889, an even more impressive Exhibition was organized; an Exhibition that the Prince of Wales not only attended on its opening-day, but to the British section of which he had given his personal attention. The 'star-turn' of the Exhibition was, of course, the famous cast-iron Tower designed by the most socially presentable (for all that he was just on sixty)

Gustave Eiffel, who, fêted by President, Prince and all Society, was the very Lion of the Hour.

No matter what the technological advances of a decade, ordinary affairs continue, in the ordinary way, and attract as much attention as though scientists were not splitting atoms or conquering Space.

The case of Sir George Chetwynd, in 1889, interested the public far more than the statistics of the Eiffel Tower, which had just been erected in Paris; far more than the report that a British and a French 'experimenter' had succeeded in producing 'animated photographs'.

Libel actions in High Life were a consistent feature of the late Victorian scene; and what made Sir George Chetwynd's libel action so much more interesting was that the defendant was the Earl of Durham, who, only five years earlier, had 'hit the headlines' with his unsuccessful petition for divorce.

Sir George complained that certain statements, made by the earl, in writing, and relating to Sir George's racing transactions, were libellous. The plaintiff claimed £20,000 damages. Society—and lesser folk who could get in—flocked to the hearing.

After some litigation, and much discussion in Court, the case was referred to the Stewards of the Jockey Club for arbitration.

Mr James Lowther, M. P., the Earl of March (heir to the Dukedom of Richmond and Gordon) and Prince Soltikoff heard the complaints and rebuttals, and made their award. They found that Lord Durham had indeed libelled Sir George Chetwynd, and they assessed the damages at—one farthing.

Further to emphasize their opinion of Sir George, the Stewards ordered each side to pay his own costs.

Though the Stewards acquitted Sir George of the graver charges that the earl had laid to his account, they found the plaintiff guilty on the minor charges; he was duly censured, and asked to resign from the Jockey Club: Victorian social life knew no more terrible stigma.

The Victorians, though they had no wireless or television, had their theatres, their music-halls, their lectures, their concerts, their spectacles of all sorts, from Poole's Myriorama to Moore and Burgess's 'coloured' Minstrels. They had innumerable card and other games, they had the stereoscope, they had the Berlin wool-work patterns that such journals as *the Queen* used to give away, free, each week.

But they also had the newspapers, and what they found in the newspapers took the place, in Victorian times, of our wireless and television. The papers were, generally, bigger, and the accounts of events, particularly of civil and criminal trials, proportionately more detailed.

All actions-at-law interested them; but they liked Sex, Money and Rank, just as we do, and, like us, they enjoyed reading about these things, especially when they were the causes of other people's troubles.

As Money meant almost as much to the Victorians as Rank, they liked cases which concerned money, even where no titled persons were involved.

Such a case as, for instance, the Whalley will case gave the Victorians of 1883 talking-material for months. It was described by contemporaries as full of 'incredible incidents', which meant something to a Victorian journalist.

In the fifteen-days trial, the public heard all about a forged will, a fraudulent compromise proposed by the defendant, and all the other irregularities which revolve about a determined attempt to lay hands on money which does not belong to one.

There must have been a remarkable amount of champerty practised in Victorian times, seeing that there was no 'legal aid' for litigants, and yet so many apparently propertyless persons were able to engage in costly litigation. The Law must have realized that third parties were financing these litigants; but suspecting is one thing, proving it another—and the prosecution of those guilty of champerty[5] was a custom more honoured in the breach than in the observance.

One wonders, for example, how Mrs Weldon, a famed late-Victorian litigant, managed to get together the cash to enter upon her long and (to her) costly series of court appearances.

Mrs Weldon had been committed, by a typical piece of Victorian family intrigue, to the lunatic asylum. The obliging 'family physician' in the case was a Dr Semple: he signed the certificate of lunacy, which enabled the family to have Mrs Weldon shut up.

Mrs Weldon got out; and the Law says that a person escaped from the confinement of a lunatic asylum who is able to avoid recapture for a fortnight has (in a legal manner of speaking) regained his or her sanity, and can be re-committed only after the Law has once again enquired into the escaped lunatic's sanity.

As a now sane person, Mrs Weldon sued Dr Semple for having wrongfully signed a certificate imputing lunacy to her. She won the case, and the doctor was ordered to pay her £1,000 damages, as well as the costs of the action.

There were other people involved in the plot to deprive Mrs Weldon of her liberty; and she went methodically after them all. Unfortunately,

---

[5]Champerty or 'maintenance' has now been legalized under English law.

she began her attacks outside a court of law, and one of her victims, Monsieur Jules Prudence Rivière, took *her* to court instead. This time, the Law found Mrs Weldon in the wrong, and sentenced her to serve six months' imprisonment for having said what she had said about Monsieur Rivière.

The new Law Courts in the Strand (they had been opened in 1882, three years earlier) began to know Mrs Weldon very well indeed. The Law treated her with the utmost impartiality, sometimes giving her the verdict, sometimes not—but never denying her the use of the Courts by reason of her barratry.

Thus some three months after Mr Justice Hannen had refused a divorce to Lord Durham, Mrs Weldon appeared in the Strand, suing Mr Gounod for £10,000 in damages. She won.

Then in the November of the following year (1885), we find her claiming damages from Sir Henry de Bathe for alleged slander. Again she won, damages being assessed at £1,000.

But when, in 1888, the indefatigable Mrs Weldon brought another action against Monsieur Rivière and some others, the jury found for the defendants.

This sort of 'serial' law-suit was something peculiar to the Victorian legal scene. We do not have them to-day; not, I feel, because people have less money or less time— they are on the whole richer, and have far more leisure—but because that burning sense of injustice which impelled the Victorian litigant to Court is missing to-day. We have seen so much—and such terrible—injustice perpetrated through two world wars, and in the 'peace' which followed both, that we may think ourselves lucky to scratch out over-taxed livings in the Welfare State, seeing that so many millions of others have innocently endured starvation, torture, the gas-chamber and death. Small legacies, 'rights of way', what-So-and-So-said—all these things may, perhaps, be again as important as they were to the Victorians— provided that a future world may know the real peace that the Victorians knew.

The 'Eighties ended on a confused note.

On the one hand, there was the 'imperialistic' sentiment which focused upon the Queen as the nation prepared to celebrate her first fifty years of sovereignhood in the usual manner—reception of the Diplomatic Corps, reviews of troops, loyal addresses, 'treats' for the school-children and hand-outs for the poor.

Much against her will, the Queen was persuaded to drive to St Paul's for a solemn service of thanksgiving—and the cheers of the crowds, as she passed through the expensively decorated streets, must have astonished 'even more than they touched' her. But most of the burdens of the official side of the Jubliee fell on the shoulders of the Prince and Princess of Wales, both popular for a number of reasons only faintly connected with their personal qualities.

Never in human memory had there been a summer like that of Jubilee Year; for six weeks not a drop of rain fell in the British Isles, though just as the authorities were getting panicky in the prospect of drought, the rain fell as though God had never sent a rainbow to reassure Noah.

But it was in a dreary rainstorm that the unemployed, in that same Jubilee Year, converged on Trafalgar-square, and made the day sadly memorable as 'Bloody Sunday'.

The Mob still held the streets; though something was happening in Spring-gardens which was to mark the end of almost-gone mediaeval London, including such relics of its past as the Mob.

In 1888, the London County Council took over the rule of the capital from the Metropolitan Board of Works and the Vestries, though the latter were to enjoy some limited powers until the end of the century.

The establishment of a municipal monopoly-authority over a city and its suburbs housing more than four million people was a piece of socialist legislation far more daring than any proposed by the street-corner speakers of the Social Democratic Federation, the Socialist League or the Fabian Society—representing the three social 'castes' in the 'classless society' of British Socialism.

But no one seemed to see it at the time as socialist: not the Socialists, not the others.

Yet Socialist—state-socialist—it certainly was; and its inherent socialism became apparent almost at once, as it began to take over, from private enterprise, those services that the County Councillors deemed to be the care of the city-state. The L.C.C. naturally was given charge of the free-education system, formerly run by the London School Board—but the schools necessitated kitchens and bakeries and laundries; and the night-schools necessitated workshops.

It was not long before the L.C.C. found itself running a score of enterprises formerly unconnected with any governmental body.

What it has never managed to do (which is why it is now powerless to prevent its suppression) is to gain control of the Metropolitan Police, though it has assisted the police in clearing the streets of the Mob.

By building 'night-refuges', 'hostels', lodging-houses, for the poor, the L.C.C. provided alternatives to nights in the Adelphi Arches or on the Embankment benches. At first the homeless were invited to use these shelters; now they are compelled. Here again, the L.C.C. took over an idea from private enterprise: Lord Rowton, Disraeli's ennobled Private

Secretary, devoted his money and his time to establishing well-built and properly run lodging-houses for the homeless throughout London. These 'Rowton Houses' set a new standard in 'twopenny flops'; and only to-day are the last of them making way for something more in keeping with our Affluent Society.

For those, of course, who could see only the surface, there was plenty of reason for looking on the dark side; plenty of material for writing the sort of *In Darkest London* books which had a big sale because there is an impulse in humanity which rather enjoys being reminded of its faults—of omission as well as of commission.

Through the streets of London, 'General' William Booth led his 'Hallelujah Band' of ragged men and women—and behind them marched a scarecrow collection of layabouts and ragamuffins, the 'Starvation Army,' jeering and mocking the Boothites, and drowning the godly music with a cacophony played on old saucepans and dust-bin lids.

The Salvation Army's motto, 'Blood and Fire', meant something then. God not having heard the Hallelujah Band's prayer for patience, the Boothites halted and turned on their scoffers. The police, impartially, waded in and carted off both the Godly and the Ungodly to the lock-up.

It seems a little unfair that in many towns, from Bristol to Gravesend, the 'Army' was charged with having incited to riot; but this Diocletian-like persecution of the embryo 'Army' did it no harm. It put it on the side of the People, to whom the adoption of military rank and uniforms was not originally acceptable.

Thinking of the gas- and naphtha-lit streets of the 'Eighties, and of the seething undercurrent of riot which was always perceptible, whether or not there was 'trouble', I am reminded of an instrument of coercion no longer seen, but which was a commonplace up to the beginning of the 1914 war.

This was the 'bier', a flat wooden platform on two wheels, similar to the 'barrer' from which costermongers sell their wares. Provided with straps, it was wheeled rapidly to the scene of disorder, the offending citizen was thrown down upon its hard surface, fastened with long straps, and wheeled off, generally with a murmuring rabble to keep him company, to the police-station.

Horse-dung and cobblestones; plumes of the naphtha-flares making the shadows quiver; acrid sweetness of sarsaparilla and aniseed and paregoric; shrill Cockney voices; dusty velvet and feathers; the nacreous gleam of pearl-buttons; high-heeled cloth-topped boots for men and women; rattle of hansom and growler and horse-bus; sirens hooting and howling on the fog-bound river; violet and patchouli and Jockey Club; the shine of toppers; the whiff of a Sullivan and Powell; the shrill peep-peep of a doorman's whistle; Johann Strauss coming gustily on the damp night air from the Temple Gardens; the smooth clatter as the Continental Express crosses the thundering ironwork of Hungerford Bridge; cigars, the sparkle of diamonds, the crimson silk lining of an evening cape; osprey, *mousseline de soie*, cut velvet; brown fog; jet-trimmed bonnets; boas; the clop-clop-clop of hooves . . . hooves . . . hooves. . . .

But it was changing; the 'Eighties began to change it. Fundamentally, out of all recognition.

The 'Seventies had seen new streets cut through the City; now the 'Eighties were to make new (and, it must be admitted, very ugly) streets through the West End: Charing Cross-road, Shaftesbury-avenue; the new Coventry-street connecting Piccadilly Circus with Leicester-square.

By the end of the decade, the electric trams which had been a 'scientific novelty' at Brighton in 1881 (they are still running there to-day) were about to replace the horse-trams which somehow survived until after the 1914 war, in such dismal places as the Burdett-road. But the horse-drawn tram, generally, could not put up much of a battle for survival against the electric tram, which did much to develop the London suburbs in the hillier districts.

In the parts around the Crystal Palace and Highgate, an attempt had been made to introduce a steam-tram: the 'residents' (more powerful then than they are now) objected; and the poor old horse was brought back, to crack its heart in attempting these alpine climbs. But there were slopes up which horses could not draw a full bus-load, and these made the districts to which they led inviolate from development, until mechanical transport arrived in the shape of the electric tram.

As soon as it was possible to get from central London to such-and-such a place, such-and-such a place had its land snapped up by real-estate speculators, and building 'development' soon followed. The pattern of London's development has always been accessibility first, settlement afterwards.

It was the tram, first horse-drawn, and then electrically powered, which opened up the south-eastern suburbs; by the time that the northern suburbs were able to be conquered (by the tram) the motor-bus was almost at hand to assist in cracking the last stronghold of 'privacy'.

P·A·R·T F·O·U·R

The Fourth Decade

Threatened war between Great Britain and a now firmly united United States was averted by the "unconstitutional" action of the Prince of Wales, as the threatened war of 1861 had been averted by the Prince's dying Father. Whether a good thing for Britain or a bad, the Prince shewed that his almost total abandonment to pleasure (the husbands of some of his mistresses and the lovers of some of his mistresses were beginning to cut up rough) had not impaired a sharp political sense, nor the ability to be "unconstitutional" at need—a happy augury for the days, still apparently far distant, when he should be King-Emperor.

The Daimler-Benz 'horseless carriage' had been available in the last decade, but not until the latter half of the Nineties, with the Prince and his noble friends making it fashionable, did the Motor-car come to stay. Powered flight had to wait until the beginning of the next decade, but the principles of aeronautics were being studied seriously and scientifically with the man-carrying glider, by Lilienthal in Germany, Pilcher in Britain, and Chanute in America—serious experimentation which would be studied by the Wright Brothers, and make their success possible. The modern Scientific World was hurrying to meet the present: Marconi was ready with his wireless-telegraphy in 1894, and had transmitted to Newfoundland by the century's end. Fessenden, in 1900, had succeeded in broadcasting the human voice by electric-arc. London was being rebuilt. Britain and the Kaiser's Germany were engaged in a costly arms-race. In South Africa, the immigrant "Uitlanders", hungry for money, whether gained through diamonds or gold (or, preferably, both) were heading for trouble with the Boers, mostly Fundamentalist Farmers of Dutch origin. First-class to New York by any of the luxury liners was £10–£50. American heiresses were coming the other way, to marry (mostly impecunious) British noblemen—or, more precisely, men with titles. Trouble with the Boers, after General Sir Herbert Kitchener had destroyed the power of the Khalifa in the Sudan, broke out into open warfare, with the British suffering defeat after defeat, until Lord Roberts and Kitchener went to South Africa to put the Boers in their place. Future trouble within the Empire was fortunately avoided when the completely unsuitable Duke of Clarence, next-in-line for the Throne after the death of his Father (still the Prince of Wales) conveniently caught 'influenza' and died, to leave the Succession to his steady, firmly heterosexual brother, Prince George, Duke of York (an admirer of Sherlock Holmes, by the way) who later ascended the Throne as King George the Fifth.

In 1897, the Queen celebrated her Diamond Jubilee, with ceremonies which brought troops from all over her vast Empire, and Emperors, Kings, Princes, and Presidents from all over the world, to pay their respects. The Service of Thanksgiving at St Paul's marks for us (as it marked for the sharp-eyed Kipling) the apogee of Empire, which, so far as the war in South Africa was concerned, was to end the decade in shameful military defeat.

In no way different from past and future Decades, that of 1891–1901 had its scandals, of which the most notorious was the Wilde affair of 1895, though the efforts of the 'Gay' community to 'avenge poor Oscar' is directly responsible for the official tenderness towards that community shewn by most governments to-day.

The British Admiralty purchased its first submarines, designed by the American engineer, Holland. The Prince found his last mistress: a massive lady, the wife of one of his naval officers. Her name was Mrs Keppel, who was to outlive him by many years, indeed beyond the Windsor-Simpson affair, on which Mrs Keppel is said to have commented that 'we did things better in my day'.

BEFORE 1890, the changes, improvements and growth of London had been mostly initiated by and carried out through the efforts of Private Enterprise, whether that Private Enterprise was associated with the Crown, with a Joint-stock Company, with a Ducal Landlord or with a small builder, backed by a building-society or the local bank.

But with the establishment of the London County Council in 1888, state-control at second hand was about to show not only its taste for power but its ability to exercise it.

Between Temple Bar and Charing Cross as the eastern and western limits, and between the Strand and Holborn as the southern and northern limits, was a curious survival of late mediaeval to pre-Restoration London known as 'Clare Market'. It was exceedingly picturesque—and proportionately unsavoury. The district contained several well-frequented theatres, including the Olympic; but mostly it consisted of small shops, taverns, lodging-houses and tenements which, by the kindest reckoning, could only have been classified as slums. The most 'respectable' streets—Holywell-street and Wych-street—were so because of the good business done by the dozens of booksellers who sold their dubious wares here; the class of work in which they dealt may be judged by the fact that, as I have said, Holywell-street was commonly known as 'French-letter-row'.

Much of this picturesque district had been swept away when the new Law Courts were built in the 'Eighties; and, to the west, more of it went with the building of Charing Cross-road. But the 'hard core' between Charing Cross and Temple Bar remained, and in 1891 the London County Council passed the final plans for its demolition.

Those plans called for the widening of the Strand between Waterloo-bridge and St Clement Danes; the construction of a curved 'by-pass' at the back of the Strand (later named 'Aldwych') and a broad street connecting this curved road with Holborn. North of Holborn, Southampton-row was to be widened to connect this broad street (later named 'Kingsway') with Woburn-place and the Euston-road.

This was not an L.C.C. plan; the old Metropolitan Board of Works had evolved it as early as the 'Fifties; but the M.B.W., though wielding much power, had not the desire to usurp private enterprise—and the L.C.C. had, right from the beginning of its reign.

South of the Strand at this point, much reconstruction of the Duke of Norfolk's London estate (Surrey-street, Arundel-street, Howard-street, and the rest) had followed the decision not to place the new Law Courts on a river-site at the eastern end of Temple Gardens.

Many of the old houses on the Norfolk estate had been pulled down in expectation of the building of the Law Courts (including that in Norfolk-street in which Peter the Great had lodged), but when the decision was made to build the Law Courts on the site of Butcher's-row, in the Strand, the empty plots were filled with houses of heavily-carved red brick which are only now giving place to newer (though not more beautiful) buildings.

Only on the southern side of the Strand did the old buildings remain: they are Crown property, and came under the protecting influence of Somerset House. Even to-day, there are at least twenty houses which, though they have been refronted at various periods since the reign of Charles II, belong undoubtedly to his period.

The City had already begun to take on a new look with the construction of Queen Victoria-street and the re-construction of Poultry, at the end of the 'Sixties; by the 'Nineties the City was full of iron- or steel-framed stone-faced office-buildings, uncompromisingly, 'business-like'; and breathing the very essence of Joint-Stockery.

But London, even then, was so vast, that no matter how many new buildings went up, the 'look', the 'feel' of London were still those of a city far removed from the present. Up such alleys as Pope's Head-alley or Change-alley, the bow-fronted chop-houses—Baker's, the George and Dragon, Simpson's—still maintained eighteenth-century standards in an eighteenth-century atmosphere. How well I recall, as a boy, my wonderment at seeing the gentle up-and-down movement of the silk hats, as the 'City gents' munched their chump chops, charred from the silver grill.

Not until 1907 did the last of the 'Clare Market' houses come down; but work began in 1891; and it was important as marking the first big incursion of the L.C.C. into a sphere of activity hitherto reserved solely to private enterprise.

In 1890, the aged John Tenniel (immortal as the artist of *Alice in Wonderland*; unknown as the artist of *Happy Families*) was given the opportunity to draw, not only his most memorable cartoon for *Punch*, but one of the handful of cartoons which have achieved world-fame.

Tenniel's cartoon, *Dropping the Pilot*, showed a self-satisfied Kaiser William II (as the Captain) watching the Pilot, Bismarck, descend the cat-walk, to the cutter which waits below, to take the Pilot into retirement and impotence.

With their usual contradictoriness, the British were saddened by the Kaiser's dismissal of a man who had given Britain more to worry about than had even Napoleon the Great.

On the other hand, they knew Bismarck . . . while the Kaiser was still an unknown quantity. Perhaps it was not so much a question of contradictory sentimentalism, as a question of 'the Devil you know'.

As one old man's tribute to another, Tenniel's *Dropping the Pilot* marked not only the summit of the artist's fame, but the summit of Bismarck's. From now on, until the débâcle of 1918, the All-Highest would control the destinies of the Reich—'Ein Volk, Ein Gott, Ein Kaiser'.

Germany, even in the last days of Bismarck, had entered the race for colonies—'Germany's Place in the Sun', the Teutonic propagandists called it. Germany gained her colonies, lost them to Britain, France, Portugal and South Africa, and now they are reverting to the heirs of the Blacks from whom they were originally filched. The whole process has taken only little more than a century.

Germany, even by the 'man in the street', was seen as the Enemy as early as the mid-'Eighties. Those infallible indices of public opinion, the boys' adventure stories, never tell of desperate resistance to the French Invader—only to the German. But the specific choice of Germany as the Enemy was based not so much on a shrewd assessment of Germany's political ambitions, as upon a quite irrational dislike of the German Kaiser. (Or was it so irrational. . . ? The Kaiser was very 'English'; and there is much to be said for this instinctive mistrust of 'English' Americans: Franklin Delano Roosevelt, the most intractable enemy that Britain has ever had, was an 'English' American.)

It is regrettably true that Britain would have armed, whether or not the Kaiser was pro- or anti-British: whether or not there was a Kaiser. But because there was a Kaiser, and because his ambitions seemed to be of a sort likely to clash with 'Ours', then Britain armed specifically against him. The Kaiser, acting through 'private' explorers, as King Leopold of the Belgians had acted through 'private' explorers, had carved out a good chunk of Africa for the Reich, and so Britain began to concentrate on the building of long-range warships. Ships of the class of H.M.S. *Benbow*, rated at 10,000 tons and developing 11,500 horse-power, date from the early 1890s. British troops' experience of jungle warfare was extensive; but small-arms and light machine-guns, as well as light, quick-firing, highly portable artillery, were also developed for the battles which seemed inevitable in the area of tropical 'spheres of influence'.

The British Army of 1890, in fact, was almost as well-armed as the British Expeditionary Force of 1914. It lacked the motor-transport and the primitive aeroplanes of 1914; but it had the Lee-Metford .303 magazine-rifle (the one with the cut-out and the annular back-sight), the Nordenfeldt and Maxim machine-guns, firing up to six hundred and sixty .303 rounds a minute; it had the Vickers-Armstrong quick-firing six-pounders, and heavier armament. It had good field-telegraphy and heliograph, even spotter balloons. It was well equipped to deal with the Enemy. What was more, it was in constant training—there were still nearly a hundred small wars to be fought before British and Germans met at the Marne.

Nothing, of course, of a war-like nature showed in Britain's social life. The upkeep of a trained army and a well-found navy called for no sacrifices on the part of the public.

Life went on as usual; and the Upper Ten continued to supply that entertaining scandal which is the product of idleness.

The Prince of Wales had had a good Press for over ten years—ever since the Rosenberg libel case, to be exact.

His friendships were not commented upon save in such journals as *Judy*, *Fun* and the *Tomahawk*, all of whose editors had clearly taken the lesson of the Rosenberg case to heart.

All his actions—and of course, his friendships—were widely reported, in both the 'respectable' and the 'smart' Press; but there was little comment of an adverse nature; those who could read between the lines did so—for the rest, the comment, such as it was, bore no derogatory meaning.

During both the Mordaunt and the Rosenberg cases, the Pious—generally Nonconformist—Press had thundered or nagged, according to the temper of the editor, against the Prince's choice of friends—just as, sixty years later, it was a hypocritical attack on the King's friends which was to precipitate the business of the Abdication.

However, there is this to be said about self-appointed critics of the Famous: they are quick to take credit for any change in the behaviour of the person criticized.

Whether they wished to or not, those critics were now under a certain obligation to compliment the Prince upon his 'changed ways'—which really boiled down to little more in his favour than that his friends were not getting into trouble these days.

But with the Tranby Croft scandal, all the dormant criticism of the Prince woke up, and once again he found himself splashed in the newspapers for reasons other than that he had opened a new hospital or been made a Bencher of the Middle Temple.

The case has been written up so often that it is necessary here to describe it only in the briefest detail.

At Tranby Croft, country house of a rich shipowner, Mr Arthur Wilson, the Prince of Wales was spending a week-end.

The Princess of Wales was not one of the house-party, which consisted mostly of men. If there were any 'particular friends' of the Prince—ladies—their very presence at Tranby Croft was concealed throughout the legal proceedings which followed on, and arose from, this apparently most respectable house-party.

Among the other guests was a Scottish baronet, Sir William Gordon-Cumming, Colonel of the Scots Guards.

The Prince was fond of cards, especially of card-games which involved gambling. A game of baccarat was proposed, and later Wilson's son confided to Mrs Lycett Green that he had detected Colonel Gordon-Cumming in the act of cheating—specifically, of placing his bet after the first cards had been played.

Challenged, Sir William did a curious thing: he hotly denied that he had cheated in the manner described, but agreed to sign a promise that he would never play cards again.

In return for Sir William's written promise, all the members of the party agreed not to mention the matter, either outside or even among themselves.

Of course, Somebody Talked—Somebody always does.

The stories which were running around London were of such a nature that only one course was left to Sir William: to seek to re-establish his good name by bringing an action for slander against Mr and Mrs Lycett Green.

Much has been said of the 'injustice' of the verdict, which went against the plaintiff; but although it is true that the visual evidence of cheating depended upon the declaration of one person, who 'thought' that he had seen Sir William move his counter after the game started, there was the much more damning evidence of the Colonel's written promise. If he was not guilty, why did he sign such a paper? If he was innocent, and consented to put his reputation in jeopardy by signing the paper, then he deserved to be condemned for folly worse than any dishonesty.

The verdict 'broke' Sir William. He sent in his papers; he resigned from his clubs; his loyal fiancée insisted on marrying him (and it would be pleasant to record that their marriage was a long and happy one), but she was the only defender that he found.

But if the outcome of the Tranby Croft affair 'broke' Colonel Sir William Gordon-Cumming, it also did much to wipe out the good impression that the Prince had made on the more touchy of his mother's subjects. It was the revelation that baccarat had been played—a *Foreign* gambling game, to make matters worse!—which shocked the Unco' Guid most.

The Free Church hacks got out the 'scathing' leaders from the Mordaunt affair, and subbed them to fit the present case: they didn't need much subbing.

What an example to give to his future subjects! No need to quote the editorials: we have seen the same thing in our own time.

The Tranby Croft scandal was soon over; though the Prince could have wished that attention be shifted from him in a less distressing fashion.

In 1892, the Duke of Clarence—'Eddy'—died. The bulletins described his illness as 'influenza'; there were not many bulletins before the illness proved fatal.

'Eddy' was the Prince's eldest son, and thus Heir-but-one to the Throne. He was dearly loved by his parents, in spite of (or, possibly because of) certain wayward tendencies which were savagely mocked, week after week, by Henry Labouchere, in the pages of *Truth*, where the Duke 'featured' as 'Collar-and-Cuffs'.

This was no national scandal: if the provinces read *Truth*, they didn't know who 'Collar-and-Cuffs' was—and those who did know knew far more about the Duke of Clarence (if only by common London gossip) than Labby dared print in *Truth*, even by the most shameless innuendo.

As is not unusual with parents who have come to the sad realization that their son has developed certain abnormal tastes, the Prince and Princess of Wales were overjoyed when Princess May of Teck, a great-grand-daughter of George III, and thus 'Eddy's' cousin, consented to marry him. The parents believed that, in marriage, 'Eddy' would forget his inverse inclinations, and settle down to a normal sexual life.

Well . . . that might have happened. Who can say?

But 'Eddy' died, deeply mourned by his parents, though not by those, with a more realistic appreciation of facts, who felt that 'Eddy' might well have involved the Crown in its worst scandal since Edward II.

In the year following 'Eddy's' death, Princess May became engaged to her dead fiancé's brother, Prince George, Duke of York, who, with his brother's death, was in the direct line of succession.

Prince George was, like his brother, a 'Sailor Prince', in that both the Princes, as boys, had made the voyage round the world on H.M.S. *Bacchante*. Public sentiment, which is generally pretty sound in these matters, recognized that what had happened had happened for the best, and that George had the makings of a king which were absent in 'Eddy'.

Yet is was only at the end of his reign, and at the very end of his life, that the generally unsympathetic view of the King changed to one of respect, and, subtly—and suddenly—to deep affection and profound love. The honest, hard-working, affectionate, simple, God-fearing man whom no one outside his family and his immediate circle of friends had ever properly understood, came, at his life's end, into his reward of his people's love. There was never a King—not even the beloved Edward VII—who was mourned as King George V was mourned.

But even this guiltless man was not spared the attacks of scandal, and it was as King that he had to bring an action against a slanderer to defend the royal honour and the royal name.

The first attack, though, belongs to this decade under review—and though it belongs to the end of the decade, we shall examine it here.

Admiral Tryon, commanding the Mediterranean Fleet, was the central figure of one of the most notorious maritime scandals of all time, which was, as well, one of the sea's greatest mysteries. To this day, no one has explained how Admiral Tryon came to act as he did.

The final manoeuvre of the Fleet exercises, which had lasted several days, was a review of the entire Mediterranean Squadron 'in line ahead'.

This means that the Fleet divided itself up into two lines of ships, which steamed ahead, one thousand two hundred yards apart. Admiral Tryon, flying his flag in *Victoria*, led the starboard line; Rear-Admiral Markham led the port line in *Camperdown*.

Now these two battleships, of the latest design, needed a minimum of six hundred yards in which to turn; this fact must be borne carefully in mind—it was certainly in the mind of every navigating officer in the Mediterranean Fleet, although apparently not in that of Admiral Tryon.

When the two lines of ships had steamed ahead for some distance, Tryon ordered his Staff-commander—in the presence of Lord Gifford and Flag-Lieutenant—to make the signal for the two lines of ships to turn inwards, and steam, on parallel courses, in the reverse direction.

Both men saw at once that this manoeuvre would be impossible: if the two leading ships were to turn inwards, with a distance of only 1,200 yards separating them, and they needed at least 600 yards each to make the complete turn, they were bound to collide.

Gifford had the temerity to question the order, but Tryon was so emphatic that, reluctantly, Gifford sent out the signal, quietening his misgivings by assuring himself that Tryon had some 'card up his sleeve'.

From *Camperdown* there came no immediate acknowledgement to Tryon's flag signal. Could the message possibly be right?

Angrily, Tryon insisted that the message be repeated back—he would brook no querying of his orders. The two great ships began to turn inwards; thirty thousand tons of armour-plate joining themselves at thirty miles an hour.

The whole Fleet watched this strange manoeuvre with more astonishment than alarm—though there was alarm enough, and in plenty. Everyone thought that at the last minute Tryon would give countermanding orders, instructing the lead ships to break off, and to resume the 'line ahead' formation.

They waited . . . and waited . . . and waited.

And at last, risking the severe penalties that any infringement of the strict naval discipline might bring about in his promising career, Gifford dared to defy the Admiral's wrath and point out that the 'point of no return' was almost on them—but even as the young officer spoke, the point was almost past.

Then, and then only, did Tryon seem to awake to the horrible possibilities of his . . . what? . . . error . . . pigheadedness . . . misappreciation of the facts?

'Oh, my God!' he is reported to have said. 'What have I done?'—and to Gifford's fevered questions: 'Yes, yes, it is entirely my fault!'

But the orders came too late. On both ships, the telegraphs rang frantically: but fifteen thousand tons of steel cannot be braked as one brakes a bicycle. With the screws thrashing violently—at first full-speed ahead, then full astern—the ships continued to approach each other; they were now so close that nothing could have kept them apart.

Tryon had abdicated all authority; a stricken man, he could only watch while more active, cooler-headed juniors leapt to save what might still be saved from inevitable catastrophe.

Men were ordered to action-stations aboard each ship; they ran to the davits to ready the lifeboats; they broke out the rafts from their covers. Each ship's company watched the approach of the other ship. And, at last, *Camperdown's* armoured prow sheered into the side of Victoria. For the men below, in the stoke-holds and engine-rooms, nothing could be done.

The Fleet watched as the *Camperdown* dug deep into the doomed *Victoria*. Boats were lowered, men jumped overboard—but Tryon was not among them.

When last seen, he was standing on the bridge, his eyes fixed on some point ahead. He was not visible for long: the doomed ship settled by the head, so quickly that all was over within ten minutes.

No one at the time could explain the tragedy—no one has explained it since.

But a curious rumour crept around London: that Tryon had chosen this infamously lunatic way in which to commit suicide.

His daughter, They said, had contracted a secret marriage with the Duke of York (then Prince George of Wales)—at Malta, They said. And the Duke, having married Princess May, had broken the hearts both of Miss Tryon and of her father.

It is not an easy task to reconcile two exact, and apparently contradictory, aspects of the century's last decade: on one hand, the picture of a light-hearted, easy-going decade—the 'Gay Nineties', if not precisely the 'Naughty Nineties"—with the grim unrest which affected almost every stratum of society save the genuinely Idle Rich.

It was a decade in which Mr A. J. Balfour seemed to be more often playing golf on Hayling Island, with his friend, Lord Winchilsea, than in dealing, as Irish Secretary, with the still violent disorder of our Sister Island.

It was a decade in which the world of entertainment reached heights of achievement never since touched: in the music-hall, the theatre, and 'spectacle'. At Olympia, the Hungarian impresario, Imre Kiralfy, was putting on shows which were not unfairly compared with the lavish, cost-ignored spectacles of ancient Rome.

London was going to concerts, seeing exhibitions, listening to oratorios and brass bands. But London was also seeing the unemployed menacing law and order; experiencing the strike, week after week, threatening the very bases of the nation's economy.

Earnest men were speaking at street-corners; as earnest, but far more efficient, men were busy in modest offices, organizing the workers into trade-unions, preparing to launch a new industrial power into men's consciousness.

Parnell died, at the age of forty-five, in 1892; but that did not mean peace for Ireland. Salisbury's government had been busy 'organizing' Britain: the Act dividing up England and Wales into sixty-one 'county boroughs', including that of London, was one more bureaucratic step towards bringing all the nation under the control of Westminster; it seems curious to us that the Socialists of the 'Nineties—Webb, Shaw, Wells and so many others—did not realize that they were not merely going to get their Socialist Paradise; they were actually getting it—the first instalments coming from both the Liberal and the Conservative governments.

Gladstone was voted back into office in 1892; and despite the most violent opposition of the Conservatives, he forced through the Irish Home Rule Bill, giving virtual autonomy to Ireland. It was a measure whose 'statesmanship' does not need to be discussed; one which under the circumstances of the day rendered the only solution possible to the festering Irish problem.

By 419 to 41, the stupid Lords threw the Bill out—and, for the first time, Reform of the Upper House appeared on the Liberal agenda; it was a Liberal policy which was to be inherited by the Labour Party.

Gladstone, since, as a very young man, he had left the Conservative Party, had based his career on three aims: world free trade, electoral reform and Irish Home Rule.

Free trade had come—but it was already being attacked, as an economic system, by that reformed Republican, Joe Chamberlain, and his Imperialists; electoral reform had come—by the inevitable processes of historical development, rather than by the efforts or convictions of any one political party; Irish Home Rule was doomed never to become law. The statesmanship of the Lords was sadly lacking, though it is not difficult to sympathize with their intractability in Irish affairs. The activities of the Land League, the Irish National League and the Irish American League (when the last-named met in the Horticulture Hall in Philadelphia, on 25th April, 1883, over five hundred 'delegates' were present) were not calculated to soothe their political opponents into tolerance. I have called the action of the Lords in rejecting the Home Rule Bill 'stupid', and so it was; but it was understandably human, for all that.

There were many of the Peers who voted in 1894 who remembered well the night of 15th March, 1883. Big Ben struck nine, and as the last stroke died trembling on the sharp night air, a tremendous explosion rocked the Houses of Parliament: it was yet another reminder—too near home to be neglected—that O'Donovan Rossa, President of the Irish American League, was in active opposition against the British Government.

The Lords were stupid, yes, to reject the offered settlement of the Irish question; but the heart has its reasons that the head cannot understand; and to sympathize with those who could not make peace with the Irish dynamiters, assassins and traitors, one has only to remember the howl which went up at any proposal to come to terms with Soviet Russia, in the years immediately after the 1917 revolution—and, so far, the Russians have never been accused of planting bombs in railway-stations, post-offices, letter-boxes and elsewhere. The Irish did so, consistently, for nearly thirty years (and began again just before the last war).

Gladstone retired in favour of his Foreign Minister, Lord Rosebery, a maladroit handler of foreign affairs who showed up no better when handed the responsibility of running the empire.

Rosebery was popular with the masses because he was a successful racehorse-owner; but the masses were not represented in Westminster, and here Rosebery contrived to make enemies in all parties, including his own. He declared himself the defender of the policies of Gladstone in regard to Ireland—and promptly alienated the Irish by a monumental tactlessness, in proposing a statue of Cromwell, the traditional Demon King of the Irish pantomime. The rocky family fortunes having been restored by Rosebery's marrying a wealthy Jewess, this financially Semiticized Prime Minister then busied himself with the Disestablishment of the Church of Wales. The masses, who liked his race-horses, were affronted when he lopped 'good drinking time' off 'licensed hours', and the well-to-do were horrified when this son-in-law of Abraham instituted Death Duties.

All parties ganged up to chuck out this ineffectual nonentity; and in 1894, Salisbury, who could not stand up to the French, but who could fairly well dominate the Houses of Parliament, returned to power.

Salisbury came back with a huge majority (411 Government seats against 260 of the combined opposition), and he needed it all.

Foreign affairs were not more disturbing than usual—in May 1895 an expeditionary force was despatched to Chitral, to put the Badisha El Oomra Khan in his place; in the Sudan, Kitchener was preparing to embark on the third and final stage of the Egyptian War begun in 1882. The most disquieting aspect of foreign affairs was the new—and extreme—pugnacity of the United States of America, of which the doctrine of Pan-Americanism was at once the cause and the result.

There had been a time when France was this country's 'ancient, inveterate enemy'; France's place, as Ancient, Inveterate Enemy Number One, had been taken by the United States of America—which still remains the intractable opponent of Britain, and all that Britain stands for.

What makes, and has made, this American enmity so dangerous is that successive British governments have adopted a traditional policy of wishful self-deception, and while admitting, at times, the enmity of France, Russia, Germany and some other countries, have refused to admit that the United States, whether considered as a people or a government, is anything but friendly.

In 1893 Lord Rosebery, then Foreign Secretary, received an odd communication from an address in West 134th-street, New York City.

Rosebery had pencilled on this letter: 'Do we know this man?'—and a further pencilled note, in an unknown hand, says: 'I seem to remember the name. Ask Spain if she knows anything.'

Finding out who the writer was cost Great Britain much humiliation at the hands of the Messiahs of Pan-Americanism.

The letter in question, bearing an immense coat-of-arms at its head, informed 'Monsieur le comte de Rosebery' that the writer, Baron James de Harden-Hickey, had taken possession of the uninhabited islands of the

Martin Vaz group (six hundred miles due east of Bahia, Brazil), that he proposed to set up his capital on the principal island, Trinidad; that he would rule the group as an absolute monarch; that he would build a lighthouse, harbour and port-installations; and that he declared himself Sovereign of the group, with the title of Prince: James the First, Sovereign Prince of Trinidad.

By the next post, a letter arrived from the Turkish Minister (Rustum Pasha, a Christian), stating that he had had an extremely odd communication from a certain. . . . And there was a letter from the Spanish Minister . . . and one from the Portuguese.

By this time, a Foreign Office clerk had looked up both Trinidad and James de Harden-Hickey.

The islands of the Martin Vaz group had been discovered by the Portuguese in the early 16th century; charted, but not settled.

Then in 1700, Edmund Halley, the astronomer and Fellow of the Royal Society, landed on Trinidad, and 'claimed' it in the name of His Majesty King William the Third.

In the early years of the 19th century, Portugal had settled convicts on the main island; but after some years the convicts had been taken off, and since then no one had visited Trinidad save the members of various expeditions hunting for the treasure of Lima Cathedral, supposed to have been buried there.

As for Harden-Hickey, he was a Frenchman of Irish descent, born in San Francisco. Educated in France, he had been a cadet at St Cyr when the Franco-Prussian War broke out; he had left the military college, and joined up. After the peace, he had returned to St Cyr, to complete his studies. On his father's death, he had inherited—and spent—his modest fortune; taken up with the Count of Chambord, Pretender to the French Throne; edited a pro-Papal, pro-Bourbon journal, *Le Triboulet*; married twice (his second wife was a daughter of Flagler, the American oil-king); fallen foul of the French authorities over the articles in his journal; fled from France; taken a trip around the world; and ended up in New York, where the Flaglers, father and daughter, would have nothing to do with him.

By 1895, it was apparent that Prince James the First of Trinidad was not to be forgotten as easily as the filed-away letter in which he had announced his annexation of the Martin Vaz islands.

The well known London firm of Stanley Gibbons offered sets of 'Trinidad' stamps for sale; and when they withdrew them from their catalogue, offering to refund the money to purchasers of the stamps, the *Daily News* sarcastically commented upon a 'Bogus Prince'—and had to pay heavy damages when the Prince took them to court for libel.

Although Trinidad, as far as anyone knew, produced only land-crabs and rabbits, it won two gold medals at the Vienna International Exhibition of 1895 for 'natural products'—which were not either tinned rabbit or tinned crab.

Reports from Texas showed that the Prince was shipping out Chinese coolies to work on the harbour-installations; and judging by the quantity of stone, cement and other materials being loaded in Texan ports for Trinidad, it looked as though Trinidad was being 'developed' seriously and speedily.

Britain stepped in.

First, H.M.S. *Barracouta* was sent out, in July 1895, to reaffirm Britain's ownership of the island. Then other British ships went to take off the coolies and other workers, and ship them back to Texas.

Then Britain, having declared her ownership of Trinidad, leased the island to the Anglo-Brazilian Telegraph Company, as a cable-station. (The Foreign Office file, explaining the intricate intrigue, makes splendid reading!)

Brazil, having peacefully dismissed her Emperor seven years earlier, was now in the middle of a civil war. But both the Brazilian 'governments' rounded on perfidious Albion for having 'stolen' some of the 'sacred territory of Brazil'—the Martin Vaz islands.

A Brazilian mob sacked the British Legation in Bahia—then the capital of Brazil; but it was the United States' reaction to the situation which ought to have alarmed, as it certainly humiliated, Great Britain.

Washington, itching to 'get even' with Whitehall ever since the redcoats had burnt the White House and sent Dolly Madison scuttling for shelter, now intervened in the Anglo-Brazilian-Trinidad dispute—but not on Prince James's behalf. ('Fellow's some sort of crank,' the U.S. Foreign Secretary is reported to have said, as he threw the Prince of Trinidad's original letter in the waste-paper basket.)

The British Government did not get merely a rebuke from Washington; it got a plain ultimatum. There was no attempt, on the part of the roughneck American 'diplomats' (whose Minister to the Court of St James had recently been convicted of fraud) to wrap up the threat in the terminology of traditional diplomacy.

Washington said: Get out of Trinidad. If you don't, we shall support Brazil's 'just claims' by any measures, even to war.

It is extraordinary, looking back, to see how preoccupied British foreign policy was with the imperialism of Russia, Germany, Austria-Hungary and France—and yet never saw, in this sudden and unprecedented ultimatum to Great Britain, the first declaration to the world that a new empire had staked its claim to recognition.

Of course Salisbury, who had knuckled under to France in the matter of the Burma-Indo-China border dispute, was not likely, twelve years later, to show any more courage in the face of American threats.

He suggested arbitration, and the King of Portugal, whose ancestors had once included Trinidad in their possessions, offered to mediate. The King was tipped off to make the decision most pleasing to the United States; and the King dutifully obliged.

The Martin Vaz islands were 'awarded' to Brazil; the installations of the Anglo-Brazilian Telegraph Company were dismantled and removed; and from that day to this, only the rabbits and the land-crabs have had the slightest interest in the former demesne of Prince James the First, who, ignored by the Powers, shot himself in a seedy hotel in El Paso, in 1898.

It was at home, though, that Salisbury found most to cause him alarm.

Trade-unionism, given its legal basis, was now establishing its power by testing, to the very limits of legality, the powers of combination, bargaining and intimidation given to it by law.

The strike is still the trade-union's favourite bargaining-piece; in those days it seemed the trade-unions' *only* bargaining piece. In the dockers' strike, it had astonished millions that the rich, the well-to-do, the bourgeois and the petit-bourgeois supported the strikers almost as wholeheartedly as did the non-striking workers themselves: in terms of actual help, the 'non-worker' did more, because he had more money to give.

Having got over their wonder at finding that public opinion, far from being shocked by strike-action (as the trade-unionists' jargon had it), seemed almost to welcome it; the strike-organizers and strike-leaders organized and led yet more strikes.

There is, of course, a law of diminishing returns in this sort of activity as in any other; and if one strikes too much, one inevitably produces a condition in which it is not possible to strike at all, no matter what public opinion holds. (This condition was to be brought about in Russia, in the following century.)

But our trade-unionists of the 'Nineties were not troubled by the imminence of that law's braking effect. So far, strikes had produced nothing but an amelioration of the workers'—the *trained* workers', be it noted—lot; the improvement in the condition of untrained or unskilled workers was being brought about by the Bills of various private members of Parliament—such Bills as led to shortened hours, to Early Closing, to the various Factory Acts, and the like.

As 1897 was the year of the Diamond Jubilee, it was inevitable that there should have been serious social unrest; as the year of the Golden

Jubilee had been marked by 'Bloody Sunday', so the year of the Diamond Jubilee, when the Kings and Princes of the Earth assembled to pay homage to the Queen-Empress, was marked by one of the most important strikes so far experienced: a six-months strike of the engineers.

Even more important was the inevitable suggestion, arising out of this strike, that the trade-unions should declare a general strike. Both sides—the employers and the trade unions—believed (or said that they believed) that such a strike would paralyse the entire economic life of the nation; and until a general strike should be called, each side might hope or fear that it would have this plenary disruptive power.

It is certain that even among the most 'revolutionary' of the trade-unionists and the Socialists who were coming more and more to control 'Labour', there were many—perhaps they were in the majority—who believed that the value of a general strike to the unions lay only in its being always a threat; that were the leaders foolish enough to call a strike, they would, inevitably, call their own bluff. Public opinion, it appeared, would not support strongly coercive measures against groups of strikers; public opinion would have no say were a general strike to compel the Government to 'take over', and thus act as strike-breakers.

Salisbury was in power by virtue of the fact that he belonged to a family which had risen to power in the reign of the first Elizabeth; the first Cecil had made his own fortune; this late 19th-century Cecil could not have done so.

Apart from his birth, he had little to recommend him as the leader of a country passing through one of its most revolutionary periods. Fortunately there were others, not so well born, who could not only see what was happening, but could take effective steps towards remedial measures.

Joe Chamberlain was a Midlands manufacturer whose sound 'Chapel' upbringing had early given him the ambition to 'mix with the Nobs', though the strict anti-episcopal bases of his dour Midland religion led him, at the beginning, into opposition to Monarchy, the Established Church, the Aristocracy, Ritual—and, indeed, all those outward signs of inward grace by which we recognize the British Constitution.

At an early age, Joe Chamberlain was a rich man; it was not only in America that great fortunes were being made by young men in a short space of time. He was a large employer of labour: a fair employer by the still harsh standards of Midland commerce.

He itched to rule other men—men whom he didn't pay. He got himself elected to the Birmingham City Council; soon, as an Alderman, he was elected Mayor—Lord Mayor. It was Joe's first title: the only one that a man wedded to Republican principles might accept without loss of face.

Joe met his Nobs: they were Republicans—which is why they welcomed Joe's approaches—but they were Nobs, for all that.

Their leader was a baronet of a very new creation (Charles Dilke's father had been given his title for work in connection with the Great Exhibition of 1851) but he was a baronet; and in becoming his ally and friend, Joe made his first step, out of Midland politics, into national affairs.

By 1878 Republicanism, in Britain, had reached its apogee—everywhere there were people discussing the Republic as though it were not only imminent, but inevitable.

The movement had brilliant men to back it and guide it; not book-theorists, visionaries, but men of purpose and power.

The British Republicans' position reminded many of General Boulanger's position in France: power was so surely his, that he had only to stretch out his hand and take it.

But Boulanger did not stretch out his hand; he hesitated; and his followers, awaiting the order to march, grew bored with waiting; bored . . . and disillusioned. The man who could have had France for the asking ended his career by falling on his mistress's grave, his own bullet through his head.

Just so the British Republicans waited too long: they talked, but they did not act. Their movement did not break up through internal quarrels; it came to a standstill through the leaders' inability to translate speech into action.

And then the *coup de grâce* was given to the movement when, in 1886, Donald Crawford, Liberal M.P. for Northeast Lanark, cited Sir Charles Dilke, Under-secretary of State for Foreign Affairs, as co-respondent in a suit for divorce.

A divorce action would have been enough to jeopardize Dilke's parliamentary career; but this particular action was of a sort to bring personal ruin as well. It was not only full of what the Victorians called 'painful details'; those painful details were of a nature to make the pious blush and the ribald chuckle.

Dilke—as Oscar Wilde, almost a decade later—was to acquire that odious accolade, given only to those men those tragedies move others more to sneers than to tears: he became the subject of errand-boys' doggerel.

> Charlie Dilke
> Spilt the milk,
> On the way to Chelsea. . . .

The divorce action marked the end of Dilke's power; so it marked the end of the Republican Movement in Britain.

Joe Chamberlain, whose Birmingham connections would not have permitted him to continue in any sort of intimacy with a man who, justly or unjustly, had been accused in the High Court of teaching young Mrs Crawford 'French practices' (*Sensation in Court!*) dropped Dilke and dropped, at the same time, Republicanism.

By the early 'Nineties, Joe, who had adopted many of the outward marks of the music-hall 'gent'—silk-faced frock-coat, single eyeglass, orchid in buttonhole—had become as staunch a supporter of royalty as that other Joe—Stalin—was to become in his late years. Joe Chamberlain became a Conservative; and anything that the Liberals supported, he opposed.

He was thus against Home Rule for Ireland, Free Trade, Peace with the Boers. Joe was not only the first great Imperialist that Britain produced—the historical pattern made him, as it happened, the last.

Where Salisbury did not know what to do in the face of the rising power of the half-socialist trade unions, Joe did.

Much of his ability to deal with this rising socialism depended upon two facts: he was born 'Chapel', and he had been a socialist—or, at least, a republican—himself.

In the modern phrase, he knew what made these men like Will Crooks, Keir Hardie, John Burns, 'tick'. He knew, too, how to use the classic, as well as the modern, ways of diverting popular unrest away from the domestic economy.

In his earlier political years, Chamberlain had pleaded such 'revolutionary' ideas as universal suffrage and the payment of Members of Parliament. It is not unjust to credit any man with the ability to see to what his proposals must inevitably lead; and assuming that Chamberlain had the ability, his ideas, even as a Cobdenite Radical, stamp him as a man working to achieve the totalitarian system under which we live to-day.

He proposed universal suffrage; but in also proposing payment to M.P.s he was proposing that this 'universal' electorate should be without power, since a *paid* M.P. cannot be an *independent* M.P.; he is nothing but a Parliamentary vote at the disposal of his Party's whips.

If we look at the facts like this, we can see that there is no difference at all between Chamberlain, the Great Radical, and Chamberlain, the Great Imperialist; any more than there was much difference between Hitler, the Socialist, and Hitler the National Socialist.

Trouble at home. . . ? Take the minds of the people off that by diverting their attention to trouble abroad.

We shall see what form that trouble took.

At home, among those classes not preoccupied with striking the Millennium into being, there was a restlessness expressed in less anti-social activities. There was a revived interest in Art; there was an enthusiasm for Literature bordering on the fanatical; there was a desire to 'get away from things' expressed—according to one's means—either in taking up the 'winter sports' that the English had invented in order to give Switzerland a Tourist Trade, or in bicycling. (Not until the latter half of the 'Nineties did a new means of transport, the Motor Car, appear.)

Bicycling was a 'sport', a 'craze'; but it was something so much more than either of these that it deserves—as one day it will surely get—a book to itself; and this book will show how deep were the social pressures which produced the 'craze', and how deep and widespread were the 'craze's' influences.

In the preceding decade, two fundamental improvements to the old 'penny-farthing' or the equal-wheeled bicycle (the latter was the earlier-invented of the two) had given the world the modern bicycle: the 'safety' (diamond) frame, and the pneumatic rubber tyre. The 'Nineties refined even this almost perfect bicycle by means of such 'extras' as the Sturmey-Archer epicyclic gear, the 'free wheel', the wooden-rimmed racing wheel, the acetylene lamp, and so on—but for all practical purposes, the modern bicycle was in full production by 1893.

It took people out of London; it enabled people to use the 'new' week-end, as given to them by the Factory and Shop Acts, in a way different from those employed when one could only walk: for one thing, people 'cycled'—but not to church.

The coming of the railways between 1825 and 1840, by linking the *principal* cities and towns of the country, had cut off the purely rural districts. In this respect, the introduction of the steam locomotive had been a retrograde step. The villages no longer linked with the towns by coach were cut off from the main stream of economic development, and Rural England, by 1890, was almost more rustically primitive than the Rural England of Cobbett's Rides.

The actual linking up of the rural districts with the urban came only with the full development of motor-transport, but it was the bicycle which began the linking.

But it was as an expression of the deep, almost frenzied need for personal freedom that the Bicycle (it needs a capital letter here) is most significant for the social historian.

Mrs Amelia Bloomer had sought to introduce her Rational Dress for Females thirty years earlier; but the life of the 'Sixties had not provided the support—as it had not provided the need—for women's adoption of the trouser (or their divesting themselves of the cumbersome skirt).

But the 'Nineties, in introducing the bicycle (or, to be more precise, the Bicycle Craze) had made the adoption of Mrs Bloomer's 'bloomers' possible, as it could be shown that the adoption was necessary.

They look very odd to our eyes, these London shop-girls, dressed up in men's tweed golfing-suits, with feather-trimmed Homburgs and starched linen collars to go cycling. They did not look so odd to their contemporaries, for apart from the 'bloomers', the same exaggeratedly masculine type of dress was being adopted by the 'New Woman', whether or not she went cycling to gather the bluebells at Dorking or Cobham.

At all times in the history of Social Man, there has been a strong mutual influence between Clothes and Ideas. With their tailor-made Harris-tweed coats and skirts, their no-damned-nonsense brogued boots and high Melton-cloth spats, their quite hideous Homburgs, with half a partridge clamped to the side, their 'drain-pipe' stiff linen collars, with four-in-hand silk ties secured by a gold fox's-mask pin, the 'New Women' made it clear that they stood for some pretty revolutionary ideas. They wanted Equality with Men—and they took the first instalment of the Equality by sharing Men's clothes with them.

The shop-girls and female clerks who dressed in masculine clothes to go cycling on Saturday afternoons and Sundays were not of necessity 'New Women'—at least, not consciously so. It was 'the thing' to wear this male garb when one went cycling: after all, one could argue a good case for it; but though not 'politically conscious', the cycling girls, by introducing this male clothing, gave more politically conscious females the opportunity to develop its wearing as a sumptuary profession of faith.

All revolutionary movements tend to mingle, and thus to demonstrate the truth that all revolutionary movements, however much they seem to differ in aims, are but many aspects of one revolutionary impulse.

This truth was never more clearly seen than in the 'Nineties, when Anti-Vivisection, Roman Catholicism, Socialism, Cycling, Spiritism (with 'Theosophy'), Women's Education and Female suffrage, and a score of other excuses for making a noise and dressing up oddly, were merely the varied parts that Revolt, One and Indivisible, was playing.

That all revolutionary trends are evolutionary trends must be a fact acceptable even by those who are not Marxists (and I am certainly not one). In order to take the development of the Super-State one step farther, the Apparat introduced the necessary opportunity by releasing and cultivating, among its (usually innocent) agents, 'revolutionary' ideas. Once these ideas have taken hold of the Mass, the 'Government' permits itself to be 'pressed' into adopting these ideas.

That 'revolutionaries, in all times, have been the convenient catspaws of an immortal System, does not argue against the burning sincerity of the 'revolutionaries'—so long as they are revolutionaries. When a few of them, as a reward for their work in making themselves the midwives of Change, are taken into the Apparat, and to them the secrets of Rule are revealed, they cease, naturally, to be 'revolutionaries', and must become conservators of the Change—until such time as another Change is needed.

They are not less sincere, as ex-revolutionaries, than they were as revolutionaries: their eyes have been opened, that is all.

Now one of the reasons for the 'burning sincerity' of a Revolutionary is that he believes that he is acting, fighting, *for* some improvement in social conditions, whereas he is always fighting *against* a condition which appears to him to limit his freedom of action.

When the well-to-do and successful writers of the 'Nineties—mostly women—went over to Rome, as the saying went, they were not supporting the Church of Rome; they were defying the Church of England. Of course, such a 'smart' writer as 'John Oliver Hobbes' could have found other ways of being 'different' than in becoming a convert to Romanism; but in her mind, as in the minds of others, a smack at the Established Church was a smack at the British Government—and all that it stood for. (And what it stood for, in the narrow view of the New Woman, was rigid opposition to that Progress which would make her the social and economic equal of Man.)

Economically, the time was not yet ripe for Equal Pay and Equal Opportunities; and because the time was not yet ripe economically, Public Opinion was not on the side of the New Women.

What a Progressive can never see is what lies under his or her (often too sharp) nose. The fact that women had had the vote in some parts of Australia since the 'Fifties and that they now had it in both Australia and New Zealand, as well as in Arizona, should have solaced the Progressives at home with the reflection that it was on its way for the Home Country, and would come at the proper time.

But in truth it mattered little what people were fighting for in the 'Nineties: the important historical truth is that they were suddenly aware of a universal dissatisfaction with Things As They Were; they wanted change; they did not quite know how that change was to be effected; but they felt themselves bubbling over with enough energy to change a dozen social systems, and remould them nearer to their hearts' desires.

For every Reaction, says the great Newton, there is an equal and positive Reaction; and the violent expressions of the New Freedom brought, inevitably, the equally violent defensive measures to suppress that Freedom.

The trials of Oscar Wilde in 1895 were, in effect, the staging of a battle between the Progressives and the Reactionaries. That this was realized by the Progressives is shown by the fact that many women writers, of whose sexual normality there can be no doubt, sympathized with Wilde. 'John Strange Winter', the fantastically successful author of *Bootle's Baby*, is an outstanding example; she defended and befriended Wilde, not because he was a sodomite, or even because Sodomy may be interpreted as a Revolt against conventional usage, but because those who prosecuted him represented the Establishment.

Wilde's trials have been so often described, in the fullest detail, that there is no need here to describe them again.

But one point, which I made in an article written many years ago, has not been picked up by the more recent biographers of Wilde.

That is that all the actions of Lord Queensberry, including the leaving of his visiting card at Wilde's club, speak the careful planning and continuous guidance of brains far more astute than Queensberry's.

Much has been made of the 'ignorance' of the noble Lord, who could not even spell 'sodomite' correctly. I have argued that the mis-spelling was intentional; had matters gone differently, Queensberry could have claimed that he had not called Wilde a 'sodomite'—but a 'somdomite'; and is that word to be found in the dictionary?

The facts are clear: there were any number of people out to 'get' Wilde. Wilde was not a 'martyr', as several generations of homosexuals, working hard, have almost managed to convince the public was the case. Nor was he, in the strict sense of the word, a 'victim', except for the fact that we are all the victims of our own weaknesses. But he was a 'symbol', and was so selected by those who thought that Freedom, as expressed in the Wildean way of life, had gone a little too far, and needed a temporary check.

It was because Wilde was so well known, so successful, that he was selected to represent Freedom-Which-Has-Gone-Too-Far; and not because he was a sodomite. They were not at all rare in the London of the 'Nineties.

Frank Harris has described how, as soon as the result of the first trial was known, and it became evident that Wilde, having lost the libel action against Lord Queensberry, was now about to be arrested and charged with unnatural vice, the boat-trains out of London were crowded with first-class passengers, all seeking the more tolerant shores of France.

The Wilde Scandal should have had more adverse effect upon the popularity of the new school of writing than it did. We have heard how the plays of Wilde were not withdrawn, but a piece of paper was gummed over the author's name. *The Yellow Book*, the 'arty' journal that the ex-railway-clerk-turned-publisher, John Lane, had successfully launched in 1893, did not long survive the Wilde trial, so closely did it seem to mirror forth the news and views of Sodom, even though Wilde had never contributed.

But all the contributors to *The Yellow Book*, including its Russian-Jewish editor, Henry Harland, not only went on writing—and mostly with success—but where their style was effeminately ornate (as was Harland's), they made no attempt to render it more Hearty. (Perhaps they tried, and failed?)

With the exception of the wretched Frederick Rolfe, 'Baron Corvo', who now that he cannot possibly benefit by the sales of his work has been made into something of a modest best-seller, all *The Yellow Book's* contributors went on to fame and financial success: Max Beerbohm, Henry Harland, Hubert Crackanthorpe, G. Bernard Shaw, H. G. Wells, J. S. Fletcher, Arthur Machen. The Author was still doing well in the 'Nineties, as he had done well in the 'Eighties; it was the age of the one-man publishing house, run by a director who loved Literature and admired Authors, even if he was prepared to make money out of them.

These publishers found their authors; encouraged and subsidized them; turned them into best-sellers. The 'sausage-machine' element in Publishing had not yet arrived; and if failure eventually awaited such publishers as Grant Richards, Eveleigh Nash, T. Fisher Unwin and George Greening, while they were active and financially solvent they launched many a remembered and forgotten—but in each case temporarily successful—name.

The spirit of Revolution, too, was manifest in Art; but the curious fact to ponder is that '*Art Nouveau*' affected neither painting nor architecture, and only mildly sculpture. The furniture of the 'Nineties—as well as the small accessories of the household (lamp-fittings amongst them)—were the artistic products affected by the New Art. Where it affected buildings was not in the general 'line', but in the style of the decorative friezes which were applied to buildings harking more and more back to the Classic. From 1890 onwards, the districts to the west of Sloane-street were developed, and houses of a vaguely François Premier style began to go up, as well as a pleasing and exciting experiment in Modern Gothic—though not in Sloane-street and Pont-street.

This Modern Gothic—as different from Manchester Town Hall Gothic as Manchester Town Hall is different from, say, Milan Cathedral—was frankly Romantic, and frankly reactionary. It was as heartfelt a gesture of defiance to Joint-Stockery as *The Blessed Damozel* was; though it could not have existed without Joint-Stockery to inspire it. Not much was built: a few private houses, of which the majority have been pulled down—fewer business premises, of which one, built for Bostell's Sanitary Fittings, is to be found at the top of Whitehall, opposite Drummond's Bank; another—with a longer lease of life ahead of it, is the Middlesex Guildhall, hard by the Westminster Abbey—a building which is, to architecture, what Frampton's fancies are to sculpture.

But Gothic, whether of the new 'Framptonesque' style or the Midlands Monastic, was on its way out: Waterhouse, turning from late Victorian Gothic, and the up-and-coming architects were bringing back the Classic, which was to hold its own (debased though much of it was to be) until the influence of Gropius and Corbusier encouraged architects to forget architecture altogether, and to turn builders instead—and not very inspired builders, at that.

The new Classic architecture was far more 'in sympathy' with the new business activities that it was designed to house. The Principle of reducing, by 'amalgamation', the volume of opposition, had already been introduced: the Big Banks were coming into being through the absorption of the provincial bankers by the London houses which had formerly been those country banks' London agents. The near-failure of Barings, in 1894, had provided some welcome support for the advocates of Bigger and Better Banks; and another aspect of Magnitude, in commercial practice, was seen in the vigorous growth of both the Chain Store and the Department Store in the last quarter of the century. Skilful publicity has persuaded too many people that Britain's first department store was Selfridge's, opened in 1909; but in truth the department store is very much older even than Marshall & Snelgrove, whose present premises in Oxford-street date from 1878. Swan & Edgar, doing business in Piccadilly Circus, were established as a department store when Piccadilly Circus was opened in 1812. (It was then called 'The Regent's Circus'.)

Even in the more modern sense of the department store (selling everything, not merely women's clothing) Whiteley's antedated Selfridge's by forty years, as did the modern Harrods, though only by some thirty.

As for the chain-store, Tommy Lipton, the yachtsman-grocer ('I understand,' said the Kaiser, 'that my Uncle Edward has gone yachting with his grocer') had already established a nation-wide chain of shops before the 'Nineties; and he was not the only one to do so. But even where goods were not sold through chains of retail outlets, goods were now being produced and sold on a national scale, thanks largely to the advertising which, for the first time, was being handled on a truly national scale.

Modern Advertising—with a capital A—dates from the 'Eighties; and through this Advertising, the Public was made aware of, and made to feel a need for, such 'necessities' as Pears' Soap, Sunlight Soap, Hudson's Soap, Epps' Cocoa, Veno's Lightning Cough Cure, Stephens' Ink, Bovril, Oxo, Mellins' Food, and a score of other 'essentials to living'.

What gave this Advertising the means to show its mettle was the development of Popular Journalism, so bitterly deplored (in writing, anyway) by H. G. Wells, though it is hard to see how he would have made his fortune without it.

The mechanism of printing and paper-making had reduced the costs of printing to unprecedented low levels; the spread of literacy had created a vast new market for any kind of printed matter.

Such men as the Harmsworth Brothers, C. Arthur Pearson, George Newnes, John Cassell, with his partners, Petter and Galpin, cashed in on low costs and huge demands. Wells distinguished between those who set out to 'educate' (like Cassell and his partners) and those who set out simply to 'drug' (Wells's phrase, not mine).

But this distinction is untenable: the men who, in the late 'Eighties, stepped on the publishing trail that Samuel Beeton had begun to blaze as far back as the 'Fifties, all had the desire to 'educate', even the Harmsworths, who came in for Wells's bitterest denunciation.

The fact is that where such publishers as Cassell catered for those who wished to educate themselves, Harmsworth and Newnes catered primarily for those who wished to 'read'. But the earliest numbers of *Tit-Bits* or *Answers to Correspondents* are certainly a good deal more 'educative' than are their descendants of to-day. It could be borne in mind that R. L. Stevenson's *The Sea Cook* (better known to us as *Treasure Island*) first appeared as a serial in the penny-a-week *Boy's Companion*—a journal of the type that Wells sneeringly called 'errand-boys' reading'.

In the higher grades of periodical publishing, the influence of the American 'family journals' may never be overestimated. As far back as the 'Forties, such American publications as *Godey's* and *Graham's* were setting standards in both editorial comment and production which set them far above their contemporary European rivals; by the end of the century, such journals as *Lippincott's*, the *Century* and *Harper's* were showing British publishers what could be achieved in the production of really first-class magazines.

On sale in Britain, especially in London, these American magazines inspired British publishers to raise their own standards, though, save for such journals as the *Studio* (founded 1893), the *Tatler* and the *King* (1897), nothing produced in Britain came anywhere near to rivalling American magazine-production.

Lippincott's, for instance, sent their agents to Europe, to commission work from rising young authors, and both Wilde's *Dorian Gray* and Conan

Doyle's *The Sign of the Four* appeared in *Lippincott's* in 1891 in response to a commission from the publishers.

Only recently have the 'comics', established at the end of the 'Eighties or the beginning of the 'Nineties, to be sold at one-halfpenny to schoolboys and older readers of juvenile tastes, been discontinued. *Comic Cuts, Chips,* the *Union Jack* (in which that 'Errand boy's Sherlock Holmes'—as Dorothy Sayers called him—Sexton Blake, made his first appearance) and dozens of others, so well known to anyone over fifty, are all products of the enterprising mass-market publishers of the 'Nineties.

From halfpenny-a-week and penny-a-week journals, Harmsworth turned to half-penny-a-day newspapers: his first, the *Daily Mail*, appeared in 1896. Then he bought the already fairly successful *Evening News*, one of London's eight 'evenings', and on these two newspapers built up the great Harmsworth newspapers empire.

The illustrated journal and illustrated newspaper date from the 'Nineties; the half-tone (photographic) process of engraving was invented in 1827, but it did not become a practical commercial proposition until the very end of the 'Eighties.

In its perfected form, it made possible the reproduction of photographs in publications printed in tens, in hundreds of thousands of copies. It made the 'picture-paper' possible.

Illustration by wood-engraving had been brought to a high degree of perfection; such journals as the *Illustrated London News*, the *Graphic* and similar weeklies could turn drawings or photographs into wood-engravings with a speed almost incomprehensible to us. But the coming of the half-tone process, which enabled the actual photograph to be reproduced in the pages of a journal, ended that respected and highly-paid member of the Art Department: 'Our Special Artist', whose 'impressions' of *The Amateur Bicycle Match at Lillie Bridge* or *The 59th Regiment Storming Sebundi Pass During Sir Frederick Roberts's Afghan Campaign* gave the public the facts of victory overlaid with all the embellishments of the artist's romantic fancy. The Kodak 'snaps' of the war-correspondent, reproduced by the half-tone process, presented life in a new—and, generally speaking, a drearier—aspect.

In the early 'Nineties, news came out of France that the carriage propelled by the internal-combustion engine had passed the experimental stage, and was now on the market. The firm of Panhard, which made these 'automobiles', appointed an agent in London, and soon people began to talk about the new 'horseless carriages'.

Soon, a few people had actually seen a Panhard, pop-popping its fifteen-miles-an-hour way in a cloud of mingled dust and benzine vapour.

The new motor-cars were alarmingly reported to cause horses to bolt—and this was literally true; horses were to bolt, right enough, out of the class of essential things.

Now in the matter of Automobilism, the 19th century had lagged behind. The rapid development of the automobile had been halted, because, as I have said earlier, too much public money had been poured into the building of railways, and railways had to be protected from all competition if the public was to be protected from loss. (As it was, the big railway companies, even though guaranteed by Government, were paying only 1¼ per cent on their capital by the end of the century).

Stephenson, the designer of the first really practical steam-locomotive, had been against running locomotives on railways, which had existed for decades before steam-traction came into being.

What he had wished to do was to build a *road* from Liverpool to London, and run steam-coaches on it; the directors of the project overruled him, and a railway was built instead. Then, when nearly all Britain was covered with railways, the competition of the existing well-developed automobilism had to be suppressed. Britain, though it travelled from town to town by steam train, moved within its towns by the antiquated horse.

The first half of the 'Nineties saw the beginning of the change which was to bring automobilism into the towns, and eventually to confine the horse to the hunting-field and the race-track, and military parades.

What gave the Motor-car its flying start was Royal Patronage. The Prince of Wales and his brother, the Duke of Edinburgh, with their intimate friend, the Duke of Sutherland, had been given, even as middle-aged men, to driving railway trains (a taste afterwards shared by King Boris of Bulgaria). The Prince Consort had liked all things mechanical, and his sons all shared that addiction.

Now, when the mechanical carriage arrived, the Prince of Wales, though well past fifty, welcomed it with all the enthusiasm of a small boy with a new toy; and soon a number of the more sporting members of the aristocracy had joined the Prince as car-owners.

Lord Winchilsea, Lord Howard de Walden and the Hon. F. Scott Ellis were joined by such rich members of the newer aristocracy as Lord Burnham (né Albert Levy) in taking up the motor-car as a hobby.

The Law did *not* insist that a man walk with a red flag before a motor-car—but that fable will, I am afraid, outlive me. What the Law did do was to insist on a speed-limit of six miles an hour (the limit permitted to steam-rollers and steam traction-engines, of which there were a few on the road, though they were rarely seen within city boundaries). Mr Ellis, in being fined again and again, did good publicity work for the Motor-Car.

'In 1896,' says the anonymous author of *Society in the New Reign*, 'the motor was introduced to the English public at an international show of horseless carriages at the Crystal Palace. The novelty, the complexity, and, above all, the costliness of the new invention soon secured for it acceptance at Court. In his youth, Edward VII and his friend, the Duke of Sutherland, had often acted as amateur engine-drivers on English railways. The warm welcome given by the Sovereign to these latest apparitions on his own highway implied therefore a sort of return to a first love. Whether in town or country, the motor has become as much a part of the courtier's baggage as is the cigarette-case. The secret of the thing's popularity is its intricacy, quite as much as its expensiveness. The King not only knows all about the mechanism and the working of the locomotive [sic] himself, but he expects his fashionable subjects to be able to discuss its internal arrangements with the same knowledge that they once possessed or affected of the pedigree of the royal thorough-breds.'

This was written in 1902; and the author is slightly inaccurate.

For one thing, the King (as Prince of Wales) drove trains until he was well beyond his youth; for another, royal interest in the motor-car had been aroused long before the 1896 exhibition.

What the exhibition did was to prove to Britain that a motor-making industry had grown up, and was able to meet the needs of an important market: the need now was to develop that market.

In the November of that same year, enough motor-owners were in existence for Lord Winchilsea to organize a run from the Metropôle Hotel, Northumberland-avenue, to the Metropôle Hotel, Brighton. This historic run is celebrated every year (usually in the same sort of historic weather, of cold rain falling through the grey mist!) and commemorates the actual beginning of the Motor Age.

As Charles Fort once pointed out, every exile, emigrant, colonist—call him what you will—is a social misfit. His leaving his own country may be explained by any of a dozen 'good' reasons: he can't find work, he can't worship God in his own way; he can't stand the political climate; he's the victim of racial prejudice—it doesn't matter: he can't get on with Society, and so he leaves to try his chances with another land.

Now it is obvious that the more 'difficult' a social environment is, the greater the number of people there will be who cannot 'fit in'. In spite of what we have heard about the thousands who have sought new lands to find religious and political freedom, the major causes of emigration have been poverty and hunger. So that it is obvious that, as the general standard of living rises, the number of 'misfits' will diminish, and emigration diminish proportionately.

When the 'misfit' is regarded, by Government, as a 'misfit', Government will encourage emigration, though usually to a land under its control, where, once the 'misfit' has rendered himself employable, and thus taxable, he can contribute to the Imperial exchequer.

An important truth became apparent to the economists of the late 19th century: it was revealed to them as they studied the curious phenomenon of 'colonial enterprise'.

How was it, they asked themselves, that paupers—many of them without trade or even minor artisan skills—could take ship, and (seemingly by the mere fact of their being transported, in considerable discomfort, overseas) achieve the status of 'solid citizens' ?

It was a matter of great interest to the economists, for they were struck by the fact that the rate of growth, so far as economic prosperity was concerned, was faster in the Colonies than in the Mother Country.

The answer took some time in coming; but it came at last.

And it was this: there is no special merit in a sea-voyage to make a pauper into a hard-working wage-earner. Give the pauper the same chances as the Colonies will give him, and he will enrich himself at home—and the State can have his taxes.

Experimentally, diffidently, clumsily, the economists began to toy with the formula suggested by the answer: they began to rough out the plans for the Welfare State—and that meant the end of Colonization.

For if the 'misfits' thought that there was even a chance that things might improve at home, they would not go forth to brave all the rigours of pioneering life in order to seek the bread denied them in their own country.

Another thing: colonies must be 'replaced'. The better that a colony does for itself, the faster that it moves from the pioneer stage to that of the established state, the faster does it come to the point at which it closes its doors against the penniless immigrant, come 'to compete with the citizen'.

America had not yet closed her doors to the emigrant (or immigrant, depending at which end of the traffic you find yourself), but any subject of Her Britannic Majesty who went to the United States of America was lost for ever as a taxpayer. Australia was on the verge of becoming a federal republic owing a nominal and sentimental allegiance to the Crown. She was about to become quite as independent a state as was the U.S.A.; and, her origins having made her somewhat touchy on the subject of immigration, Australia had passed the stage at which she could be used as a dumping-ground for Britain's 'misfits'.

Colonies, in short, are profitable to the Home Country only in their first, their pioneering, stage of development; when the Home Country, in return for military protection and economic help and governmental 'guidance', pays lightly for the colonies' raw products, sells them manufactured goods dear, and taxes with no delicate touch.

And now that so many other countries were on the move to get new colonies before their own people were too 'spoilt' to face emigration, it behoved Britain to seize while there was still something for the seizing.

In 1877 Disraeli had tried to annex the Republic of the Transvaal—and had failed. In 1881 Gladstone had acknowledged the failure of the attempt, and had signed a treaty recognizing the independence and all-but-sovereign condition of the Republic.

Both sides knew that the treaty was but a temporary measure; that, sooner or later, the uneasy peace would degenerate into something worse.

There were, in fact, two 'independent' South African republics: that of the Transvaal and that of the Orange River—the so-called 'Free State'. Both might have retained their grudged independence had not several things happened, the principal of which was the discovery of diamonds and gold on their territories or 'within their spheres of influence' . . .

The Boers of the Transvaal and the Orange Free State were, however, against any union with Britain; and it was obvious to both sides that persuasion would achieve nothing.

A violent Press campaign, carried out with all that skill which enables the historian to see that modern Public Relations practice is no new thing, prepared the British public for what was intended to happen. The rapacity of the Boers was denounced; their taxes on imports were decried as an obstacle to industrial progress; they were blamed for having held up the progress of the mining industry (diamonds, gold, coal, copper); they were vilified as Bible-thumping hypocrites, who flogged the male Negroes and raped the females; they were described, in a variety of ways, as a species sub-human and anti-social, an obstacle to Human Progress, from whom power ought to be taken as quickly as possible. It was widely reported that, for all the disgusting aspects of the harems of black slaves that most Boer farmers kept, even this practice had some recommendations in morality, seeing that most Boers had a tendency to practise incest with their daughters.

(It is regrettable that this 'moral' approach to a political showdown was not confined to British diplomacy; on the other side of the world, some American 'settlers' in Hawaii had deposed Queen Liliuokalani, and established a republic, because of the Queen's 'moral turpitude'. The Settlers'

'Independent' Republic once proclaimed, they 'asked' the United States to take over. Unlike British control over South Africa, U.S. control is still maintained over Hawaii.)

The British High Commissioner, Sir Alfred Milner, whose racial origins are even now a mystery, asked for an interview with Kruger. The two men met at Bloemfontein on 1st June.

Milner was a passionate and mystically dedicated Imperialist; because, whatever he was—he was not British by race—he was more British than the British. You don't have to be British to uphold the mystical doctrine of 'Manifest Destiny', as Russian, German and American leaders have proved within the last generation. Milner upheld this doctrine: he met Kruger to put the next phase of the 'Destiny' into operation.

Milner demanded that the 'Outlanders' settled in the Transvaal should be given full rights of citizenship at the end of five years. Both men knew that this demand was merely a pretext for aggressive action on Britain's part; nevertheless, Kruger affected to consider it on its face-value, and suggested that seven, and not five, years should be the period of 'preparation for citizenship'. Milner would not agree, and Kruger consented to make the period five years.

But, said Kruger, if I grant citizenship to these foreigners settled amongst us, I must have firm guarantees that the independence of the Transvaal be respected.

After the Jameson Raid of New Year's Day, 1896, Kruger could hardly have asked less. Chamberlain, all the same, refused to give the guarantee he wanted.

A famous French historian has called these negotiations of 1899 'a masterpiece of duplicity', and one is reminded of the Fuehrer's negotiations with the unhappy Czechs.

While Milner was arguing with Kruger, heavy reinforcements were pouring into British South Africa, principally into the Cape. Warships were steaming into Simonstown, and the guns being daily unloaded from the cargo-ships were heavier than any which had so far been fired in Africa.

At last, Krueger presented his ultimatum: Britain to state precisely what her demands were in regard to the 'Outlanders'; the total cessation of troops and material being conveyed to the Cape—or war.

On 22 October, 1899, it was war.

All wars are the same; all wars are the shooting stage of an economic struggle; all wars have to have their 'excuse', since the public doesn't understand the economic motives of war. All wars are wars of 'Jenkins' Ear'.

But sometimes the excuse sounds better—nobler—than at other times; and on this occasion, it sounded weaker than ever.

The persons concerned in its origins were not of the sort of which history should—or could—make heroes; and though there were acts of bravery in the conduct of this war, there always are. But the people who make the wars do not perform the acts of bravery.

It is astonishing, to look back, how 'popular' the war was; in other words, how well the Government propagandists had done their work.

As soon as the news of the defeats began to come in—generals like Methuen and Buller trounced by a pack of farmers!—the civilians, in their tens of thousands, presented themselves at the recruiting offices; small boys wore celluloid buttons of a 'patriotic' nature; and all the newspapers 'ran' the despatches from the Lady War Correspondent and from Lord Randolph Churchill's son. (Never was the ungentlemanliness of the incestuous Boer so clearly displayed as when they attributed Winston's escape from internment to his having broken his parole. The boors!)

What caused the Government concern was not the number of recruits, but the fact that fifty percent of the recruits had to be turned away for medical reasons—usually undernourishment.

In South Africa, the great exponents of the doctrine of 'containing' the enemy found *themselves* 'contained'; Rhodes was locked up in Kimberley, Colonel Baden-Powell was locked up in Mafeking, General Sir George White was locked up in Ladysmith: the small forces besieging these men were just not large enough to force the siege.

Methuen was entrusted with the relief of Kimberley; Buller with that of Ladysmith. Neither succeeded; and not until the British Government woke up to the fact of its South African generals' total incapacity, and decided to replace them with the ageing Roberts, with Kitchener as his principal assistant, did the tide of battle turn in the war.

The same mentality which in 1940 saw Dunkirk as a brilliant victory was enchanted when, at long last, Ladysmith and Mafeking—particularly Mafeking—were relieved. There is a verb, 'to maffick', which dates from the night when the news of Mafeking's relief came through, and all London went mad.

Traffic ceased throughout the great city, as street-wide mobs, arms linked, sang and danced from Bow to Chiswick. The 'toffs' in their toppers linked arms with 'Arry and 'Arriet in their pearls and fevvers; and not a soul in that drunken, dancing, hysterical mob remembered—if one had ever known—that against the Boers' 80,000 men-at-arms (a third of the entire male population) were ranged no fewer than 206,000 British troops, armed with everything from Maxims to Sir Hedworth Lambton's naval 14-inch guns, towed to the battle-front on railway-bogeys.

By September 1900, victory had passed from the Boers; Roberts and Kitchener had arrived at the Cape in the previous January; it had taken these two brilliant soldiers just nine months to reverse the situation. The war went on for two more years, ending in guerilla warfare; but by the end of 1900 victory was assured to the British.

These later victories (even Redvers Buller had recovered his grasp of events, and had helped to defeat the Boers) did nothing to assuage the bitterness and grief that the initial defeats had inspired in the Queen.

The war had, literally, killed her. It may be that the Queen could not see sufficiently far ahead—or it may be that she could see too far ahead: to a time when all this fighting, no matter whether it led to victory or defeat, would be shown for a tragic waste of time.

Perhaps she did see that far ahead. . . .

She insisted on visiting the wounded soldiers; and she had to be taken away from the hospital, before she had completed her rounds, since the sight of so much suffering, by simple, innocent soldiers, brought a paroxysm of weeping that she could not withhold.

On the news of Roberts's first successes, she consented to drive through London to a thanksgiving ceremony at St Paul's, but in the following year it was only with a great effort that she was able to receive Roberts, on his return to England. That was on 2nd January, 1901. Three weeks later, the Queen was dead.

If, in invention, the 'Nineties had been a decade inferior to earlier decades, it was one in which the experimental work of earlier decades was shown to have practical possibilities.

In 1894, the first practical demonstration of wireless telegraphy was made by a young Italian engineer, Guglielmo Marconi, who brought his ideas to London, where he hoped to find the financial backing for his work. He was not disappointed.

The naval manoeuvres of 1897 included ships equipped with the Marconi apparatus, and by the end of the decade Marconi had succeeded in sending his wireless signals across the Atlantic, from Poldhu, in Cornwall, to Cape Race, in Newfoundland.

At those same naval manoeuvres, another young engineer, half Irish, half Jewish, the Hon. Charles Parsons, showed his mettle. Having failed to get my Lords of the Admiralty to look at his steam-turbine, he fitted out a small launch with the new engines, and as the Grand Fleet was solemnly steaming past Portsmouth, Parsons took his *Turbinia*, at 30 knots, and—literally—danced rings around the Fleet. There was nothing that the affronted officers and ratings of H.M. ships could do—they could hardly fire on Parsons; so he executed figures-of-eight around the Fleet, which could only turn a collective Nelsonian blind eye on his impudence.

The London public had been able to see a cinema film of the Queen, taken as she rode in her open landau to St Paul's; they might buy a gramophone record of the late Poet Laureate, Lord Tennyson, reading

Maud and *The Charge of the Light Brigade*: he had died in 1892, but his voice had been immortalized by the miracle of the Gramophone.

Very many public buildings and hotels and not a few private houses were now fitted with electric lifts—Apostoloff, who had invented the dial-telephone in 1892, had also perfected the automatic, press-button, self-levelling electric lift in the same year.

The first license to be given to a 'mechanical Clarence', as the Scotland Yard authorities quaintly call a motor-cab, was issued in 1897: it was in respect of an electric taximeter-cabriolet. The gas-lamps all over London were being dimmed by electric light: outside the stores, not only of the West End, but of the suburbs—Brixton, Camberwell, Peckham, Penge—the hissing, clicking arcs shed their blue-white radiance into shop-window and over pavements of the new Stuart's Granolithic.

In Austria, the Empress was assassinated, and the Crown Prince shot first his mistress and then himself. In more 'democratic' America, the President got the same treatment as an Empress had received.

Edison was working on a device to print the sound-track on the cinematograph film; in 1900, the Prince of Wales's favourite brother, and companion in hundreds of escapades, died, as did his favourite sister, the Dowager Empress of Germany. Both died of cancer. The unprecedented marched in step with the eternal.

No one knew, in that last year of the 19th century, that Britain would begin a new decade with a new sovereign; any more than even the Wright brothers guessed that, hardly into that new century, they would succeed, at Kitty Hawk, in realizing Man's ancient dream of mechanical flight.

Yet even those who had no interest in Science or Invention were aware of something *different* in the air, as the world approached the Twentieth Century.

Nothing had quite happened yet—but something, everyone felt, was on the verge of happening. On the surface, things appeared very much as they had been for a long time; there were still big houses, still filled with servants. The classes still preserved striking distinctions of dress, no less than of speech: in his preference for suits with short jackets, the Prince of Wales was followed, not by his contemporaries, but by the younger 'bloods'. The Masher was still extant, and the silk-lapelled frock-coat and the silk hat were the standard dress of every adult male above the class of shop-keeper (and even he wore this uniform on Sundays).

When a Great Personage died, the funeral was as splendid as though a whole century of invention and social change had not intervened since the 18th century. The troops now wore khaki—though most of the senior officers stuck to blue—but not at home, where the traditional scarlet jacket still marked Tommy Atkins, and the black 'frock' with braided frogs still marked the officer.

There was still a vast body of men and women living without work, or the pretence of work: they were the rich, the 'well-do-do'; money could be safely invested at 5 per cent; and even by 1900, people of modest capital could still be well supplied with domestic servants at five to seven shillings a week and their keep.

Such great commercial magnates as Tommy Lipton had not only opened chains of shops to sell their groceries; they had—still commercially, and not politically—intervened in the economic development of distant lands, with results which, seen to-day, make them appear not so much 'Captains of Commerce' as Empire-builders of far more permanent authority than a Disraeli or a Chamberlain.

In their search for plentiful and stable sources of raw material, the Liptons developed their vast tea-plantations in Ceylon and Assam, bringing down the price of tea to within a pauper's reach, and making of Britain a nation of tea-drinkers; the Vesteys built up huge empires in South America, whereby they might ensure the constant supply of meat and fruit to Britain; the Australian meat-trade, made possible by Harrison's invention of refrigeration, kept pace with that of the Argentine and Uruguay; and the name of Liebig began to dominate the hoardings.

The change was just beneath the surface, and just about to be apparent.

In laboratory and workshop, the scientists and inventors were fashioning a new world which was to be born with the new century.

Becquerel's observation of the odd behaviour of pitch-blende in 1888 had resulted in the Curies' discovery of the cause of that odd behaviour: the radio-active substance that they named 'radium'.

And even as the Curies were discovering natural radio-activity, Roentgen discovered how to produce the phenomena of 'radiation' by artificial means—the so-called 'X-rays'.

The effects came first; the causes were explained later; but the work both of the Curies and of Roentgen put other scientists—notably J. J. Thomson—on the search into the true nature of matter.

It was obvious now that the 'atom', not of Democritus or of Aristotle, but of Dalton, was not the 'building-block of the Universe', but that particles made up the atom, as the atom made up the molecule. Thomson's enlightening tool was the Geissler tube, that scientific toy which had so entranced Frederick the Great.

By seeking to explain the effect of the Geissler tube, Thomson came inevitably upon the theory of sub-atomic matter—the particle that he named the 'electron'.

Scientifically, that decade of the Nineties was an age of giants: J. J. Thomson, William Thomson (Lord Kelvin), Lord Rayleigh, Sylvanus Thompson, William Crookes, Oliver Lodge—why, this half-dozen alone would serve to glorify a nation over an entire millennium; they did their outstanding work within the short space of ten years.

They studied Light, and they studied Magnetism; and they proved— by proving the identity of the two—the fundamental identity of all matter. With J. J. Thomson working in Britain, and Planck working in Germany, it became almost inevitable that a young engineer named Albert Einstein should have propounded his General Theorem of Relativity in 1905—and that the Atom-bomb of 1943 was as inevitable, too.

In Germany, the Lilienthal brothers were experimenting with gliderflight, and proving eminently successful; in England, Percy Pilcher was achieving an almost equal success, when his glider 'stalled' and the young aeronaut was killed. In America, Octave Chanute, was even more successful—and luckier, too, in that, unlike Pilcher and Lilienthal, he did not kill himself. His glider served as the model for the aeroplane to which the Wright brothers fitted their petrol-engine, and were thus enabled to make the first man-carrying mechanical free flight.

Or were they . . . ?

The French have always maintained that Clément Ader made the first such flight with his *Avion*, in 1897—which is why the name 'aeroplane' was officially changed, in French, to that of 'avion'.

And there are still those who maintain that it was Samuel Langley, and not the Wrights, who took the first flying-machine into the air.

The fact is that whoever may claim the actual precedence as the first aviator, Flying was imminent. The poets first, then the novelists; then the writers of fantasy, then the writers of boys' tales; they had all taken Flying as one of their principal themes, which proved that Flying was about to become a reality.

The first electric underground railway had been opened in London in 1890; right at the decade's end, in 1900, a much more ambitious electric 'tube', the Central London Railway, was opened—and this was to mark the end, within five years, of the steam engines used on the District and Metropolitan underground systems.

The great mansions still lined Piccadilly, and there were still private houses in Oxford-street. London was still more residential than commercial, the more so as ring after ring of suburban building took the limits of Greater London farther and farther from the centre.

Yet so much had not altered: the traffic was still entirely horse-drawn; the women still drew up their long skirts to avoid the dung that little boys chased with bucket and brush, to sell to garden-loving householders at tuppence the bucket.

The Belgians had wrapped their table sugar, and the French and Americans had bottled their milk for decades; London still used unwrapped cube-sugar (it still does!) and delivered its milk by jangling chariot bearing a vast pewter churn, on which a brightly polished brass oval bore the name of the dairyman—more often than not a Welsh one. Outside a hundred thousand front-doors or area-gates, the pewter, hinged-lidded pots or—in humbler households—the cloth-covered pottery jug, would wait for the morning milk.

Flies were everywhere in their disgusting millions; and the gutters were choked with foul water after every rainfall, even the smallest.

Outside the luxury of the 'shopping streets' of the West End (and never has shop-keeping attained such luxury as in the years between 1890 and 1914) the old London persisted with a dogged refusal to change. Gaslight and naphtha-flares, and street after street lined with stalls. Whelks and cockles, humbugs and tiger-nuts, sarsaparilla and everlasting-strips; Widow Welch's Pills for Female Irregularities and Union Jack paste for corns; the *Police Gazette* and *Home Notes;* and everywhere, under gaslight or arc-light, under the new Swan lamps or under the old naphtha-flares, London persisted unchanged.

As one's hansom bowled over the new patent wood-block paving of the West End or rattled over the dirt-strewn cobbles of the East End, it was impossible to realize—even to know—that not far off Professor Thomson was making the Atomic Bomb possible.

P·A·R·T F·I·V·E

The Fifth Decade

The last of the Five Decades, which covers almost completely the brief reign of King Edward the Seventh, was one of a deliberate intention, with every social class to "have a good time"—and organized entertainment: the theatres, the music-halls; the concert-halls; the football- and cricket-grounds; the cycle-meets and the motor-races; all offered the determined-to-be-happy at all costs at least the temporary means of entertainment. That this determination to enjoy themselves sprang from a feeling of apprehension; a conviction that "it was too good to last"; did not make the search for pleasure any less purposeful. The decade had begun with the century. Three weeks after that new century had begun, the old Queen had died after a record sixty-four years on the Throne. And it was rumoured, and not unjustly believed, that the spectacle of the British defeats in South Africa had hastened, if not actually caused, her death.

With that death, the whole Nation did, indeed, go into mourning—but for all the threatened social upheaval (the Liberals were set to give battle to the Lords, and to tax the "Rich")—the Nation responded to the exciting novelty of the new century. Everything seemed to be happening, and everything was novel. For the first time in history, Man had achieved man-carrying, heavier-than-air flights. Marconi's wireless was extending its range farther and farther; cars were getting faster and faster (100 miles per hour on an American track in 1903). As the decade moved on, so did Flying—always, to suit the mood of the Reign, offered as a public entertainment—make unbelievable strides. By 1910, Count von

Zeppelin, who had been impressed by the North's observation-balloons in the American Civil War, had flown five thousand fare-paying passengers in the prototype of those 'Zeps' which were to bomb Britain only five years ahead. And it was at a 'flying display' at Winton Aerodrome in 1910 that the Honourable Charles Rolls—partner with Henry Royce in designing and manufacturing the famous (even then) Rolls-Royce car—was killed in falling two hundred feet from his "plane". I saw that, as I had seen Rolls come in at Dover, two months earlier, after having flown the Channel both ways. (Blériot had been the first to fly the Channel, one way, the year before.) Politically—especially internationally—it was an exciting time. The years-old dream of the King had come true: there was now an Entente Cordiale between France and England—and about time, too, people said, when the Kaiser, in the last year of our decade, sent a gunboat, The Panther, to Agadir in Morocco; and war looked imminent. The Suffragettes made noisy nuisances of themselves; chaining themselves to the railings of public-buildings, kicking up a row in the Stranger's Gallery of the House of Commons, pouring acid into the slots of pillar-boxes. To the cheers of an immense crowd, the King's horse, Minoru, won the Derby.

Self-indulgent as any Tudor or Hanoverian King—both Henry VIII and George IV spring to mind—the King, a glutton at table, was, and had been for years, grossly overweight. At last the too-heavily-burdened heart gave up the unequal struggle, and, with his last mistress at his bedside (the generous Queen Alexandria had sent her carriage for portly Alice Keppel), the King died, as I remember well, on 6th May, 1910—one of the hottest summers within my memory. He was an immensely popular King–as well as a lucky one. Throughout his brief, nine-year reign, Britain had been building Dreadnoughts for her Royal Navy; overhauling her Army (which had done so badly in fighting the Boers), and making strides with her underwater fleet. The lucky King died before the war, for which all this arming was the preparation, broke out. In 1906, Aubrey Fessenden, using the Lee de Forest thermionic valve, broadcast Handel's Largo from the National Telephone Company's experimental station at Brant Rock, New Jersey, on 21st December—another "first" for the last decade.

MOST CENTURIES, over the past thousand years, had begun with England's finding herself involved in war—internal or external.

The twentieth century was no exception. The beginning of a century, too, in English history, usually finds the nation at the end of a war, or at the end of the first stage of a war: the politicians who welcome in the new century may usually promise Peace—and keep their promise.

Again, what gives the ever-hopeful Public the deceptive belief that a new century seems to give the assurance of a complete change in human affairs—and always for the better—is the fact (and it is a fact) that the closing of a century usually coincides with the closing of a monarch's reign; the beginning of a century heralds in a new one.

No sovereign ever ascended the throne of Great Britain with more popular welcome than did Edward VII—'Teddy', to the upper classes; 'Good Old Ted', to the less polished. There was something more than a little Solomonesque about the portly, sixty-year-old King: if he had the not undeserved reputation of having chased (and been chased by) innumerable beautiful women, he had Solomon's other reputation, too, of sound commonsense. Teddy's popularity was based on many qualities, actually possessed by him, or attributed to him by common rumour; the principal were a light-hearted sexuality, entirely without viciousness (what used to be called 'gallantry'), and an ability to assess and to solve problems by the exercise of the Common Man's point of view. Teddy was popular because his simple and enjoyable life seemed, to all but the case-hardened wowsers among his subjects, the sort of life that they would have led had they had the King's opportunities. The fact that he did not appear to suffer any penalties through his unremitting search for pleasure appeared to confirm the popular view that there is nothing fundamentally wrong in the philosophy that Marie Lloyd expressed in one of her most popular songs: 'A Little of What You Fancy Does You Good!'

It may be, too, that the British public of 1901 were drawn closer to traditional British institutions by the fierce animosity that Britain's foreign policy had aroused in almost every other country. There was not a state, big or small, near or remote, whose public we had not offended in some way.

For the first time in human memory, the British found themselves thoroughly and universally disliked.

On 3rd April, 1900, Edward, then still Prince of Wales, left for Copenhagen with the Princess, to spend their customary three weeks' holiday with the Princess's family. As their train was leaving the Gare du Nord, in Brussels, a fifteen-year old Belgian youth named Spirido leapt on to the running board of the carriage and fired four times at the Prince and Princess. One of the bullets went into the partition between their heads.

The train stopped, Spirido was seized by the station staff, the Prince jumped out of the carriage, and calmly but authoritatively told those who held Spirido not to harm the lad.

Spirido and his three adult accomplices turned out to be 'members of an anarchist club cherishing anti-British and pro-Boer sentiments. Spirido explained that he regarded the Prince as "an accomplice of Chamberlain in killing the Boers".'

The Prince was less excited by the incident than were his friends—and enemies.

To Frank Lascelles, the Prince wrote:

> The bullet was found in our carriage today; though a small one, it was quite capable of doing serious mischief if it had struck a vital part. Fortunately Anarchists are bad shots. The dagger is far more to be feared than the pistol. . . . The Princess is none the worse, and bore everything with the greatest courage and fortitude.

And to Lady Londonderry, he dismissed the whole episode in the jocular phrase, 'Fortunately, "All's well that ends well"!'

In more serious vein, he wrote to Lord Spencer:

> It was fortunate that the miscreant was so bad a shot, as it seemed inconceivable that he should have missed me at two yards. Dr. Leyd's propaganda had borne fruit in the Anglophobism that he has produced in the Foreign Press, and the anarchists are profiting by it, as they look on England and the English as the enemies of mankind in oppressing the poor Boers!

What the Belgians thought of the attempt was clear: the three adult accomplices of Spirido were acquitted of any intention to kill, while all that Spirido got was a period of detention in a House of Correction, release on bail to prepare his appeal, and a facilitated chance of escape into France—which was taken.

The Kaiser was furious—not because he liked his uncle, but because he disapproved of leniency towards those who shot at kings-to-be.

The behaviour of the Belgians in the Spirido affair is simply outrageous, and people in Germany are utterly at a loss to understand the meaning. Either their laws are ridiculous, or the jury are a set of damned, bloody scoundrels. Which is the case, I am unable to decide.

Fourteen years later, the German authorities were to be able to adjust Belgian laws to conform more to the German ideal of social justice; but in 1900 Belgium was still independent of the Kaiser's rule.

The French authorities 'could not find' Spirido. Then came the most fantastic development in this odd affair: King Leopold of the Belgians, who wished to make up a coolness which had arisen between himself and the Prince, went himself to Paris in order to put private detectives to find Spirido. Leopold urged Queen Victoria to order the English Ambassador in Paris to tell the French Government that she would regard the non-discovery of Spirido as an unfriendly act, and Leopold forwarded to the Queen his full report on his efforts to find the would-be assassin.

With the Belgian King's intervention, the French authorities had to act, and Spirido was 'found' and arrested, handed over to the Belgians, and confined to the House of Correction. On Edward's coming to the throne, both Spirido and his mother appealed to the new King for clemency.

All this did nothing to make Britain or her royal family more popular abroad; and the French Press outdid its reputation for irresponsible viciousness in the campaign of vilification that it waged against Queen Victoria.

Even the Duke of Orleans, who had been born in England, and had received nothing but friendship from all members of our royal family, caught the contagion of venom, and wrote a letter to the French Press in which he approved the campaign against the Queen.

It was in such an atmosphere of anti-British sentiment that the Queen died at half-past six on the evening of Tuesday, 22nd January, 1901, and Albert Edward, Prince of Wales, ascended the thrones of Great Britain, Canada and India, as Edward the Seventh.

The motto of the Order of St Michael and St George is *Auspicium Melioris Aevi*—Things Are Looking Up, if I may venture a free translation. Only the reigns of the popes have mottoes—according to the highly legendary Prophecies of St Malachy—but had the reigns of kings their appropriate mottoes, *Auspicium Melioris Aevi* would have summed up the estimate in which Edward and his potentialities were held by the mass of the British people.

With the whole world—nations and persons—ranged against Britain, British affairs had suddenly taken on, for the British, the importance of the intimately domestic. If the affairs were of no consequence to Outsiders, they were, by that reason, doubly of consequence to the British.

On 23rd January, 1901, as my father used to recall, and as the pages of the contemporary Press fully verify, all London (its buildings, no less than its 5,000,000 inhabitants) went into mourning for the dead Queen. The rich, the poor; the idle, the industrious; the stockbroker, the shopkeeper; the housewife, the domestic servant—all went into black.

But it was an Age, rather than a Person, that the country and the empire mourned. Only the very oldest among the British, the grandfathers and grandmothers, remembered a time when there had not been a Queen Victoria on the throne; when a king's head appeared on the coins; when glasses were raised to 'The King!' and when, uncovered, men stood to sing *God Save the King!*

For sixty-three years, Victoria had symbolized Britain; and if British rule had been extended over lands which were the unknown, hardly rumoured jungle-homes of savages when Victoria came to the throne, something of a markedly Britishizing quality had come over the Crown in the sixty-three years of the reign just ended.

In 1837, before William IV had died, the King of Great Britain was King, also, of Hanover: a monarch whose realm was divided between Britain and Continental Europe: in other words, a European sovereign.

Victoria had not inherited Hanover; and though her husband had succeeded to the sovereignty of a German duchy, that inheritance had not been retained by the British Crown. The Prince of Wales, inheriting Saxe-Coburg-Gotha from his father, had passed it on to his younger brother, Admiral of the Fleet H.R.H. Prince Alfred, Duke of Edinburgh. Victoria had established the tradition that the monarchs of Great Britain were monarchs of Great Britain only—even though they had become Emperors of India.

There were still many Continental relatives of the royal family: German, Russian, Roumanian, Greek; but the royal family itself was now for the first time in our long history essentially British.

It was a British king that the people, even while they mourned Victoria, were preparing to acclaim at his coronation.

'When Victoria ascended the throne in 1837, the British monarchy had sunk low in the estimation of the world. Her coronation was apologetic in its simplicity, and the prophecy was current that it was the last that Westminster would witness. Long, however, before the end of her reign, the Queen had restored the prestige of her position, and had made the Crown both respected and beloved.' Sir Sidney Lee, who wrote this just estimate of Victoria's achievement nearly three generations ago, might have added that the Crown had been strengthened by being 'popularized'; by being made to seem part of the inheritance of all the people, instead of, as formerly, the exclusive interest of a small caste.

That movement towards the 'popularizing' of the Crown was to know no set-backs during Edward's short reign. Before he died, on 6th May, 1910, the King was to see some of the nation's most cherished institutions derided and threatened—if not actually abolished. But among them was not the Crown.

In a decade of the greatest political and social change that Britain had known since the reign of Charles I, King Edward, by his own supple diplomacy, based upon his unrivalled understanding of men, and—through that understanding—his power to sway them to his gentle will, contrived to preserve and enhance the prestige of the Crown even while he was unable to prevent the loss of some of its political power.

'He had become in a supreme degree a man of the world,' says Sidney Lee, 'in whom shrewdness mingled with benignity.'

It had not been lost upon the King that, though all foreign nations had, after their own manner, turned upon Britain because of the Boer War, the now independent nations of the empire had not done so. They had not even stood aside, but had sent contingents to South Africa to 'fight Britain's war'.

Accordingly the new Prince of Wales (later George V) and the Princess set off, in May 1901, to open the first (Australian) Commonwealth parliament at Melbourne; they left form Portsmouth on 16th March, only two months after the death of Queen Victoria.

But the Boer War, though it had passed its climax, was still raging, and a gesture was needed from the Mother Country to show its daughter-states that the 'enduring principle' of British rule was . . . enduring.

From Australia, the Prince and Princess of Wales were to go on to New Zealand, Canada and the United States, whose government had shown friendliness in its refusal to be drawn into the list of those who were denouncing Britain. (With the first instalments of the Pan-American Empire just acquired—Cuba, Hawaii, Puerto Rico and the Philippine Islands—the United States was beginning to appreciate the responsibilities as well as the prestige of Empire.)

But the King soon showed that it was not only with the feelings of Britons beyond the seas that he was concerned; his subjects at home were not less the objects of his solicitude.

He was about to be crowned, with a ritual which had its origins in ceremonies more ancient, even, than that with which Charlemagne was made Emperor of the West in Rome.

Into this ritual had been inserted some words which, however worthy they might have been thought in 1689, when the Bill of Rights was drafted, had become needlessly offensive to many of the King's subjects in the years which had passed since the Glorious Revolution.

But there was a ritual, not connected with the coronation, which contained phrases even more offensive.

Before reading the first of his Speeches from the Throne, the King was to be called upon, by tradition, to make a declaration in which he repudiated the doctrine of Transubstantiation, and further asserted that 'the invocation or adoration of the Virgin Mary or any other saint and the sacrifice of the mass as they are now used in the Church of Rome are superstitious and idolatrous.' The King was also required to vow that he made the Declaration 'without any evasion, equivocation, or mental reservation whatever, and without any dispensation past or future or possibility of it from the Pope or any other authority.'

The King, though having no leanings towards Roman Catholicism, felt that this ancient stuff had no place in his modern kingdom, and pressed his Ministers to remove it from the Declaration.

The Ministers ganged up. They 'altered' the Declaration in such a manner as to preserve all its anti-Roman bias, and all its offensiveness. Only by the King's insistence that no more of 'the Lord Chancellor's bungling' be permitted to stand in the way of this reform were the offending passages removed in time for King George V to make the Declaration in its new form; the 'necessary legislation' could not be passed in time to alter the Declaration for Edward, and the King had the chagrin of having to read the offensive passages, knowing that no one but his Ministers would realize that he had wished to delete them.

That first clash with his Ministers had ended in defeat for the King; and there were to be other clashes, in which he was to prove no more triumphant. As usual, it was against the Tories—led by Balfour—that the ancient (though constitutional) prerogatives of the Crown had to be defended by a king who was determined to be a king. Even Lloyd George did not seek to diminish the Crown's prerogatives—only those of the House of Lords.

But against that fundamental change in foreign policy that Edward, on his own authority, had been working to achieve since the end of the Franco-Prussian War—the great Entente between France and Britain—the prejudices and machinations of the King's Ministers were powerless to act.

The King had made himself so popular with the French—in ways uncomprehended by his Ministers, and even by his subjects—that not even a Fashoda or a Boer War could stand in the way of the gradual and (as we now see it) inevitable rapprochement.

But if Edward needed the buttressing of his popularity, Fate was about to lend a hand.

The preparations had been made for the coronation—and no such 'apologetic' coronation as had been arranged for his mother in 1837. London was 'buzzing' with excitement; the Boer War was over, all but the last few guerilla skirmishes; Peace was with us again, and with Peace, a promised restoration of that popularity, in Europe's eyes, that most Englishmen believed that they had once enjoyed.

The nation had had to hold its breath again, when, only four months after his accession, the King had narrowly escaped being crushed to death by a falling mast on Tommy Lipton's yacht, *Shamrock*. The King had escaped Spirido's bullet, Lipton's mast—now the superstitious were going to have to ask themselves: 'Will the King's luck hold out the third time?'

The coronation had been fixed for 26th June, 1902; but only two days before that date, the announcement was made that it had had to be 'indefinitely postponed'; the King was seriously ill, and his principal medical men, Sir Francis Laking and Sir Frederick Treves, had ordered an immediate surgical operation.

In 1902, hardly anyone had heard of 'perityphlitis', that inflammation of the vermiform appendix which had first been operated upon by Henry Hancock, surgeon of Charing Cross Hospital, in 1848. Few surgeons since had considered the condition operable, preferring to treat it with a mixture of opiates and (to us) violent cathartics, so that except where Nature herself effected a cure the patient died. Léon Gambetta, the great French politician, died because his doctors did not know how to treat his 'perityphlitis'.

The King protested bitterly against his doctors' diagnosis: he, too, read the newspapers, and knew what costly preparations all ranks of his subjects were making to celebrate the coronation with an enthusiasm literally without precedent.

'Can't you put it off?' the King asked querulously. 'Can't you keep the thing dormant? Just for a little while. . . ? Just until after the coronation. . . ? '

Treves, the clever, worldly Jew who was a blood-relative of the Duke of Norfolk, Earl Marshal of England, saw the need for uncompromising bluntness—even uncompromising brutality.

Plainly, he told the King that the choice was a simple one: either a postponement of the coronation—or death. There were no two ways about it. Which was it to be?

Reluctantly the King consented, though he insisted that the coronation itself should be postponed, and not those ceremonies which were traditionally performed on the eve of a crowning. And the King insisted that all those honours that he had conferred, and which were to be made public at the coronation, should not be deferred.

The King was more tired than he knew; the generals—in particular Kitchener and Redvers Buller—had been more than usually irritating, indulging their prima donna 'temperaments' to the scandalizing of everyone but those who understood what general-officers are usually made of.

The operation was successful—*and* the patient recovered. The King's gratitude towards all those, doctors, nurses, attendants, who had served him through his illness, was not only marked, but alluded to by him in public addresses. The King had not feared death; but he had been less hopeful of surviving that he had admitted, even to himself.

As soon as he was able to get up, he left for a sea-cruise, and when he returned to London, some weeks later, he was as completely recovered as a man of his age dared to expect.

The coronation was fixed now for 9th August; and the postponement had effected a curious alteration in the character of the distinguished assembly of guests.

On the announcement that the coronation was to be postponed, all the more notable of the distinguished guests had returned to their home countries; only those minor royalties who were lineally related to the King remaining. Of the special missions only that of Ethiopia had stayed in England.

Again, chance had taken a hand in underlining the essential 'family' element of the new relationship between the King and his people. 'From the Dominions, Colonies, Dependencies and Protectorates came representatives of the armed forces of the Crown. Every race which acknowledged allegiance to the British Empire was represented—Maoris from New Zealand, Dyaks from North Borneo, Chinese from Hong-Kong—from the four quarters of the world came contingents to prove the solidarity of the Empire. The most impressive of the native contingents came from India, whose members represented a vast array of races and creeds. Besides such official guests, tourists from America, Australia, India, South Africa, Canada, and Western Europe crowded the London streets.'

After going on to describe the actual order of procession to the west door of the Abbey, Sidney Lee continues:

> . . . At last came the famous eight cream-coloured horses, drawing the antique golden coach, through the crystal panels of which could be seen the King and Queen. All lingering doubts as to the health of the King were set at rest when he was seen looking radiant and well, acknowledging with his Queen the acclamations of his people. Popular enthusiasm knew no bounds, and a mighty roar of continuous cheering

echoed from the Palace to Westminster. It seemed as if the pent-up anxiety of the nation had burst forth into a great shout of triumphant acclamation at the recovery of their King from what might well have proved a fatal illness.

The King himself had never felt better. Two days later, he told Lord Grenfell that his only anxious moment was when he had thought one of the archbishops would collapse, and that made the King 'slightly nervous' during the service.

Without in any way departing from the high standards of dignity inherited from his parents and inherent in himself, the King had contrived to please more people at his coronation than had ever been pleased before, and this he had done, not only by extending the patronage of the impersonal Crown, but also by warm acts of personal kindness.

In 1911, on the accession of King Edward's son, the number of honours awarded—peerages, baronetcies, privy councillorships, knighthoods and decorations—was 515; a figure which was further diminished to 313, in the New Year's Honours of 1913. At King Edward's coronation, the number was 1,540.

The King was aware that many of his subjects, who would gladly have accepted some mark of distinction, had a 'conscientious' objection to one which carried with it a 'title'.

The attitude of former sovereigns to this objection had been either one of irritation that a subject could hold an honour in little esteem, or that hardly less agreeable attitude which may be summed up in the phrase, 'Please himself!'

King Edward, whose brain was always directed by his heart, saw no reason why the Crown should not recognize service, even in one who held 'conscientious' objections to a title.

So the Order of Merit was founded in 1902, much against the 'advice' of Lord Salisbury and the heads of the War Office and the Admiralty. Though it had been pointed out to the King that the heads of the Service Departments were against this Order's being awarded to military and naval leaders, Roberts, Kitchener and Wolseley were offered it—and accepted it; but Art, Literature, Science was also honoured, in the persons of such distinguished men as Kelvin, Lister, Rayleigh, Morley, Lecky, Watts, Alma-Tadema and Meredith.

The lesser servants of the Crown were not forgotten by this warmest-hearted of our kings since George IV—and Edward VII was not forgetful, where George, unfortunately, was.

To reward the members of the administrative or clerical branches of the Civil Service, both at home and throughout the Empire, the King instituted the Imperial Service Order.

It was the happiest of all coronations—only the Tories were uneasy: they not only mistrusted the King, they mistrusted their ability to 'control' him—and that, in the Tories' opinion, was something worse.

The City which had grown, over two thousand years, from the village of Llyn-dun, had now reached its apogee. It was to grow bigger, as mere numbers of inhabitants went: indeed, though its rate of growth is slowing down, it has not yet reached the limits of its population-growth.

But it passed its apogee when it ceased to be an Imperial Capital, and the last king to reign over an empire of which London was truly the capital was Edward VII.

Little of the imperial architecture which was inspired by the nation's imperial condition survives—little, in fact, was built; the reign of the last King of a British Britain was too short.

Selfridge's remains—'vulgar', they have called this imposing relic of Edwardianism; and vulgar it probably is. But seeing how assured it is, it could hardly be otherwise than vulgar; for to be self-assured is to be bold, and to be bold is to be noisy, and to be noisy is . . . well, yes, vulgar. There is not a more vulgar piece of architecture in the world than the Arc de Triomphe, in Paris; and the explanation of its vulgarity is to be found in the names of those splendid victories which run down the great walls which flank the central arch.

One magnificent piece of Edwardian architecture you will be able to see only in that grim *memento mori*, the London County Council's *Survey*. This was the building on the south side of the Strand, hard by St Clement Danes church; a building originally erected for the Temperance and General Insurance Company, and latterly used as the offices of the *Illustrated London News* and its associated journals.

The splendid Byzantine interior, with its golden mosaics, for months lay bare to the dusty winds which blew in from the Strand; the bronze candelabrum, of Etruscan, rather than Byzantine, design, hung from the towering ceiling; it was not worth the removal, so greatly have our tastes changed. The splendour shames us: we shall be more comfortable with the Kliptiko packing-case which has replaced this relic of more assured times.

Across the road is a still-surviving building of the same period, though it was not built until Edward's reign ended: Australia House, which stands on the site of the old Sun Inn, at the junction of Holywell- and Wych-streets, that they began to pull down as Edward ascended the throne, and had demolished completely in the year that the Kaiser came to England, and stayed with Colonel Stuart-Wortley at Highcliffe Castle.

One magnificent building in this now exceedingly rare architectural manner happily survives on the Victoria Embankment: the only surviving example of Edwardian Baroque. This is the office of the Church Commissioners. In Moorgate, the former offices of the Eastern Telegraph Company survive, though they really belong more to the last years of Victoria than to the first years of Edward.

And though the 'new' Gaiety Theatre was pulled down a few years ago, 'because of woodworm', the old Gaiety Restaurant next door—built by the same architect, at the same time, of the same materials—survives: it is now the offices of the English Electric Company, that corporation whose exquisite taste commissioned the modeller, Charles Wheeler, to erect the two worst pieces of 'sculpture' which ever defaced even a building in the modern mode.

I had watched, with a lively and sympathetic interest, the gallant efforts of the late Lupino Lane to preserve the Gaiety Theatre, that George Edwardes made one of the principal centres of Edwardian theatrical brilliance.

Lane, as we know, failed to get the demolition order rescinded, and the heart-broken man had to watch the destruction of his beloved theatre—'because of woodworm'.

I use the phrase, 'had to watch', in a purely metaphorical sense. But I actually watched the demolition with my own eyes; every day I passed the theatre, and saw the workmen tear it down, piece by piece.

And—except for the timber framing of the dome—there was not a piece of structural woodwork in the whole theatre.

It was a modern building, with steel girders, brick walls and stone facing, and I am sure that the entomologists of the world would be enraptured to find a 'worm' which could threaten the strength of steel, brick and stone.

The facts of the demolition of the Gaiety are, I must feel, part of a great London mystery, which will probably not be solved in my time.

There is the sombre new wing of the British Museum; there is the post office in Newgate-street, built on the site of the old Christ's Hospital, and as they found when erecting the modern building—over Bastion XIX of the first Wall of London.

Edwardianism, so far as architecture is concerned, had hardly time to get into its stride before the Empire fell, and Imperial taste passed with Imperial sentiment.

As I said, London reached its apogee in the brief reign of Edward VII.

It was not exactly a shabby city, for the strict covenants that the great landlords were able to enforce in those days caused buildings to be painted by their tenants every four years (and, in the case of the Duke of Westminster's Belgravia property, every year).

But it was still a city of small, homely buildings; there had been nine-storeyed warehouses along Queen Anne's Thames; but nine storeys were not to be reached again until after 1920, save in the case of the unique Queen Anne's Mansions.

The seven- and eight-storey buildings of Victoria-street were the tallest in London—usually six storeys marked the limit of height.

Along the Strand, save for the new and splendid Cecil, Savoy and Grand hotels, all the work and play—newspapers, theatres, shops, restaurants—did their business in the refronted three-storey houses of Charles II's day.

Some of them are still there, but the gaiety and glitter has departed from the Strand, as it has departed from all the other streets of London.

When I look back at the 'luxury' of Edward's London, I must qualify, I find, that word, 'luxury'. In the first place, there was something essentially 'comfortable' about Edwardian good living; the word 'luxury' too often conveys something open and windy and far too public: something like Hollywood's idea of a Roman pageant. Edwardian 'luxury' was personal, intimate, domestic.

In the second place, it was widely scattered. There were still slums, and terrible slums they were, too. And certainly the mass of Londoners did not share in the rich living which went on at the Top.

But far more had access to the good things of life than is the case to-day.

Perhaps what made London so luxurious a city in the Edwardian era—may only ten years be an 'era'? I think so—was the multitude and perfection of its restaurants, its theatres and its shops.

The perfection of its restaurants was something to be credited only to London's wealth, which had brought over the foreign hoteliers, chefs and waiters: the Edwardian restaurant, whether that of the Carlton or that of Pagani's, was good because it was foreign. There were many 'old English chop-houses', but they provided comfortable, rather than luxurious, eating: they belonged to the City man. There was luxury, or the clever imitation of it, wherever you found a foreign restaurateur, even though he was providing a two- or three-shilling six-course dinner at the Florence, the Cavour, Gatti's, Pratti's or Pinoli's.

An inherent sense of the fitness of things produced the 'right atmosphere' as no former or succeeding generation did.

Electric light was new, but the Edwardians handled it with genius, softening it until it had all the warm, gently golden friendliness of candlelight. To come from the theatre into a restaurant full of the glow of pink-silk-shaded lamps shining softly on white napery, was to be filled with the promise of deftly-handled luxury. And the promise was never unfulfilled.

The Carlton, now gone to make way for that greenhouse in which the New Zealand High Commission must refrain from throwing stones, was slightly pre-Edwardian, but the Ritz, the Piccadilly and the Waldorf—all happily spared 'modernization'—are pure Edwardian.

The shops, too, were of a now inconceivable luxury; for polished and gilded wood gives an air of luxury that chromium-plate and polyvinyl sheet cannot.

There were some big stores—Harrods, Whiteley's, Marshall & Snelgrove, Barker's, and many others—but mostly the shopping was done in small, exquisitely fitted shops, where the service flattered the customer into a purring extravagance which still did not bankrupt even the spendthrift.

And the theatres. . . ! When I heard that Lily Elsie had died, I wondered if her last thoughts had been of that magical night in 1907, when she and Joe Coyne had waltzed up and down the great staircase on the stage of Daly's, and she had sung the Waltz Song in Lehár's most famous light opera.

The Merry Widow, The Chocolate Soldier, Peter Pan, The Arcadians, The Dollar Princess, False Gods, The Speckled Band, The Man from Toronto, Pygmalion, Sherlock Holmes: are there any of these Edwardian successes which are unknown to even the least looking-back of the present generation?

And the playwrights, working so well rewarded to supply the acting talent of the Edwardian theatre: Henry Arthur Jones, Pinero, Shaw, Somerset Maugham, Monckton Hoffe . . . well!

And on the more homely level, there was a music-hall of unexampled vitality and achievement; and think of the names which have come down from that: T. E. Dunville, Little Tich, George Robey, Marie Lloyd, Albert Chevalier . . . need I go on?

The motor-taxi—it was a single-cylindered Unic—had arrived in London in 1903, three years after the Tuppenny Tube had been opened, to connect Shepherd's Bush with the Bank. For two-pence, anyone west of Piccadilly could get to the theatres and restaurants. The hansoms and growlers did not vanish, before the competition of the taxi, until the Cavalry needs of the first world war made horses more valuable than petrol.

Then, in 1904, the London General Omnibus Company put its first motor-bus into commission in London—it took only seven years for the last horse-bus to be taken off the roads, though I saw a horse-tram in Burdett-road as late as 1918: it must surely have been the last.

Cheap travel, cheap dining-out, cheap theatres and music-halls: almost anyone could have a taste of luxury, even though, for many, it was only a taste. But taste it they all could.

The winds of change were blowing, right enough; but in that cozy Edwardian afternoon, most people were aware only of the curtains moving a little, of a faint rattling of the door.

The curious aspect of Edwardianism is not that there was so much evidence of impending change; but that so few people indeed accepted that evidence at its face value—which made it, for them, no evidence at all.

Though the world's Press was reluctant to admit that the Wright brothers had actually flown at Kitty Hawk (and the U.S. Department of the Army flatly refused to credit the report) the truth gradually forced itself upon the world that Flying had come. Nearer home, there were other signs of fundamental change: militant women, organized in what we should now call a 'para-military' body, set out to gain the Vote, using as tactics and strategy Woman's immemorial ability to make a damned nuisance of herself in a Good Cause (that is, the achievement of something that she desires).

Considering that Australia and New Zealand had given women the Vote (in Victoria, as far back as 1858) there was no reason why women should not have had it in Britain; and considering, too, that the more widespread the electorate is, the more responsibility the 'people' appear to assume, and thus the less odium settles upon government, the wonder is that the Suffragettes needed to indulge in their grotesque tactics to get the Vote.

In one respect, the strategy of the Suffragettes was masterly; and it is in this one respect that they have never yet been praised.

This was in the choice of their Commander-in-Chief.

Since the whole strength of the Suffragettes' strategy depended upon men's inability to fight them on their own terms, it was a masterly stroke to choose an attractive, completely feminine woman to represent the Campaign for Women's Suffrage. The Edwardians, who loved their King because he loved their women, simply could not find it in themselves to fight Mrs Pankhurst as brutally as she was fighting them.

A gang of hockey-playing Sapphists would have lost the battle in the first year; Sylvia and her pretty young women—all as normal as a Denise Robins heroine, save in this matter of the Vote—could hardly lose.

Their behaviour, though shocking, was normal, too. They were as shameless in the pursuit of the Vote as any normal girl is in the pursuit of a husband; though it is easier to explain why a woman wants a husband than it is to explain why she should want the Vote.

They chained themselves to railings—especially to the railings of No. 10, Downing-street and other notable buildings; they dropped explosive and corrosive packets into the pillar-boxes (a trick that they had learnt from the Irish); they 'demonstrated' in public—in restaurants, in theatres, in churches; breaking the well-bred hush with a hurried, shrieking, 'Votes for Women!' before being chucked out by the scandalized waiters, ushers, sidesmen. They travelled all over the country, heckling political speakers; they wrote innumerable letters; they lay down on pavements, during the homeward-bound evening rush; one 'martyr' even went so far as to throw herself in front of what should have been the Derby winner—she certainly called attention to herself, not only getting herself killed, but, which was to many people far worse, injuring the jockey and causing a fine racehorse to be shot.

All the same, these Suffragettes, though employing the grossest exhibitionist tactics, must be seen as something very different from the Committee of One Hundred and their supporters, with whom we are at present familiar.

The Suffragettes' behaviour might have been outrageous; their appearance was not. They did not adopt grotesque clothing; above all, they washed. That alone should save them from the ignominy of being likened to Canon Collins's Beggar's Opera.

Still, for all this evidence of change, the Edwardians were happy in the certainty that the good life would continue.

On the political front, there were dark clouds; and internationally the prospects looked anything but peaceful.

But in the social life of the nation, result seemed to yield naturally to cause; men could still hope to reap what they sowed; work still brought its rewards, and money could still yield a five per cent which was as safe as the Bank of England.

Periodical publishing flourished, though now the half-tone had almost completely displaced the wood or steel engraving, save in the scientific and technical Press.

One result of the introduction of the half-tone engraving around the year 1900 was the ability to reproduce the artist's work very much as he had drawn it; and the effect of the half-tone was to encourage the artists to draw in a manner which had been barred to them by the limitations of wood or steel engraving.

Hand-coloured steel engravings may reproduce, in a stiff, wooden way, pen drawings of rigid dresses; half-tone can reproduce water-colour paintings of soft—and especially diaphanous—fabrics. For the first time, because their water-colour paintings could now be reproduced by mechanical means, the artists turned to water-colours, and used them to paint, again for the first time, not merely the soft, clinging outer garments, but those lace-trimmed and frilled under-garments which were produced now merely because they could be attractively illustrated.

It had long been permitted to illustrate, even in the most respectable of journals, a woman in corset; the grim functionalism of the wood engraving robbed the illustration of any erotic character; the picture of a corset was just about as 'suggestive' as the wood-engraved picture of a steamhammer.

But encouraged by the perfect fidelity of half-tone reproduction, the artists now got more and more daring; and underclothes (I am astonished that Mr James Laver hadn't noticed all this) were used as the means of making the privately erotic a public affair.

The Gibson Girl—profitable invention of the American artist, Charles Dana Gibson, whose 'straight' work had included the hysterically romantic illustrations for *Rupert of Hentzau* and *The Prisoner of Zenda*—not only seemed to symbolize the Edwardian Age; the artist's dream became incarnate in the person of Miss Camille Clifford, whose charms merit some analysis here, for they not only pleased the Edwardians, they reveal the Edwardians to us.

Camille Clifford was a young woman, but her fashionable corsetière, by thrusting her breasts up and forward, and her rump down and out (giving Camille *the* Chic Shape of 1902 onwards), created the curious illusion that Camille was a woman well on into middle age who was trying to get her figure back into youthful lines. Young men do often try to ape the appearance and mannerisms of more sober years; it is rare, indeed, in the world's history that Fashion dictates that young *women* shall try to make themselves look like older women trying to look younger. (It says much for the corsetières and the hairdressers of the post-coronation years that they usually succeeded in this extremely odd imposture.)

Camille, then, corseted into a quite unnatural shape, her hair piled high and thick on her head (over horse-hair pads), dressed in black velvet, tight above, full and trailing behind—imitating age even to the concealment of the throat—looked like a magnificently preserved woman of fifty and more.

What bizarre psychological trick lay behind this 'image'?

The answer, I feel, is not hard to find. All Fashion's 'images' are inspired by hero- or, rather, heroine-worship. What Fashion seeks to do is to make every woman look like the woman most admired at the time. We have seen the corpse-white *pauvres petites*, hair *en bouffant*, eyes ringed with black, emaciated bodies wrapped in skin-tight black leather: and, upon my soul, they do look like Brigitte Bardot—all of them!

The ideal of the post-Coronation years, so far as women were concerned, was the rich, well-groomed, middle-aged-to-elderly woman-of-the-world of whom the King was so fond (this included his beautiful, just-on-sixty-year-old wife).

The Edwardian woman of the upper class had almost everything: both security and freedom; all the privileges of Woman with a complete social equality with Man. The young women were still not quite emancipated; the middle-aged were almost completely so. They rode to hounds, they played bridge, they drank, they shot, they were Great Hostesses, they had lovers, they attended race-meetings, they motored, they went up in balloons (those of them who wished to go up in balloons), they wrote novels, they served on committees, they went abroad, they had everything.

No wonder that all the other women, young or middle-aged or old, wished to look like them.

The fashion-designers met this desire by creating the female shape, and the clothes to cover it, which were so admirably displayed by Miss Camille Clifford, the Gibson Girl.

There were male heroes, too—and not all of them created for the delectation of schoolboys. There was Prince Ranjitsinghi—'Ranji'—the one-man campaign against colour-prejudice; the Indian who was also a first-class cricketer; the Prince who was the hero of the working man. 'Ranji' ran even the great W. G. Grace neck-and-neck in the popularity stakes. (I am quoting now.)

There was Jackie Fisher—Admiral of the Fleet Sir John Fisher—the man who wished to take the North Sea Fleet to Kiel and blow the German fleet, without any declaration of war, out of existence. It is interesting to speculate what would have happened had Britain, and not Germany, adopted the *Blitzkrieg*: we should still, in all probability, have been in an Edwardian golden age.

There were lesser, but not much lesser, heroes: Lieutenant Mueller, the Swedish Physical Culture Messiah, come to teach us how to make our 'daily dozen' regenerate us, warding off disease and death.

There was Eustace Miles, the High Priest of Vegetarianism, at whose London restaurants you could eat a four-course dinner, complete with nut-steak and soya-bean chicken cutlets, for under a shilling. Though it was Miles's noisy anti-meat campaigning, and not his restaurants, which put him in the news.

There was an American anti-booze, anti-sin termagant, Mrs Carrie Nation, who was closely rivalled in noisiness by another middle-aged lady with too much time on her hands, Mrs Ormiston Chant, who sought to save our Youth by violent attacks on the Empire and the Leicester Lounge—a theatre and a pub in Leicester-square; both the resorts of prostitutes. Mrs Ormiston Chant used to promenade London carrying placards and banners; and she is linked with the Suffragette movement in that one of her main arguments was that men should suffer the same legal penalties for going with prostitutes as the prostitutes suffered for soliciting the men to do so.

Gipsy Smith was an evangelist, offering a short cut to God, to a Britain which has always fought shy of the mediator; though after the spell of the Gipsy Smiths has worn off, it often seems that God, no less than the mediator, has disappeared. But Gipsy—who chose the Crystal Palace as his favourite Mount of Olives—had a large following.

There was that fellow-Scandinavian of the Mueller persuasion: Sandow, the World's Strongest Man, another prophet of the Keep Fit cult, who was quickly taken over by the sales-promotion men, so that every schoolboy and clerk had a set of Sandow spring muscle-developers in the bathroom. Sandow, just after World War I, killed himself by attempting to lift an overturned car from a ditch—but that was a long way off when Edward was on the throne.

All this hero-worship was heavily plugged by the schoolboys' journals, whether of the Top (*Boys' Own Paper* and *The Captain*) Middle (*Chums*) or Basic (the *Gem*, the *Magnet*, *Boys' Friend*).

The world was still sufficiently civilized not to have turned over its basic juvenile literature to those who couldn't write at all: Max (afterwards Sir Max) Pemberton wrote his *Iron Priate* for *Chums* (of which he was Editor), and a young bank-clerk named P. G. Wodehouse was writing stories for schoolboys in *The Captain*.

No matter for what class of reader these boys' journals were designed, public-schoolboy or errand-boy, they all insisted that the schools in their stories be public schools (complete with fags and Latin cribs) and that their sentiment be Royalist and Imperial. There was no damned Liberalism about the stories: all coloured men—save 'Ranji'—were 'natives'; and all 'natives' were savages. All heroes played cricket—well—and not only had British names, but were British by race. (This is significant, in view of the hundreds of thousands who were pouring in from the ghettoes of Poland, White Russia, Roumania and Turkey—*they* would later have British names, be public-schoolboys, and play cricket—well: but they would not be British by race.)

These journals did not regard any Churchmen as heroes save those who were successful missionaries or cricketers. They never mentioned such popular figures as Father Bernard Vaughan, who filled Farm Street Jesuit church with fashionable congregations, come to hear him thunder against the Sins of Society. (Vaughan was credited with having converted Edward VII on the King's death-bed; but this is pure wishful thinking on the part of those who would have liked to think we had done with the Reformation.)

There were other writers, too, making a handsome living outside the profitable field of boys' journalism.

Following in the wake of the ever-more-daring illustrators of corsetry and lingerie, the novelists came up with the Bedroom Novel. The short word which made *Lady Chatterley* famous—indeed, provided the only literary justification for that novel—had already appeared in print, in 1905: you may find it in Henley's and Farmer's *Dictionary of Slang*.

But the novelists did not need naughty words to get their 'hot stuff' over; and reading the 'hot stuff' to-day, one wonders what all the fuss was about.

Victoria Cross—pen-name for one of the three talented and unconventional daughters of an Indian Army colonel (the others were 'Laurence Hope', who wrote the *Indian Love Lyrics*, and Amy Woodeford-Finden, who set them to suburbanly unforgettable music)—wrote *Anna Lombard*, which went rocketing into the best-seller class, and helped the author to sell a total of five million copies of her books.

H. G. Wells, turning from science fiction, had a go at the 'realistic' novel, and shocked the Edwardians of 1908 into making his *Anne Veronica* the best-seller of the year. Though Florence Barclay remembered that an even surer recipe for literary success than plain Sex is Sex-plus-Religion: her *Rosary* was the best-seller of 1909.

Not all the novelists were as socially successful as Hall Caine, who entertained the King and Queen on their visit to the Isle of Man in Coronation year, and made King Edward laugh with (I use Caine's own words) 'some quaint Manx tales'.

But they all did very well: Britain was reading more than ever, since the cinema was still a rather vulgar penny-gaff, and wireless was what ships sent out distress signals with.

Theirs was a simple art; Cubism, Fauvism, Dadaism had all crept into painting, altering its traditional modes, and distorting it often beyond normal recognition as a familiar art-form. But the writers, though they had quickened the rate of their narrative, were still writing what, essentially, had been written in Smollett's, Sterne's and Fielding's day.

There have been greater writers both before and after Edward VII's day; but no period in our history can show so many first-class storytellers. They were masters of plot, men and women; 'literary' and 'popular'.

Without having to turn up the records of the time, I can list dozens of the names whom the fruitful temper of the day made into successful writers, and who gave something—much—to the unique character of that brief, golden day.

I list them in no order of merit: but see what memory calls up. H. G. Wells, Arnold Bennett, Joseph Conrad, John Galsworthy, A. E. W. Mason, Seton Merriman, H. de Vere Stacpoole, Bettina von Hutten, Mrs Belloc Lowndes, Douglas Sladen, Erskine Childers—a great name built upon one great, though slender novel—Thomas Hardy, Henry James, Conan Doyle, 'Raffles' Hornung, E. Phillips Oppenheim, William le Queux, Richard March, Una Silberrad . . . there's a publisher's list for you!

No King of Great Britain had travelled so widely; nor did the travelling stop when Edward came to the throne.

Denmark, Sweden, Greece, Germany, France, Italy, Russia: all had visits from the King. He believed in his power to soothe politically-inspired susceptibilities, and, since on several occasions the threat of war in his reign had come to nothing, the King seems to have justified his self-confidence.

But though he was much absent, his country—and especially his capital—saw much of him.

He was indefatigable in both 'official' duty and in those less arduous duties which were not the less important because they linked the Monarch with his People, rather than the King of Great Britain with the comity of Monarchs.

When Napoleon III said, to the eager seekers after riches, 'Gentlemen, help yourselves!', he was setting a precedent that King Edward followed. But it was to pleasure, rather than to wealth, that King Edward invited his subjects to help themselves—and he set them a heart-warming example.

He loved life; he loved being alive. He loved people—all sorts of people, and if he sometimes, though rarely, shared the prejudices of his people, he never shared their snobbishness.

He had as many, and as intimate, friends among the Socialists of France and Britain as among those of the Right; as many friends among the self-made, the parvenus, the arrivistes, as among those of many quarterings. Introducing the 'eminent financier', Terah Hooley, who was extremely lucky not to have followed some other 'eminent financiers' of late Victorian and early Edwardian days to the 'cooler', King Edward said; 'I wish you to meet my particular friend, Mr Hooley.'

When Arthur Lynch, an Irishman who had commanded an Irish Brigade in Kruger's army, was arrested after the Boer War, and, after trial for high treason, was sentenced to death, King Edward first got the sentence commuted to imprisonment, and then quietly set about giving Lynch a pardon.

The clemency was not misplaced; Lynch wrote thanking the King; and that the ex-'traitor' ended World War I as a colonel in the British Army says much for Edward's shrewd commonsense, as well as his innate kindness of heart.

His people loved him. Even Socialists, when attacking the monarchy, were always careful to separate the person of Edward from his kingly function. This affection of almost all for the king had some astonishing manifestations: when the Civil List came up for revision, immediately after King Edward's accession, and the usual criticism of the sums to be voted followed, it was that old die-hard of Socialism, Keir Hardie, who spoke up for raising the Queen's personal allowance—and nothing could more have touched the King's heart than a gesture of friendliness and respect for his beloved wife.

He was, indeed, nearer to his people than any monarch before him had ever been, and he set the seal on his popularity by winning the Derby—though his popularity did not need that greatest of all popular triumphs.

As he led Minoru through the paddock, men and women of the working class were observed to pat him on the back, crying 'Good old Teddy!' (His son came to be among the most beloved of British kings, but one simply cannot imagine any member of the public, even intoxicated, shouting 'Good old George!')

The matchless quality of King Edward may be appreciated when we consider how all this familiarity on the part of his subjects was never held, by him or by them, to diminish in the slightest degree the respect in which they held him, and the dignity that he preserved in himself.

He ruled over a country and an empire which were managed by possibly the most irresponsible gang of politicians since Lord North's government had successfully achieved the loss of the American colonies.

When it seemed that the Lords might—or would—reject the Budget of 1909, as they not only had the right to do but indeed the constitutional and moral duty to do if they did not approve its terms, the Ministry (Campbell-Bannerman had resigned, and Asquith had taken his place) resolved to carry their Budget and destroy the Lords at one and the same time.

In a speech made at Leigh on 15th July, Lewis (later first Viscount) Harcourt had this to say:

> The black hand of the Peerage, which holds its secret sessions at Lansdowne House, has issued edicts of assassination against too many fair measures desired by the people and passed by overwhelming majorities in the only House in which the people are directly represented.

The King protested against Harcourt's use of the word 'assassin' in relation to any member of the Upper House, and pointed out to Harcourt that he particularly deplored this unseemly demagogic nonsense (my phrase, not the King's) immediately after the King had been Harcourt's guest.

Harcourt did not apologize. He said airily that 'the metaphor might be rough, but is not unfair; and the facts I stated are absolutely true'.

The Budget put new duties on landed and other property, upped the Income Tax, gave £3,000,000 extra to the navy to build battleships, and £8,000,000 for the Old Age Pensioners.

All this added up to a deficit of £12,000,000 for the forthcoming year; so the Chancellor—Lloyd George—proposed to cover this sum by further taxing alcohol, estates and legacies. The Lords threw the Budget out, and there was a General Election: Winston Churchill, Asquith, Lloyd George, Harcourt and all the other 'democrats' now presented the nation with the choice that they had so carefully engineered: A 'democratic' Government— or an unchanged House of Lords.

It was not only the people and the Lords who were presented with the Liberals' ultimatum; the King had one, too.

Either the King must create a sufficient number of peers to ensure the passing of the rejected Finance Bill—or he must be 'advised' to surrender his royal prerogative of creating peers, and to hand that prerogative over to Margot Tennant's husband and his fellow 'statesmen'.

The King died before he had to make the bitter choice—and in the year of his death, his son, George V, made the right choice: keeping the royal prerogative by agreeing to create the necessary number of peers to pass Government measures.

The Lords sought to retain their own traditional and constitutional powers by giving in to this political blackmail; but in their case, as in later cases, appeasement did not save them. The Ministry went on to pass measures which effectively deprived the Lords of any real legislative power, and concentrated all political authority in the Commons.

In the meanwhile, the new world was taking shape, not in the chamber of the House of Commons or in the drawingrooms of the still powerful society hostesses.

The gramophone, the cinema, the telephone were being perfected, and were being ever more widely used. In 1904, Fleming, in England, and Lee de Forest, in America, simultaneously invented the thermionic valve, which was later to make, not only radio-telephony, but television, possible. At Brant Rock, New Jersey, on 21st December, 1970, Aubrey Fessenden demonstrated, before officials of the National Telephone Company and representative Pressmen, his perfected radio-telephony. Seven years earlier, he had succeeded in broadcasting sound over a mile or so; but the sounds had been garbled, and almost inaudible against the high-pitched whine of the electric arc which was sending the signals. Now, in 1907, the sounds were clear and pure, and Handel's *Largo*—the first music ever to be broadcast—went out over the air.

Flying had made tremendous strides since the Wrights had gone aloft in 1903. Once it had been demonstrated that flying was possible, a score of inventors, in France and England, got to work designing their own machines: Blériot, Farman, Voisin, in France; Hawker, Moore-Brabazon, Sopwith and Rowe in England.

There was one man, though, who enjoyed a unique fame as a popular hero, the rich Brazilian, Santos-Dumont, who began with dirigibles and went on to aeroplanes. The public on both sides of the Channel loved this plucky little amateur inventor; but it was Blériot, in 1909, who crossed the Channel by air, and would have made anybody but generals ashamed that they had turned down the Channel Tunnel scheme only three years before.

Though the car-industry was still controlled by the French, the British were making great strides in catching up; and the pride of the 1909 Motor Show at Olympia was the elegant and powerful Rolls-Royce Silver Ghost; the King's patronage of motoring seemed to have found its complete justification in this triumph of British car-design, the creation of two men: the Hon. Charles Rolls and Sir Henry Royce, who had set out in partnership with the declared intention of producing 'the Best Car in the World'.

The American, Yerkes, had taken over the development of London's underground railway system, buying existing lines, projecting new, and handing over to his successor, Stanley (afterwards Lord) Ashfield, an English-born American, an almost complete monopoly of London's underground traffic.

As I wrote these last pages a quarter-century ago, the news came that Sir Bruce Ingram had just died, still the editor of the *Illustrated London News*, which he became in 1901. He gave G. K. Chesterton a job in 1904, paying the great 'G.K.' £4 10s. od. a week. Money was still worth something, even when Edward VII died, six years later.

The King had been ill, on and off, for some years; but his death was foreshadowed in a curious way.

He died on 6th May, 1910; on 2nd May, the Postmaster-general authorized the issue of some stamps with unfamiliar colours, an experimental issue.

The penny stamp, then the most commonly used of all the values, had had its normal red changed to a sad blackish-purple.

At once the news ran around London that the King had died, and that the 'mourning' stamp had been rushed out to mark his passing. There was no connection between the King's death and the choice of colour for the penny stamp: the stamp was printed weeks before the King was taken ill. But four days after the rumour of the King's death had shocked London, he was dead in all truth. His son just had time to tell his dying father that his horse, Witch of the Air, had won the Spring Two-Year-Old Plate at Kempton Park that afternoon.

Someone had already given the King the news, but when the Prince of Wales, not knowing this, told him, Edward roused himself and said, 'Yes, I have heard of it. I am very glad.'

Just before this great and good man passed into his last coma, he said, 'No, I shall not give in; I shall go on; I shall work to the end.'

He did not give in, even though he never spoke again.

At a quarter to midnight, as Big Ben was striking, Edward the Peacemaker went to his rest. The last voice that he heard was the voice of London—the gaslit London which passed with him.

I·N·D·E·X

Aerated Bread Company 27
Airplanes 192, 193
Alabama claim 75, 76, 78
Albert, Prince 25, 26, 53, 87, 100
Alexandra, Queen 113
Army 61–70
Asquith, N. H. 192
Ashanti (see Colonial Wars)
Austin, Alfred 11
Automobiles 157–159, 193
Aylesford, Lord and Lady 92, 105, 122

Baker, Col. Valentine 82–83
Bazalgette, Joseph 11, 12
Becquerel, Henri 117
Beeton, Samuel Orchart 30, 85
Bell, Laura 19–22
Bicycle 150–151
Bloomer, Amelia 150–151
Bloody Sunday 98, 127
Blunt, Wilfrid Scawen 19
Boer War 93, 94
Booth, William "Gen." 128
Boothby, Guy 118
Bradlaugh Case 94
Burns, John 97–99

Cambridge, George, Duke of 66, 67
Campbell
    Lady Colin 92
    Lord and Lady Colin 106
Chamberlain, Joseph 149
Chambers, Sir William 6

Channel Tunnel 73, 74
Chesterton, G. K. 193
Chetwynd, Sir George 124
Churchill
    Lord Randolph 84, 122
    Winston 192
Colley, Sir George 93, 94
Colonial Wars 114–115
Corelli, Marie 118–119, 121
Clare Market 133
Clarence, Duke of 92, 132, 138
Compton, Spencer (see Devonshire, 8th Duke of)
Cook, Kate 105–6
Crimean War, The 53–54
Crompton, Colonel 95, 111
Crystal Palace, The 96, 129
Cubitt, Thomas 5, 7

Devonshire, 8th Duke of 19
Dickens, Charles 16, 51–53, 121
Disraeli, Benjamin 79–82, 94–95, 99, 127
Doyle, Arthur Conan 106–7, 118–20, 156–57
Dryden, Vaughan 120
Durham, Earl of 92, 105, 124, 126
Dynamiters 109–10

Education 58–60
Edward VII, King 171–80, 190–91, 193–94
Electric

195

current 116–17
light 91
Electric Lighting Act of 1882 95
Elephant Man, The 111–13
Eustun, Lord 92, 105–6

Fessenden, Aubrey 192
Fort, Charles 107
Fuzzy-wuzzies (see Colonial Wars)

Garrett, William George 91
Gas 3, 4, 91
George V, King 192
George, Prince, Duke of York 132, 138–39
Gibson Girl 186–87
Gifford, Lord 139–40
Gladstone, William Ewart 21, 22, 58, 75–76, 78–79, 81, 94–95, 97, 99, 111, 121–23, 141–43
Gordon-Cumming, Sir William 92, 137–38

Gordon, General George 111, 123
Grant, "Baron" Albert 5
Great Exhibition, The 3
Green, Lycett 137
Grosvenor Hotel 15

Haggard, Rider 118, 120
Hardy, Thomas 118
Hate, Doctrine of 114–16
Heynau, General 35
Holloway, Thomas 28–29, 31
Holmes, Sherlock 92, 106, 111
Hotels, London 15, 32–34, 103

Ingram, Sir Bruce 193

Kelvin, Lord 4
Kensington House 5, 6
Keppel, Mrs. 132

Langtry, Lily 85–86
Lawrence D. H. 119
Lawrence, T. E. 113
Lloyd George, David 192
London 5, 6, 7, 9
   Belgravia 10
   Fleet St. 31, 32
   Hyde Park 15
   Lancaster Gate 3

Strand, The 31–33
West End, The 6, 9, 102
London underground 13–14, 91

Main drainage scheme 11
Maiwand, Battle of 92
Marlborough, Duke of 105, 122
Martin Vaz Islands 144–46
Maxim, Hiram 115
Meredith, George 17
Morris, William (Lord Nuffield) 115
Music halls 103–4

Napoleon III 53–57, 72
Novosielski, Michael 6

Paris 5
Paris Exhibition of 1887 123
Pearl, Cora 15
Pearson, Charles 13–14
Punch 10–11

Queensberry, Lord 153

Reis, Johann Philipp 87, 116
Ripper, Jack the 92, 110–11
Roberts, Lord 132, 163–64
Rolls, Charles 193
Rosebery, Lord 142
Royce, Sir Henry 193
Russell, Lord John 11

St. John's Wood 15
Salisbury 143, 146–47
Shaw, G. B. 113
Simpson's Coffee Divan 3
"Skittles" (see Walters, Catherine)
Somerset, Lord Arthur 92
Soutar, Charles 106
Sperido 172–73
Stanger, Urban Napoleon 106–7
Straus, Ralph 119
Suez Canal 77, 79–80
Suffragettes 170, 184–85, 187
Swan, Joseph 3, 91

Telephone, The 91, 96–97, 116, 192
Television 192
Tenniel, John 134–35
Thomson, J. J. 117

INDEX

Thompson, William (*see* Lord Kelvin)
Tranby Croft 92, 137, 138
Transvaal 161–62
Treves, Sir Frederick 111–13
Trinidad 144–46
Tryon, Admiral 139–41
Trollope, Anthony 52

Vanishing Londoners 107–9
Verne, Jules 118
Victorian family life 103–5
Victoria, Queen 25, 34, 36, 45–47, 53, 64, 66–68, 82, 110, 126, 164, 173, 174

Wales, Prince of 25, 82–84, 86, 88, 92, 105, 115, 121–23, 131, 136–38
Wales, Princess of (*see* Alexandra, Queen)
Walters, Catherine 17–19, 21, 25
Watson, John H. 92
Weldon, Mrs. 125–26
Wells, H. G. 118
Wilde, Oscar 132, 153–54
William II, Kaiser 135
Windham, "Mad" 22
Wolseley, Sir Garnet 70–72, 74, 93, 123
Wood, Mrs. Henry 118

Zulus (*see* Colonial Wars)